Michael Davie, who served in the Royal Navy in World War Two, has been a reporter on the *Observer* for many years. He has been Journalist of the Year, and is a former editor of *The Age*, Melbourne. He has written books about President Lyndon Johnson and about California, and edited the diaries of Evelyn Waugh.

MICHAEL DAVIE

The Titanic

The Full Story of a Tragedy

GRAFTON BOOKS

A Division of the Collins Publishing Group

LONDON GLASGOW
TORONTO SYDNEY AUCKLAND

Grafton Books
A Division of the Collins Publishing Group
8 Grafton Street, London W1X 3LA

Published by Grafton Books 1987

First published in Great Britain by
The Bodley Head Ltd 1986

Copyright © Michael Davie 1986

ISBN 0-586-07433-3

Printed and bound in Great Britain by
Collins, Glasgow

Set in Times

To Peter

Contents

Acknowledgements

My thanks are due especially to the following: Anne Chisholm, Archibald Chisholm, Sir Andrew Duff Gordon, John Grigg, Mrs Dorothy Ismay, Edward S. Kamuda, Russ Lownds, Howard Matson, Viscount Mersey, Edith Newhall, Patrick Stenson, Jesse Stoecker, Robert Straus, John B. Thayer, and members of the Halifax Maritime Museum, the Halifax Public Archives, Harland & Wolff, the International Ice Patrol, the Library of Congress, the Marine Library of the Department of Transport, the New York Public Library, the Philadelphia Maritime Museum, the Public Record Office, the Southampton Public Library, the Ulster Folk and Transport Museum, the Widener Branch of the Free Library of Philadelphia, and the Woods Hole Oceanographic Institution. Most generously, Michael Moss of the University of Glasgow made available before publication his research for the official history of Harland & Wolff.

Thanks are due to the Society of Authors on behalf of the estate of George Bernard Shaw for permission to quote the Shaw letters in Appendix Two; and to A. P. Watt on behalf of the National Trust and Macmillan London Ltd. for an extract from *Gehazi* by Rudyard Kipling from *The Definitive Edition of Rudyard Kipling's Verse*.

Copyright photographic material is reproduced by permission of the following: the Ulster Folk and Transport Museum; Harland & Wolff; Radio Times Hulton Picture Library; Beken of Cowes; the *Cork Examiner*; the *Illustrated London News*; the *Southampton Echo*; the

Mercantile Marine Service Association; the Marconi Company; Halifax Public Archives; the Woods Hole Oceanographic Institution and Associated Press.

While every effort has been made to trace the correct owners of all copyright material reproduced in this book, the publishers regret any errors of attribution that may have unwittingly occurred and will be happy to make suitable acknowledgement in any future editions.

Introduction

The keel of the White Star liner *Titanic* was laid down at the Harland & Wolff shipyards, Belfast, in 1909. She was launched on 31 May 1911 and sailed on her maiden voyage from Southampton to New York, via Cherbourg and Queenstown, on 10 April 1912. With a gross tonnage of 46,328 tons, she was the largest ship afloat; 882 feet long, 92 feet wide, 8 decks rising to the height of an 11-storey building. Four days and seventeen hours after the voyage began, at 11.40 P.M. on Sunday 14 April, she hit an iceberg and was badly damaged. Two hours and forty minutes later she sank. Of the 2227 passengers and crew, 705 escaped in twenty lifeboats and rafts: 1522 were drowned, including her master, Captain Edward Smith.[1] At dawn on 15 April the Cunard liner *Carpathia*, having heard the *Titanic*'s wireless distress calls 58 miles away, arrived at the scene and began picking up survivors. On her return to New York on the evening of Thursday 18 April, she was met by 30,000 people. Next morning, in the Waldorf Astoria Hotel, a committee of the United States Senate, chaired by Senator William Alden Smith, started to investigate the disaster: thereafter the committee moved to Washington, where its report was published on 28 May. A British government inquiry, conducted by a judge, Lord Mersey, began to sit in London on 2 May, heard 94 witnesses, and reported on 30 July. Between 17 April and 8 June, four ships chartered by the White Star

[1] These figures, not universally agreed, are the best estimates of the Titanic Historical Society.

Line recovered 328 bodies from the North Atlantic; of these, 209 were taken to Halifax, Nova Scotia; the rest were buried at sea. These are the basic outlines of the sinking of the *Titanic* seventy-four years ago.

The story has retained a remarkable power; no disaster of modern times, neither the San Francisco earthquake of 1906, nor the Colombian volcano of 1985, nor the *Challenger* space shuttle explosion of 1986, nor any of the jumbo jet airliner crashes, has excited quite the same horror and fascination. Some disasters are undeniably acts of God, but the *Titanic* sinking has always seemed ambiguous. Although caused by an iceberg, it was also man-made, the result of the state of mind – grandiose, avaricious, and self-confident – of the British and American magnates and engineers who conceived and built the ship.

A further reason why this particular disaster is of permanent interest is that it happened slowly, unlike a jet airliner crash. Nobody expected it. Everyone on board, whether rich or poor, passenger or crew, was confronted with a sudden test, and given time to fumble or meet it.

Over the years, many images from the disaster have proved indelible, and many legends and rumours have circulated. Re-investigating the story, I have found that for most people the facts and rumours are inextricably entwined. Most people recall that the ship was travelling too fast: had not the captain been urged to set a record? The band was playing as she went down: was it not a hymn, or was it a jazz tune? And the other liner nearby: was there not a ship whose captain would have gone to the rescue if he had not assumed that the rockets he saw and the music he heard wafting across the water were evidence of revelry? And Captain Smith of the *Titanic*: surely the real reason for the collision was that he was drunk, a fact that subsequent inquiries hushed up under pressure from the Board of Trade and the shipping company?

My main purpose in writing this book has been to re-examine the evidence and tell the story as clearly and comprehensively as possible, trying to sift fact from fiction. Although many books may have been written about the *Titanic*, none has told the complete story, from the background of the building of the ship to the aftermath of the disaster. The early accounts, like the one by a fluent British journalist and man of letters, Filson Young, tended to be full of rhetoric but short on facts. Survivors quickly published moving, but inevitably incomplete, accounts. The United States Senate and the British Board of Trade inquiries produced hundreds of pages of verbatim testimony. Ballads were composed; memorials erected; sermons preached. The early books mostly turned the tragedy into a triumph for Anglo-Saxon phlegm. 'Before the doomed ship was engulfed in the devouring waters,' wrote Filson Young, 'there was a drama upon her decks more wonderful in its dignity and splendour than any that has been invented by the imagination.' Such remarks sparked off a vivid exchange as early as May 1912 between two great literary figures of the time, Bernard Shaw and Conan Doyle.[2] Shaw, for the iconoclasts, pointed out the discrepancies between the tales of heroism written up by the press and the grim realities revealed by the inquiries. 'The occasion has been disgraced by a callous outbreak of romantic lying,' he proclaimed. Conan Doyle, for the conservatives and traditionalists, maintained that the captain, crew, and survivors had indeed behaved in a heroic, exemplary, and quintessentially British manner. No subsequent account has settled the argument conclusively.

[2] See Appendix Two for the correspondence.

The best known book on the *Titanic*, Walter Lord's *A Night to Remember*, simply told the powerful story of the disaster itself, blow by blow. Subsequent writers have looked behind the facts, but have tended to promote a particular line or theory: thus Geoffrey Marcus, in *The Maiden Voyage*, published in 1969, states his suspicion of all official inquiries and argues that the British commission under Lord Mersey was a whitewash designed to protect the White Star shipping line and their officers. A book by an American clinical psychologist from Michigan, Wyn Craig Wade, aims to vindicate the senator from Michigan, William Alden Smith, who conducted the US inquiry, and turn him into the hero of the story. In these books one sometimes hears the grinding of an ideological or nationalistic axe.

I have approached the *Titanic* story as a reporter, but have also tried to explain its causes and repercussions; to see how the ship symbolized the shift of power across the Atlantic from Europe to the United States, and why this particular disaster has cast such a long shadow down seven decades, becoming a metaphor for the human predicament. I have visited, in North America, Northern Ireland, and England the main places that feature in the story, including Woods Hole, where most of the scientists who located the wreck of the *Titanic* in the summer of 1985 are based. I have talked to experts and to collectors and to the families and friends of survivors. I have not gone back to the handful of remaining survivors themselves – two or three in Britain, less than two dozen in the United States; they were very young then, and are of advanced age now; long ago, they said what they had to say.

The story is not ended yet. The blurred underwater photographs taken by the Woods Hole expedition have given it a bizarre new perspective. The *Titanic* has re-appeared; and the ship itself is set to be the final survivor. The last member of the crew, Sidney Daniels, died in Portsmouth in 1983. But the *Titanic* is still there, in reasonable shape, and one of the first photographs of her showed the crow's nest in which Fred Fleet, the lookout man, suddenly yanked his bell-pull three times, telephoned the bridge, and called out, 'Iceberg right ahead!' Many years after the sinking, Fred Fleet hanged himself on a clothes post in his brother-in-law's garden, but the telephone is still intact, two and a half miles down, on the bed of the Atlantic. Precisely what else may be down there, perhaps scattered across a mile or more of the ocean floor, will not be known for years yet, if ever. Wild schemes have been published that envisage raising the ship, towing her back to Belfast, where she was built, refitting her, and sailing her off to complete her maiden voyage, on the if-at-first-you-don't-succeed principle. The *Titanic* has always inspired fantasies.

From the world's imagination the *Titanic* never alto-gether vanished. She has inspired novels, an opera, and poems – latterly of a more sardonic kind than the heroic writings that immediately followed the sinking. The disas-ter has been seen as a turning point in history, a symbol of the change from a reasonably settled world to much more alarming times: 'The event,' as John Thayer of Philadelphia wrote twenty-eight years after he was res-cued, 'which not only made the world rub its eyes and awake, but woke it with a start, keeping it moving at a rapidly accelerating pace ever since, with less and less peace, satisfaction and happiness . . . To my mind, the world of today awoke April 15, 1912.' Osbert Sitwell described the sinking as 'a symbol of the approaching fate of Western Civilization'.

Even at the time, and certainly ever since, the *Titanic*

has been seen as a prime example of man tempting fate, or technological hubris, the event that made people wonder for the first time whether man's ingenuity would necessarily produce the beneficent results he hoped and expected it would. Some thought that the disaster, because it was so plainly the result of overweening pride, would teach the world a lesson. As the Bishop of Winchester said, preaching a sermon on the Sunday after the disaster, the iceberg had the right to be there; the *Titanic* did not. But her begetters' spiritual successors, not only in shipbuilding, continued on their merry way. Nevertheless, the *Titanic* is still lodged in people's minds as a warning, even though unheeded, of the dangers of human presumption.

Travelling round, I have been surprised to find how many mysteries still bedevil the event. Did the people who built her really think her unsinkable? How can anyone have thought it safe to belt through a region of ice at high speed? Did the rich really come off best? Should the half-filled lifeboats have tried harder to rescue the drowning? Was Captain Lord of the *Californian*, the ship that failed to go to the *Titanic's* rescue, rightly condemned? What was the role of the president of the huge international shipping combine that owned the *Titanic* – J. Bruce Ismay – who unlike his skipper did not go down with his ship? What was Marconi up to, and how was the *Titanic* linked to the Marconi scandal? Was Senator Smith as incompetent as the British Government privately thought? Was there a Lord Mersey cover-up?

I heard echoes of the *Titanic* story in recent events. The dispute in Whitehall, in 1985–6, about the sale of Westland Helicopters to an American giant closely parallels the concern felt by ministers at the turn of the century over predatory American attitudes to the proud British transatlantic shipping lines. In the gigantic 'build-up shop' at Harland & Wolff, I saw posters saying 'No' to the 1985 Hillsborough agreement between Britain and the Republic of Ireland – a reminder that the *Titanic* and the Home Rule Bill of 1912 were contemporaneous, and that the 'reef' on which the final Home Rule scheme was 'shipwrecked' (the words used in the standard constitutional history of modern Britain by D. L. Keir) was the fierce provincial sense of nationality of Ulstermen – especially as represented by the Protestant workers in the Harland & Wolff shipyards who joined Carson's Ulster volunteers to prepare for armed resistance to Home Rule. Again, when part of a British Airways jumbo jet landed in the garden of a house in Boston, late in 1985, the pilot's spokesman who said that aircraft inspection regulations had not kept up with airline developments was echoing the furore which followed the revelation in 1912 that Board of Trade rules about safety at sea had been outdated by advances in shipping technology, also across the Atlantic. When *Challenger* exploded, someone at Cape Canaveral said that such an incident had been thought impossible. But the loudest echo is still of the faint sound, described by a fireman, Jack Podesta, as 'like tearing a strip of calico, nothing more', that the iceberg made as it sliced into the hull of the *Titanic*.

1

The Evil Dream

In the 1860s, British industry was entering the most expansive and prosperous era it has ever known, or is ever likely to know. In particular, shipbuilding and transatlantic traffic were growing in volume year by year. It is impossible to understand the genesis of the *Titanic* without looking at the men who conceived the idea of a giant ship; and impossible to understand them, and the reasons why they ever imagined such an extraordinary vessel, without some notion of the tortuous and ruthlessly competitive international shipping business – British, German, American – of which they were part.

The man behind the *Titanic*, as it happens, was Canadian. He was born in Quebec in 1847 as William James Pirrie, the son of A. J. Pirrie, an Ulsterman of Scottish descent. His mother was also from Ulster, a member of the Montgomery family. After the father died, mother and son returned to Ireland, where the boy was apprenticed at the age of fifteen to the shipbuilding and engineering firm of Harland & Wolff. Pirrie was a partner in Harland & Wolff by the time he was twenty-seven. During the next half century, largely thanks to his leadership, it became the greatest shipyard in the world, and the birthplace of the *Titanic*.

People these days are inclined to think that the *Titanic* was a freak; a huge ship of unique size and luxury. This misunderstanding underrates the scale of the enterprise. Pirrie's idea, conceived in 1907, was that his firm, in partnership with the White Star Line, would build not one but three monster transatlantic liners. They would sweep the opposition off the seas. The first would be named the *Olympic*; the second the *Titanic*; and the third – according to report – the *Gigantic*.

All three were built. The *Olympic* had an illustrious career, carrying more troops than any other vessel in World War One. The *Gigantic*, prudently renamed the *Britannic*, was sunk by a German mine in 1916. Nowadays, nobody outside the passionate fraternity of lovers of old ships remembers this useful pair. But the *Titanic* became, as she has remained, the best-known of all ships to the man in the street, her name springing to mind more readily than the *Golden Hind*, the USS *Arizona*, or HMS *Victory*.

It is odd that Pirrie, the bold prime mover, has disappeared so completely from the story. Had he sailed in the *Titanic* on her maiden voyage, as he fully intended, he would have been better known. He would either have drowned, in which case he would have been as closely associated with the ship as her skipper, Captain Smith, and her richest passenger, Colonel J. J. Astor; or he would have escaped, in which case he would have been as universally reviled as the chairman of White Star who got away in one of the last lifeboats, J. Bruce Ismay. As it was, his doctor forbade him to take the trip because of prostate trouble; he was too ill to testify in the much-publicized official inquiries that followed; and after their reports came out it was too late for anyone to ask him awkward questions. His role receded into the past. His hair turned white during his illness, but he remained the great shipbuilder. Indeed the business done by his world-beating yards actually boomed, because they reconstructed many ships after the disaster to make them conform to the new rules officially imposed as a result of the defects exposed in their prize product. In World War One, Lord Pirrie was in charge of all British merchant shipbuilding. He was made a baron in 1909; he became a viscount in 1921. He died at sea in 1924 from pneumonia in the Panama Canal, returning with his wife from a voyage on Harland & Wolff business to South America.

To find the source of Pirrie's grand ideas and confidence, we need to look back at the atmosphere of those early years. Belfast had a long shipbuilding tradition, but it was only around the time that Pirrie became an apprentice that Harland & Wolff started on its rapid rise to world dominance. The founding father was a restless engineering genius from Yorkshire, Edward Harland, who in 1858 bought a small boatbuilding business on Queen's Island, which is still part of the Harland & Wolff site today. Harland was no traditionalist. His main reforms, according to his successors in Belfast, were two: he replaced wooden upper decks with iron decks, thus in effect turning the hull into a box girder of immensely greater strength; and he changed the shape of the hulls by giving them a flat bottom and square bilges, thus increasing their capacity. He also did away with the relics of sailing ship days, bowsprits and figureheads, though his steamships were still carrying sails until nearly the end of the century.

The stroke of luck in Harland's career was to catch the eye, early on, of Hamburg Jews. One of them, a financier named Gustavus Schwabe, came to Liverpool and put money into a rising local shipping firm, the Bibby Line, and gave repair and building contracts to Harland. Schwabe's nephew, an engineer like Harland, became Harland's partner. His name was Gustav Wolff. In Harland & Wolff's present-day order book, which lists in numerical order the 1500 ships they have built in their hundred-and-twenty-five-year history, numbers one, two, and three are Bibby Line ships.

Harland and Wolff joined forces just before Pirrie

arrived in their yards as an apprentice. With every year that passed, their business expanded. In 1864, the gross tonnage of the ships they built was 30,000 tons. In 1884, the figure was 104,000. Pirrie's career was contemporaneous with the development of steel shipbuilding, and he himself was in the forefront of all the important advances in naval architecture and marine engineering. He took over as chairman when Harland died in 1894; so he was thirty years under Harland, and thirty years on his own as chairman.

He was more than chairman: he was a dictator. Physically, he was small and ferociously energetic. He craved public recognition. He stood out from his rivals because he was not only a master-technocrat but a master-businessman. The members of his board were ciphers. He secured the orders for ships himself, built them to his own designs with little more than a general specification from the clients, and charged them the building costs plus a four per cent commission for Harland & Wolff – a highly satisfactory way of doing business. (It was when the firm built the *Canberra* for P & O on a fixed price contract that it lost millions and virtually went broke.) Apart from Pirrie, nobody knew or was even allowed to discuss his firm's finances; one of the ship architects who inadvertently became involved in financial talks with a shipowner was summarily dismissed. When Pirrie was away from Belfast, meetings were chaired by his wife.

Though forgotten now, Pirrie was lauded in his own day, when engineers were national figures. The celebrated journalist W. T. Stead, who was drowned in the *Titanic*, praised Pirrie's 'foresight, optimism, incessant industry and selection of able lieutenants (a sure sign of superior ability)' and proclaimed that he had developed 'the greatest business of the kind that has existed in the world since men first began to go down to the seas in ships'. The verdict of the *Dictionary of National Biography* is that he was 'the creator of the big ship'.

How did this happen? The starting point may be said to have been the alliance between Harland & Wolff and White Star.

The important new figure who enters the story here is the formidable T. H. Ismay. His father had been a boatbuilder in a small way in Maryport, Cumberland. In 1869 – not long after Pirrie joined Harland & Wolff – T. H. Ismay bought, with Schwabe's financial backing, the flag of White Star, a company that had made a name on the Australian run, shipping optimistic emigrants to the goldfields.

White Star's history, as it happened, contained an odd prelude to the *Titanic*. In 1863, the company took delivery of a fine ship called the *Royal Standard*, advertised as the latest word in seagoing comfort: 'Her saloons are spacious and handsomely furnished, with everything requisite for the voyage, including bedding, linen, piano, library, etc.' She was launched in the summer of 1863 and on 4 April 1864, 14 days out of Melbourne and homeward bound, she struck an iceberg. 'Destruction seemed inevitable,' said her master. She was making ten knots under sail when she struck; the iceberg towered 600 feet above her, he said. The main and mizzen masts snapped, the starboard lifeboat was smashed, and her starboard quarter was stove in, though her hull was of iron. For half an hour the ship rubbed along the flank of the iceberg, reckoned by the master to be a quarter of a mile long, before she could break away; 35 days later she limped into Rio.

The Australian run was profitable, but it was small beer, as Schwabe and Ismay saw, by comparison with the glittering new opportunities offered by the Atlantic. The whole secret of the growth of the shipping companies and the size of the ships they built is to be found in the extraordinary expansion, unparallelled in history, of the population of the United States. During the half century between 1840, when Samuel Cunard's *Britannia* inaugurated the first transatlantic steamship service, and 1890, trade between the United States and Britain rose sevenfold, in cotton, tobacco and wheat, with Liverpool as its focus. At the same time, the population of the United States quadrupled. Cunard were not slow to realize that their business could not expand by relying on mail, cargo, and first-class passengers alone; so they also started to carry steerage passengers, cashing in on the flood of immigrants from Britain as well as continental Europe. Bigger ships and longer passenger lists were the keys to profit; but the expanding market also attracted competitors. Ismay's White Star, financed by Schwabe and building all its ships at Harland & Wolff's yards, was challenging Cunard on the Atlantic routes by the early 1870s; and by the 1880s the great German shipowners joined the battle as well.

Then came the Americans and J. P. Morgan. The impact of American capital on the shipping business had been long delayed, partly because of the American Civil War, and partly because the new breed of industrialists and financiers had been fully occupied opening up the continent with oil, steel, and railways. But when it came it was devastating. It started when a company that later became part of the Morgan combine acquired Inman Lines of Liverpool, which gave the Americans access to British shipbuilding technology. At White Star, correctly identifying the threat, T. H. Ismay attempted to assemble a consortium of British shipowners to save the ailing company, but the other shipowners would not listen to him. The issues and arguments were much the same as those of 1986, when the British Cabinet split over whether

Westland Helicopters should be sold to the American giant, Sikorsky. Ismay's warnings, like those of the Minister of Defence, Michael Heseltine, went unheeded.

It was one of the few failures of his career and one that he always regretted. Shortly before he died in 1899, leaving more than a million, an interviewer asked him about his principles of business success. He named two. First, he said, don't be too greedy; always let someone else make a bit. Second, never let a weak man go out of your trade if it means letting a strong one in. He instanced the shipowners' refusal to save Inman. 'And now,' he said, 'we have an American railway company come into the trade, with millions at its back, running under a well-known British flag, and setting us all to work building whether we want it or not.'

Morgan's aim was to establish in the Atlantic the same sort of business that he was used to at home: a monopoly. With Pirrie's help, he forced through an amalgamation with the big German lines, North German Lloyd and Hamburg-Amerika. He then launched the most vicious fare war in shipping history, offering third-class trans-atlantic passages for as little as £2. His principal target was Cunard. Having driven the company into financial trouble by his price-cutting, he then tried to buy it, and was only repulsed when the British government, alarmed by the idea of a great British asset passing into foreign hands, came to the rescue with substantial and favourable subsidies. The condition of the subsidies was openly nationalistic. 'Under no circumstances shall the management of the company be in the hands of, or the shares of the company held by, other than British subjects.'

Pirrie had quickly seen the Morgan threat. The source of much of his business, White Star, was as vulnerable as Cunard: profits reduced by the fare war, short of capital for new ships. Schwabe had died in 1890, Ismay in 1899.

Ismay's son, J. Bruce Ismay, was relatively inexperienced. Pirrie saw that unless drastic action was taken White Star would drop further and further out of the battle and build fewer and fewer ships in Pirrie's shipyards. His solution was unattractive, but practical. Instead of opposing Morgan's ambitions, he supported them. Three years after Ismay Senior died, Morgan with Pirrie as an intermediary swallowed White Star. The head of Cunard, Lord Inverclyde, acquired considerable prestige from the skilful way he exploited Morgan's bid in order to extract favourable loans from the government, while yielding none of his company's independence. But at the very time that Inverclyde was concluding these advantageous arrangements, J. Bruce Ismay was being forced to sell – not least by the pressure of his father's old ally, Pirrie.

The transaction was a financier's cat's-cradle. It had been the International Navigation Company of Philadelphia, with the Pennsylvania Railroad Company, that had acquired Inman Lines. In 1902, the International Navigation Company had changed its name to the International Mercantile Marine Company. This company, with Pirrie on the British board, acquired practically all the shares in the Oceanic Steam Navigation Company, which had always owned the ships of the White Star Line, of which Ismay, Imrie & Co. were managers. Morgan then registered the Oceanic Company shares in the name of the International Navigation Company of Liverpool, a subsidiary of the International Mercantile Marine Company, which in its turn transferred the shares to two trust companies in the United States as security for certain bonds.

Given the intricate nature of Morgan's combine, it is not surprising that the absoluteness of his control of White Star was not fully appreciated. The *Titanic* was generally regarded as a British ship. Even Lord Mersey, with his Liverpool background, was taken aback in the Board of Trade inquiry into the *Titanic's* sinking when he learned that the White Star Company's seagoing rules, under which the *Titanic*, like all other White Star vessels, had been operating, had been drawn up in the United States. Morgan had seen how his bid for Cunard had alarmed the British. All White Star ships were to be officered by British subjects and to fly the British flag. A majority of the directors were to be British. The original Ismay company of Ismay, Imrie & Co. became a shell, but Bruce Ismay remained chairman of White Star and was soon persuaded by Morgan to become president of International Mercantile. The appointment looked impressive on paper, but for J. Bruce Ismay it was a humiliation.

These were significant events in the tilting of industrial power away from Britain and towards the United States. One great British company, Cunard, had had to be baled out by the government – an early example of state intervention. Another equally prominent British company, virtually a national institution, had been taken over. The effect of the White Star deal was to bring together British technology, in the shape of Harland & Wolff, and American capital. This was the conjunction that produced the *Titanic*.

But it was not changes of ownership alone that produced the drive towards bigger and bigger ships. Despite Ismay Senior's complaint that it was the American newcomers who kept the British shipowners building whether they liked it or not, it was an economic force much more fundamental than J. P. Morgan's aggression that constantly pushed the owners forward. Once the technology was available, the growth in the size of ships was unstoppable, whether anyone wanted them or not. Taking emigrants to the United States was more profitable than government mail contracts or high-class passenger traffic. Nor was the emigrant traffic all one way. At one stage, 100,000 disappointed or homesick Britons were annually heading home. The snag was that the emigrant market was wholly unpredictable, depending as it did on famine or repression or fashion. The seesaw demand meant that the owners needed to look sharp to make the most of it; hence the fare wars; and hence the need to attract and carry more and more passengers, to cover rising costs and make a modest return on capital. As the chairman of the White Star line wrote in Lloyd's List in 1924, looking back at 'steamships of the monster type' and their history: 'This extensive third-class business has been a very potent factor in the development of the fleets of the principal companies, and has culminated in the super-liners of today.'

Influenced by narrative paintings of the nineteenth century, we are inclined to assume that the desperate emigrants who poured from the slums of Europe into the slums of New York or Chicago took any ship they could find. But the images of women on deck wearing shawls and surrounded by wide-eyed children are misleading. Cunard took most seriously a complaint from one steerage passenger, evidently representative of many, who said that he had been treated as if the company was doing him a personal favour in conveying him across the Atlantic. It was not only first-class passengers who could be attracted by extra space; so could the huddled masses. Every pressure was in the direction of size. Cunard built the *Bothnia* of 4555 tons in 1874, the *Umbria* of 7718 tons in 1884, the *Campania* of 12,950 tons in 1893. White Star replied with the *Teutonic* and *Majestic*. The Germans by the turn of the century had deployed an imperial race of four-funnelled monsters with names to match: *Kaiser Wilhelm der Grosse, Kronprinz Wilhelm, Kaiser*

Wilhelm II, Kronprinzessin Cecile. In 1899, as Ismay
Senior was dying, White Star came up with the *Oceanic*,
17,274 tons and 705 feet long, the first ship to be longer
than Brunel's white elephant of 1858, the *Great Eastern*,
and the largest steamship in the world.

In the archives of Harland & Wolff is a book of
photographs of the *Oceanic* presented to Thomas
Andrews Esq., Pirrie's nephew and later one of the
designers of the *Titanic*, with the compliments of Ismay,
Imrie. The frontispiece is of Thomas H. Ismay, his hair
slightly curled and his determined mouth in a faint smile.
The internal decor of the ship is that of an Edwardian
country house, not surprisingly since one of the architects
was R. Norman Shaw. The principal saloon featured
Ionic pillars. In the smokeroom was a representation of a
bacchanalian procession inspired by a poem of Dryden.
Carved trophies of fruit and flowers in the style of
Grinling Gibbons decorated other parts of the first-class
accommodation, and so did allegorical female figures of
Great Britain, America, Liverpool, and New York, who
is holding a rudder and a coil of rope. A Harland &
Wolff archivist has tucked into the back of this lavish
book an article from a contemporary magazine, which
featured a series of statistics and cartoons to dramatize
the size of the new ship. A hen would have to lay an egg
every day until the middle of 1967 to produce the number
of eggs carried on each trip. The volume of 'jams, jellies
and marmalade' aboard would fill a jar 6 feet high and
14 feet and 1¾ inches in diameter. Alice of *Alice in
Wonderland* was shown standing on a ladder gazing in
wonder down into the jar.

The century opened with both White Star and Cunard
in a position to move their new ships up a few notches in
size. Cunard moved first. The government had given
them the subsidies partly so that they would build two big

ships that could be turned into armed transports in time
of war. By 1907, these two were ready for service, the
Lusitania and the *Mauretania*, both of them not only
larger but much faster than anything afloat. The *Mauretania* at once became especially loved and fashionable.
Henry James crossed to England in her in 1911 and met
Thomas Edison on board; the liner lifted James across
the seas 'as if I had been carried in a gigantic grandmother's bosom and the gentle giantess had made but
one mighty stride of it from land to land'. When she was
broken up in 1935, President Franklin D. Roosevelt
presented a model of her to the Smithsonian Museum in
Washington and wrote a sentimental private memorial,
calling her an 'old dowager' and recalling the hand-carved
panels of Latvian oak in her dining-room.

This was the daunting new competition that White Star
had to beat. They were running a regular express service
from Southampton to New York with *Teutonic*, *Oceanic*,
and *Adriatic*, but these were no match for the crack
Cunarders. How was White Star to reply? It would be
hopelessly uneconomic to try to compete with Cunard for
speed. More speed would mean less passenger and cargo
space. The leapfrog must be to go for extreme size, and
attract the urgently needed extra passengers by providing
special luxury for the rich and more spacious accommodation for the poor.

It would be wrong to give the impression that everyone
was enthusiastic about bigger ships. Complaints about
size went back a long time. In 1776 William Julius Mickle
published his translation of *The Lusiad*, Camoens's epic
poem about the discovery of India by Vasco da Gama.
He described *The Lusiad* as 'the Epic Poem of the Birth
of Commerce'. But he added, in one of his voluminous
notes expounding the growth of trade, that 'the Portu-
guese historians ascribe the shipwreck of many Portu-
guese vessels on the voyage between Europe and India to

the avarice of their owners, in building them of an enormous bulk, of 4, 5, and 600 tons'. Captain Cook's two vessels, he observed, had been of 462 and 336 tons respectively. In the nineteenth century, professional misgivings surfaced when a royal commission was appointed in 1873 to inquire into 'unseaworthy ships'. One of the leading partners in Cunard, Charles McIver, told the commission about the danger of building ships that were too long in relation to their width. Another prominent Liverpool shipowner, Alfred Hold, agreed. So did McIver's sons, who were also employed by Cunard. All three McIvers were forced to resign; and Cunard set out to rebuild its fleet faster, heavier, and longer than ever.

Twenty years later, the greatest and most prophetic of American historians, Henry Adams, visited the Chicago Exposition, a display of the wonders of the industrial and artistic world. Eight or ten years of study, as he explained, had led Adams to think that he might use the thirteenth century as the unit from which he could measure motion down to his own time. What could he learn from the Exposition about the course of history, and the effect on it of the new sciences? He was especially concerned to try to understand 'the law of acceleration', the speed of progress. Fifty years earlier, he reflected, science had taken it for granted that the rate of acceleration could not last: scientists encouraged laymen to think that force would be limited in supply. It then emerged that

force was inexhaustible . . . Nothing so revolutionary had happened since the year 300 . . . Impossibilities no longer stood in the way. One's life had fattened on impossibilities. Before the boy [he meant himself] was six years old, he had seen four impossibilities made actual – the ocean-steamer, the railway, the electric telegraph, and the Daguerreotype; nor could he ever learn which of the four had most hurried the others to come. He had seen the coal-output of the United States grow from nothing to 300 million tons or more.

Adams was born in 1838, the year when crossing the Atlantic by steamship became feasible for the first time. Railroads had begun by then to radiate out from the eastern cities; Samuel B. Morse sent the first electric telegraph message in 1844. Daguerreotype, the first successful photographic process, was invented in France by Louis Daguerre in 1839. Force, or power, ruled the rate of man's progress, and society had by common accord agreed in measuring its progress by coal-output, the world's principal source of energy. The coal-output of the world, said Adams, had roughly doubled every ten years between 1840 and 1900. This rate of acceleration might seem exaggerated, but it could be tested. 'Perhaps the ocean steamer is nearest unity and easiest to measure, for anyone might hire, in 1905, for a small sum of money, the use of 30,000 steam-horse-power to cross the ocean, and by halving this figure for every ten years he got back to 234 horse-power for 1835, which was accuracy enough for his purposes.'

In Chicago, Adams studied with special attention the exhibit by Cunard.

Historical exhibits were common, but they never went far enough; none were thoroughly worked out. One of the best was that of Cunard steamers, but still a student hungry for results found himself obliged to waste a pencil and several sheets of paper trying to calculate exactly when, according to the given increase of power, tonnage, and speed, the growth of the ocean steamer would reach its limits. His figures brought him, he thought, to the year 1927; another generation to spare before force, space, and time should meet. The ocean liner ran the surest line of triangulation to the future, because it was the nearest of man's products to a unity

– the best single example of his multifarious skills.

Henry Adams published *The Education of Henry Adams*, which contained these reflections, in 1906. They were already out of date, for even he had underestimated the 'rate of acceleration'. He had written about an ocean steamer generating 30,000 horsepower in 1905. But the Cunarder *Lucania* already generated that amount of power in 1893, and the *Lusitania*, launched the year after *The Education*, generated 68,000 horsepower. (His prediction about the date of the biggest ocean liner was only a decade too early: Cunard's *Queen Elizabeth*, whose maiden voyage had to be postponed because of World War Two, was the biggest liner ever built, at 83,000 gross tons.)

The decision to build White Star's three monsters was taken as the *Mauretania* and *Lusitania* were coming into service. According to tradition, Pirrie and Bruce Ismay met one evening at Pirrie's London house in Belgravia and sketched out their plans 'over coffee and cigars'. *Olympic* and *Titanic* were to be a hundred feet longer than the Cunarders, only four or five knots slower, and at 46,000 tons no less than 15,000 tons bigger. They were to be built regardless of cost, and regardless of complaints from harbour boards that there was no room for them. New York was especially angry. To make the boards realize they were living in the past, Pirrie replied that it was his ambition to build a liner of a thousand feet long, and he did not rule out the possibility of a ship of 100,000 tons.

He certainly thought on a grand scale. At the time he was drawing up the plans, there was not only no dock big enough on either side of the Atlantic to take the new ships, but no yard big enough to build them either. Harland & Wolff had to construct specially strengthened slips to bear the weight.

They are still there. Not long ago, I went to see them, wondering what traces were left of Lord Pirrie's ambitions. I met my guide, Mr Tommy McCluskey, at the Belfast docks, in the main Harland & Wolff offices – red brick and little changed since Pirrie's day – who led me a hundred yards out of the back door and stopped. We stood surrounded by a wasteland of cracked and discoloured concrete, empty apart from a row of parked company cars and scattered piles of rusty metal. 'This is where she was built,' he said. Then he added wryly, 'The *Titanic* is one of our better known vessels.'

Away to our right rose two huge yellow gantries, known as Samson and Goliath. Like enormous goalposts, they straddle a dry dock in which four banana boats for Vestey's were recently built all at the same time, a dock so huge that it could accommodate, if a mad latter-day Pirrie required such a thing, a vessel of a million tons. So no theoretical limit to the size of ships had yet been reached? Mr McCluskey shrugged. 'A million tons is possible,' he said, 'though improbable.'

In one of the first books written about the *Titanic* after she went down, the journalist and man of letters Filson Young called her 'monstrous', and an 'evil dream', and 'unthinkable'. Standing in the concrete wasteland, I remembered his rhetoric about her construction. As his mail steamer from Fleetwood glided through the mud flats, he had heard, he claimed, a noise like bees in a giant hive. This 'sonorous murmuring', as he drew closer, turned into 'the multitudinous clamour of thousands and thousands of blows of metal on metal coming from a veritable forest of iron, a leafless forest of thousands upon thousands of rusty trunks [carrying] a multitude of pigmy men swarming and toiling amid the skeleton iron structures.' It was 'in this awful womb', Filson Young goes on, 'that the *Titanic* took shape'. At the sight of it, men held their breaths:

It was the shape of a ship, a ship so monstrous and unthinkable that it towered high over the buildings and dwarfed the very mountains beside the water. It seemed like some impious blasphemy that man should fashion this most monstrous and ponderable of all his creations into the likeness of a thing that could float upon the yielding waters . . . Yet, like an evil dream, as it took the shape of a giant ship, all the properties of a ship began to appear and increase in hideous exaggeration. A rudder as big as a giant elm tree, bosses and bearings of propellers as big as the size of a windmill – everything was on a nightmare scale.

Old photographs pinned up in the company photographer's office show that the gantry dominated the shipyard and the city. These days, the biggest structures in the yard, apart from Samson and Goliath, are grain silos, massive sheds, and a fertilizer factory. But harbours and shipyards change slowly. Ships still use the four-mile Victoria Channel between the flats, as the *Titanic* did, once. Cave Hill and Black Mountain are unchanged, except for television masts. The spire of St Joseph's, the church in Dock Road, is still a landmark. One floating relic of *Titanic* days, moored in Milewater Basin, is an old light cruiser, HMS *Caroline*, built by Harland & Wolff and a survivor of the Battle of Jutland, scrupulously cared for and used now as a training base for the naval reserves, and still with her original funnels, masts, and fighting top.

The row of huts used by the foremen who supervised the *Titanic*'s construction is still standing, though now tumbledown, with broken windows. So is the long concrete ramp some thirty feet across with a slope of four or five degrees on which the *Titanic*'s hull was built. Its purpose, Mr McCluskey explained, was to tilt the hull so that when launched it would slide easily over the greased keel-blocks wedged underneath and into the water. The bow would have projected over the end of the ramp. One could estimate where the pigmies had lifted and riveted the plates of the 300 feet of hull ripped open by the iceberg.

Other relics were embedded in the concrete: narrow rails, like tramlines, for the cranes bringing in the plates; and holes the size of half an orange. Mr McCluskey gouged the mud out of one of these holes with his toecap, and revealed a rusty iron ring that would have held the base of one of the wooden posts supporting the scaffolding's outer skeleton. We walked to the far end of the slipway where it met the water. In the old days, massive dock gates like a high wooden fence stood here to stop incoming tides from flooding the slipway. Because water inevitably seeped through, a pump was needed to pump out the ditch between gates and slipway. This pumping station, built underground, survives, though flooded; peering down into the brown water, you can see the submerged wheel that controlled one of the valves. Somebody turned this wheel on 31 May 1911, when shortly after noon, in the presence of J. P. Morgan, the dock gates were withdrawn, the hydraulic rams at the far end of the concrete ramp gave the *Titanic* a push, and the ship was launched while (according to Filson Young) the 'thousands of pigmy men who had roosted in the bare iron branches, who had raised the hideous clamour amid which the giant was born, greeted their handiwork, dropped their tools, and raised their hoarse voices in a cheer. The miracle had happened.'

Big ships are not launched at Harland & Wolff today, since – unlike the shorter *Titanic* – they would bend in the middle as the first half reached the water. They are built in the giant dry dock and then floated out. Nor are they riveted; they are welded by machines controlled by computers. In its heyday, Harland & Wolff employed 40,000 or 50,000 men; now, partly because of new technology and partly because of a slump in shipbuilding, it employs 6300, which accounts for the deserted nature of much of its 300 acres and for the silence that is the most striking difference between the yards now and the yards in 1911.

The glories as well as the decibels have declined since 1911, but it is still easy to find old men whose self-esteem is grounded on the skill they showed at the shipyards in the days when Harland & Wolff led the world.

One of them, Mr Dick Sweeney, keeps a rivet of *Titanic* vintage in his house for old times' sake, a big squat nail three inches long, made of pure iron and as thick as a man's thumb. Three million rivets like this went into the *Titanic*; some of them are visible in the underwater photographs of the wreck taken in the summers of 1985 and 1986. In his trim front room on a hillside overlooking the shipyards, Mr Sweeney, a wiry man, said he had worked in the yards for most of his life, and his uncle and grandfather had worked on the *Titanic*. Most Belfast people, he said, thought the sinking not so much a night to remember as a night to forget. 'They were ashamed it wasn't as unsinkable as they said it was. It wasn't a good achievement, was it, to build the boat and get it sunk? That's the way Belfast people looked at it.'

Remembering Joseph Conrad's simile about the *Titanic* being ripped open like a Huntley & Palmer biscuit tin, I asked Mr Sweeney to tell me exactly how its hull had been put together. The plates of the *Titanic*, he said, were of iron.

They called it steel-plate, but it was not really high-class steel in those days; it was really raw hard iron. Most ships now are made of high tensile steel, which is much tougher. I was a welder. They built the first oil rig in the world at Harland & Wolff and the caulkers – the men who trim off the steel after it has been automatically welded – couldn't cut that metal; it turned their tools. Of course the whole of the *Titanic* was hand-riveted, a massive job. They started at six in the morning and went on until half past five at night, working in squads of four. First the 'heater boys' heated up the rivets. They were called heater boys, but they might be fifty. They had a long pair of tongs and they poked the rivets into a coke brazier for three or four minutes, keeping the brazier hot by working a bellows with their foot. Then they threw the rivet to a 'catch boy' and he put the stalk of the rivet into a hole through two overlapping plates. Then a man called the 'holder up' put a big heavy hammer under the panhead on the rivet, which was of pure iron, and held on to it while the fourth man beat it and flattened it into the hole. The outside hull, the shell, was worked on by special men called 'shell-riveters', and the men who hammered in the rivets were divided into the right-handers and the left-handers who were known as 'cloot-men', cloot meaning left. They used a light sledge hammer weighing about five pounds. You didn't need to be big and tough so much as wiry, with skill in using your muscles. They'd do about 200 rivets a day in the *Titanic* time, provided it didn't rain. If it did, the wet horn would sound and they would all have to go home. For the time they had to be at home they didn't get paid; they were paid from horn to horn by the number of rivets they put in.

I asked him about the *Titanic*'s double bottom, claimed at the time to be an effective safety feature, although it only came up seven feet above the keel. The outer skin was an inch thick, the idea being that if this skin was pierced the inner hull, although thinner, would keep out the water. An inch thick, I said, did not sound very thick to me. Mr Sweeney demurred. An inch was very thick; most ships now would have a hull of $7/8$ or $3/4$ inch plate. The bulkheads of the *Titanic* were half an inch thick – the divisions inside the ship that the boilers apparently crashed through when she stood on end before sinking.

Mr Sweeney offered me a cup of tea and shook his head. 'They thought it was really unsinkable.'

Before I left, Mr Sweeney hinted at something special about the *Titanic*'s construction, something I found hard to interpret. He recalled that, at the time, Ireland was rent by the Home Rule controversy. The country was divided, he said, so it would be only natural, would it not, if the shipyards were divided also? He implied that he had heard, from his uncle and grandfather, stories of political disaffection among their fellow workers. Certainly, given that many of the men, if not most, believed that the government at Westminster was planning to betray them, they had no reason to feel pro-English, and it was an English company – or they thought it was an English company – that was building the ship. Pirrie himself cannot have been popular; he was a Home Ruler and on one occasion clashed violently with Orangemen. Was Mr Sweeney implying that political disaffection had led to sabotage, or at least that the job had not been done as well as it might have been? He retreated from any such allegation; but it hung in the air. I thought of a photograph I had seen earlier in Harland & Wolff's offices. It showed men pouring out of the yards at the end of a day's work, some smoking clay-pipes – the picture was pin-sharp – and some wearing peaked caps, led by two small boys with bare feet; in the background rose the scaffolding of the *Titanic* and the *Olympic*. The picture seemed laden with doom. The *Titanic* was doomed, and so were the men. Some of them joined the volunteer force raised by Sir Edward Carson to resist Home Rule, and later the Ulster Regiment that was cut to ribbons on the Somme. Mr Sweeney probably had heard tales of work deliberately skimped by these men, but even if the tales were true their secret protests would not have affected the *Titanic*'s fate, though the men could have thought differently, which might account both for Mr Sweeney's readiness to plant the idea in my mind and for his reluctance to enlarge on it. His hesitant testimony seemed still more interesting in retrospect, after the 1986 Woods Hole expedition reported that the *Titanic* had burst open down a seam of rivets.

He said again before I left, 'They really thought it was unsinkable.' But did they? I found it hard to believe that anyone, even at the height of Edwardian self-confidence, could ever have believed in the possibility of an 'unsinkable' ship, least of all the hard and experienced shipbuilders and shipowners of Belfast and Liverpool.

The answer, as I learned later, is that although the owners and builders were confident that they had done everything possible to make the *Titanic* safe, there is no evidence that they thought or said she was unsinkable – though plenty of other people did. One of the early journalists into the field after the sinking was Sir Philip Gibbs, a prolific popular author. In his pamphlet *The Deathless Story of the Titanic*, a paradoxical title, he quoted what he said was the owner's description of the watertight doors: 'Each door is held in the open position by a suitable friction clutch, which can be instantly released by means of a powerful electric magnet controlled by the captain's bridge, so that, in the event of an accident, or at any time when it might be considered advisable, the captain can, by simply moving an electric switch, instantly close the doors throughout – practically making the vessel unsinkable.' Gibbs said that the last five words were written in italics. They read now, he said, 'with a dreadful irony'. A contemporary shipping journal also used the words 'practically unsinkable'. The idea spread, and the qualifier was lost. Time and again at the official inquiries passengers and crew testified that they had reacted slowly to the collision because they

thought the *Titanic* unsinkable. Several people continued
to think so even after they were in the lifeboats.

The explanation of this extraordinary but widespread
delusion – nobody today could think a ship unsinkable –
must have had something to do with the spirit of the
times, the confidence exuded by believers in progress like
Pirrie, and the consequential confidence engendered in
others, whether they knew anything about ships or not.
That anyone should be drowned in a Harland & Wolff
ship was highly improbable. True, one of their ships had
been shipwrecked on her maiden voyage, but the captain
had been drunk, which was scarcely the fault of the
shipbuilders. As for White Star, the managing director
Harold Sanderson told the Board of Trade inquiry that
the total number of passengers carried in the ten years
before the *Titanic*'s voyage had been 2,179,594 and the
loss of life two; both lives – of first-class passengers –
were lost in 1902 when the *Republic* collided with the
Florida. Besides, the construction of the ship paid special
attention to safety. The wireless installation was particularly powerful, with three different sources of supply, one
from the ordinary electric light plant in the engine room,
one elsewhere in case the engine room flooded, and a
third from storage batteries in the Marconi Room itself.
The double bottom was deep enough to allow a man to
walk through it upright, and was bigger than usual, being
carried above the bilge instead of stopping short under it.
The pumping arrangements were exceptional, since every
boiler compartment had its own pumping equipment.
Finally, the structure featured plating and connections of
extra strength, and with an unusual number of watertight
bulkheads, fifteen in all.

Descriptions of the *Titanic* in the technical journals
before she sailed took pride in her sheer size. *Engineering*,

a very sober publication, called the *Titanic*'s height 'splendid': 104 feet from keel to navigating bridge. It gave the statistics of the biggest ship in the world: length overall of 882 feet 9 inches, extreme breadth of 92 feet, gross tonnage of 46,328 tons – about 1000 tons heavier than her sister ship the *Olympic* – and an anticipated 'continuous sea speed of 21 knots'. Twenty-nine boilers, the journal continued, having in all 159 furnaces, were arranged in six separate watertight compartments. She was certified for 905 persons in first class, 564 in second, 1134 in third, and a crew of 944 – a total of 3547. The machinery was exhaustively described and accompanied by many precise drawings and some photographs, of which the most startling shows a man dwarfed by a receding row of monstrous boilers. Particularly notable from *Engineering*'s point of view, apart from the size, was the combination of quadruple expansion engines operating the two-wing propellers and a low pressure turbine for the centre screw.

Having dealt thoroughly with the boilers, *Engineering* took a tour of the passenger accommodation. It concluded that the *Titanic*'s special attractions lay in the Turkish baths with shampooing-rooms, the swimming bath, the gymnasium with gym instructor, and the squash court, which was 30 feet long and 20 feet wide (still the standard dimensions). *Engineering*'s big-ship reporter was plainly not a squash player. He conceded that the court was 'an interesting development', but added that 'the game is most popular with the Americans'. He singled out the swimming bath as the new feature that 'should appeal particularly to passengers. It is arranged much on the lines of an ordinary swimming bath on land, and is fitted with dressing boxes and fresh-water sprays.' One arrangement he approved was the fully carpeted first-class restaurant in which (unlike the dining-room) you could dine à la carte, an advantage 'more consonant with modern ideas as to diet'.

After the *Titanic* went down, posthumous descriptions concentrated on her conspicuous display. In beauty and luxury she had no rival, wrote Sir Philip Gibbs.

All that the genius of modern life has invented for comfort and adornment was lavished upon her in a prodigal spirit; all that wealth and art can attain in splendour was given to her decoration. The imagination of old story tellers writing of fabulous ships paled before the actuality of this magnificence . . . Here any passenger might sit in a tropical verandah restaurant, where vines grew upon the lattice work of windows through which there streamed – artificial light! It was called the Café Parisien, and here at night the band played the gayest tunes of life . . . The dining rooms, state rooms, and common rooms were furnished in various periods and styles, copied faithfully from old models, so that English gentlemen might sit in rooms panelled and adorned like those of Haddon Hall, and fair women might have their beauty reflected in oval mirrors hanging upon walls like those of Versailles when Marie Antoinette played with her ladies. For the payment of £870 per voyage the richest man on earth would not lack a single comfort that his wealth might buy.

All this was, in a sense, true, and Sir Philip omitted the feature of the *Titanic* which seems most extraordinary today: the Edwardian opulence of the best cabins. Some of them had Adam fireplaces that burned coal in their sitting rooms and, in the bedrooms, full-size double four-poster beds. The two grandest suites, fifty feet long, had private promenade decks. Every style of architecture was represented: Elizabethan, Dutch, Adam, Louis Quatorze, Louis Quinze, Queen Anne. In the reading room there were sash and bow windows. Even the third-class (or steerage) cabins were perfectly adequate for a five-day trip, four bunks to a cabin, with washbasin. From the photographs, it looks as though the standard of comfort in the third-class public rooms was about the same as it is on a present-day cross-Channel ferry. The great difference between the third and first class was that the third class still looked like a ship, with pipes and girders showing, whereas in the first class all the construction was hidden behind panelling or tapestries.

The idea of decorating a ship so that it seemed like a very large house or hotel reached a climax in the *Titanic*. But the idea itself was not new. Beatrice Lillie's famous quip as she stepped aboard the *Queen Mary* – 'Say, when does this place get to New York?' – could have been made at the turn of the century. Pirrie visited the best hotels in England, on the Continent, and in the United States to work up the interior designs of Harland & Wolff liners. The *Liverpool Daily Post* had said the *Oceanic* would cross the Atlantic 'with the speed and certainty of an express train – the conquest of the mighty force of matter by the mighty force of mind', and then described her as 'a triumph of art, as the last thing, so far, in the way of floating hotels . . . now mahogany; now oak; now satinwood'. The lavatories were of 'costly marble. It is the literal truth to say that the *Oceanic* is the Hotel Cecil afloat.'

Boastfulness as well as decor reached a climax with the *Titanic*. No record survives of who thought of the name that has helped to make her famous. In the old days, names had been more modest; *Golden Hind* for Drake, *Endeavour* for Captain Cook. Ismay Senior started the custom of giving White Star ships names that ended in 'ic': *Oceanic, Atlantic, Baltic, Republic, Adriatic*. One, a tender, was called *Traffic* and another *Arctic*, until the line thought better of it and renamed her *Baltic*. Running out of seas and oceans, they turned to the gods.

One can see how their minds were working. Advertising, with new mass circulation newspapers booming on both sides of the Atlantic, was a significant part of salesmanship; and becoming more and more extravagant in its claims. The booklet written by Sir Philip Gibbs gives the flavour. The title page is faced by an advertisement of a man looking like Mr Asquith who is offering, under the headline 'Discard Your Truss', not merely an alleviant but a certain cure for rupture. 'Words of Wisdom to Wage Earners' recommends Mother Seigel's Syrup as a herbal remedy that will 'surely and speedily' cure indigestion for ever. Bovril claims that in recent experiments upon human subjects reported to the Medical Association, Bovril was 'proved' to produce an increase in flesh and muscle, or 'body-building power', from 10 to 20 times the amount taken. The master of the late barque *Colorado*, shipwrecked on Staten Island off Cape Horn, states that he and his crew of 25 men were kept alive for six months 'on this barren island, in a region of perpetual ice', entirely by drinking Epps's Cocoa. Similar extravagances were appearing about ocean liners. 'What more appropriate setting,' said an advertisement for the *Titanic*, 'than this dignified Jacobean room, redolent of the time when the Pilgrim Fathers set forth from Plymouth on their rude bark to brave the perils of the deep!' Large claims and grandiose words – 'conquest', 'titanic', 'unsinkable' – were in the air. Edith Wharton, in her novel *The Custom of the Country*, published in 1913, invented a fashionable transatlantic liner ironically named the *Semantic*.

The basic flaw of the *Titanic* was not technical. Her fate is better explained by the theories of Henry Adams than by drawings of her water-tight compartments. Adams saw the modern world being propelled at an ever-increasing speed by the new energies released through scientific discovery, ruled by men who worshipped the dynamo with blind faith and lacked all understanding of where they were leading mankind. Pirrie, Adams's contemporary, is a classic example of a dynamo-worshipper. But he was not alone. Faith in the dynamo was so persuasive that it infected even an old sea dog like the *Titanic*'s captain, Captain Smith.

2

'Iceberg right ahead!'

By the time the *Titanic* sailed from Belfast docks for her trials in Belfast Lough she had been visited and examined by Board of Trade inspectors, according to evidence given at the British inquiry, more than two thousand times. She performed her trials to the general satisfaction, arriving in Southampton on 2 April when she filled up with coal. In Southampton, White Star's newest triumph was received with acclamation, and not entirely because of her size. She was a source of jobs. Belfast built her, but it was Southampton that supplied most of her crew, including Captain Smith.

Southampton still regards the *Titanic* as a Southampton ship. The disaster was felt there more than anywhere else. An old copy of the *Southern Daily Echo* contains a group photograph of forty small children, all from the same school, and all deprived of a father or a brother or an uncle by drowning. The inhabitants of one short street near the docks lost thirteen relations between them. The little two-storey houses of Milbank Street have been replaced by light industry, but Winn Road, Westwood Park, where Captain Smith used to live, is still leafy and residential and recognizably turn of the century, though many of the substantial old houses have been demolished to make way for flats. *Kelly's Directory* for 1911–12 lists the houses: Ballencrieff, Lyndale, Speranza, Cranbourne, Boldrewood – and the residents, among them Rear-Admiral Charles Winnington-Ingram. Captain Smith is eighth on the list, at Woodhead. His house has gone, but the social status of the road is unchanged, with blocks of flats called Brookvale Court, Pinehurst and Sandringham Court. Captain Smith had seen service as a commander in the Royal Naval Reserve, and Winn Road still houses an RNR officer, also on the south side.

Elsewhere in Southampton are no less than seven memorials to the men who died in the *Titanic*, one of them prominent in the main square, with bas-reliefs commemorating the engineers, a neat flower bed at the foot, and floodlit at night. Until recently, an anonymous woman used to leave a wreath beside the flower bed every year on the anniversary of the disaster. The other *Titanic* memorials are a drinking fountain, a bronze tablet in the post office, a memorial in the seamen's chapel of St Mary's Church, two in Millbrook Church, and another in St Augustine's, Northam, which contains a reference that sounds sardonic now to 'her presumed indestructibility'. Captain Smith was probably one of those who so presumed.

Ships' captains came up the hard way in those days. Smith started his apprenticeship aged 16 in sailing ships. He served in the Boer War as a commander with the Royal Naval Reserve. He was sixty by the time he took over the *Titanic*, and had been with White Star for thirty years; a captain for twenty-five. Some calculated that at the time of the *Titanic*'s maiden voyage he had sailed two million miles for White Star. The company had complete confidence in him; they invariably gave him their best and newest liners; they made him commodore of their fleet. Before the *Titanic*, he had captained the *Olympic*. His salary was the highest of any man afloat: £1250 a year, while the captain of the *Californian*, the ship that failed to come to the *Titanic*'s rescue, was earning £240 a year. Newsreel film of Captain Smith survives; in his uniform frock-coat, four rings on each sleeve, and stiff collar, and with his fluffy beard, he looks upright, dignified and above all reassuring. It was as advantageous then for a ship's captain to look the part as it is for an airline pilot now.

His standing in society at large, not merely in the maritime community, is shown by what happened after he went down with his ship. Two years later, in 1914, the mayor of Lichfield decided that it would be appropriate if the town erected a memorial to him. Smith was a Staffordshire man, and Lichfield was half way between Liverpool and London. It was pointed out, in support of Lichfield's claim, that Anna Seward, praised by Dr Johnson as the 'Swan of Lichfield', had written movingly of icebergs round the North Pole in her ode on the death of Captain Cook. A subscription list was opened, and the widow of another national hero who had lost his life among ice, Captain Scott, was commissioned to produce a slightly larger than lifesize statue. The subscribers, and those who attended the unveiling, represented the higher reaches of British society. Waldorf Astor MP, elder son of the first viscount and first cousin once removed of the Colonel J. J. Astor who had gone down in the *Titanic*, was on the list. So was the Duke of Sutherland. So was the Dowager Countess of Arran. Among those who wrote tributes to Captain Smith were the Marquess of Salisbury, who was a former president of the Board of Trade, and the publisher Mr J. G. Hodder Williams of Hodder & Stoughton. Lady Diana Manners (later Lady Diana Cooper), the most brilliant social figure of the day, attended the unveiling ceremony, together with her sister the Marchioness of Anglesey. Addresses were given by Lord Charles Beresford and the Duchess of Sutherland. The navy was represented by Captain Smith's old Southampton neighbour, Rear-Admiral Winnington-Ingram.

The captain had met most of these prominent people, and had come to know them, because they had sailed in a ship under his command. Then, as now, it was an important part of a liner captain's job, if the weather allowed, to cultivate the grander passengers; for their part, a certain cachet attached to knowing the captain. On the night the *Titanic* sank Captain Smith had been entertained at dinner by Mr and Mrs George D. Widener, with Mr and Mrs John B. Thayer among the other guests: the cream of Philadelphia society. Later, a woman survivor wrote to the United States senators inquiring into the disaster to tell them that Captain Smith had been drinking at the dinner; but she had not been at the table and two women who had, Mrs Widener and Mrs Thayer, both signed written depositions saying that the captain had not drunk alcohol at all. Apart from this solitary wild traducer, not one survivor, whether passenger or crew, had anything but good to say of Captain Smith. Five conflicting accounts of the manner of his death were given; the most dramatic was that he drowned while swimming towards a lifeboat with a baby in his arms. All the accounts are creditable to Smith. The senior surviving member of the crew, Second Officer C. H. Lightoller, remembered Smith all his life – and he did not die until 1952 – as the best captain he had known.

Somewhere, though, there was a flaw. Smith said some strange things. In 1907, arriving in New York as captain of a new White Star liner on her maiden voyage, he told the *New York Times* he had never been in trouble at sea in all his long career, though of course he had seen storms and fog; nor did he expect to be in the future. 'Modern shipbuilding,' he was reported as saying, 'has gone beyond that.' Beyond what? the reporter should have asked. Five years later, the impression that Captain Smith gave both passengers and crew was of total confidence in his new ship.

His crew certainly had confidence in him. His three

senior officers had all served with him before. Captain Smith had brought over his chief officer from the *Olympic*, Henry Wilde, to be chief officer of the *Titanic* – thinking his experience of the sister ship would be valuable on the maiden voyage – which meant that two *Titanic* officers had to move down a rung, W. M. Murdoch to First Officer and Herbert Lightoller to Second.

Aboard the *Titanic* for her first Atlantic crossing, the crew numbered just over 900. Some 340 of these worked below decks in the engine department; engineers, trimmers, electricians, boilermakers, greasers, firemen. There were some 290 stewards and stewardesses. There was a window cleaner, a linen keeper, a stenographer, a fish cook, an assistant soup cook, a masseuse, an iceman, platewashers, a roast cook, several bakers, a night watchman, an assistant vegetable cook, nine 'Boots', and Italian and French waiters in the à la carte restaurant. The number of all-round seamen on board was much less than the number of crew looking after the passengers.

Of those passengers, there were 337 in first class, 271 in second class, and 712 in third class. The British well-to-do were not tempted by a maiden voyage, preferring the Cunarders, so the first class was dominated by Americans. The second class was mainly Anglo-Saxon. The third class, largely immigrants, included Armenians, Italians, Syrians, Chinese, Russians, Scandinavians, Dutch, and Irish.

The *Titanic* sailed from Southampton on 10 April shortly after noon, bound for Cherbourg to pick up more passengers. Captain Smith must have known that the latest leviathans required careful handling. Six months earlier, when he was taking the *Olympic* out of Southampton on her sixth Atlantic crossing, she had collided with a cruiser, HMS *Hawke*, whose bow had torn a jagged and ugly gash ten feet deep in the *Olympic*'s starboard quarter. An Admiralty Court held that the *Olympic* had gone too close to the cruiser and that White Star, and hence Captain Smith, were to blame for the collision. Smith had not been pleased; he wrote to a friend to say that 'we are not taking it lying down'. He meant that White Star would appeal, which they did; nevertheless the verdict was upheld. It was thought at the time that the huge bulk of the *Olympic* might have drawn the cruiser towards her. Two of Smith's officers in the *Titanic*, Lightoller and William Murdoch, who was on watch when the *Titanic* hit the iceberg, were also aboard the *Olympic* when she hit the *Hawke*.

Smith must have been reminded of the *Hawke* as he stood on the bridge of his latest command as she in her turn left Southampton. A local paper described what happened. 'The departure of the *Titanic* on her maiden voyage on Wednesday was marred by an untoward incident, which caused considerable consternation among the hundreds of people who had gathered at the quayside to witness the sailing of the largest vessel afloat,' said the *Southampton Times & Hampshire Express*. The wash of the *Titanic* caused all six ropes holding the liner *New York* alongside the jetty to part. The great consternation was among the sightseers who had trespassed on to the *New York* to get a better view, for they thought a collision 'inevitable'. A touch ahead on the port engine by Captain Smith and the rapid intervention of two tugs saved the day. But it had been very close. The *Southampton Times* interviewed Captain C. Gale of the tug *Vulcan*. 'We got hold of the *New York* when she was within four feet of the *Titanic*,' he said. The paper ended its report by remarking that the trespassers aboard the *New York* 'will doubtless retain for years vivid recollections of the first sailing of the *Titanic* from Southampton docks'. The episode showed, for the second time, that lessons still had to be learned about the giant ships' manoeuvrability.

Was Captain Smith, behind the obscuring beard, a risk-taker? Of all the characters in the *Titanic* drama, he seems now particularly hard to understand. Here was a ship's captain of vast experience, universally regarded as a highly responsible man, who behaved at times in a manner that appears, in retrospect, positively reckless. In his reminiscences, Lightoller recalls, with approval, the dash with which Smith used to take his ships into New York – 'at full speed', says Lightoller, though the word 'full' must have been an exaggeration. 'One particularly bad corner, known as the South-West Spit, used to make us fairly flush with pride as he swung her round, judging the distances to a nicety; she heeling over to the helm with only a few feet to spare between each end of the ship and the banks.' According to Lightoller, Smith as a mailboat captain was relentless in the way he pressed on despite heavy seas and fog to get the mail through on time; this was one of the reasons why Lightoller admired and respected him. Robust captaincy was a function of intense competition between rival companies. But Cunard historians maintain that the White Star Line, which Cunard eventually took over, followed a particularly bold policy.

Did Captain Smith choose a daring route across the Atlantic for the *Titanic*? Well-connected elderly English-men recall well-connected friends saying years ago that the secret of the *Titanic* disaster was that she was taking a shortened route, too far north, because she was lacking coal as a result of the great 1912 coal strike. True, the strike gravely embarrassed the transatlantic liner business. The *Olympic*, in New York on one crossing, crammed every available part of the ship with coal in order to boost White Star's reserves. The *Titanic* had to get coal in

Southampton from other ships, which were consequently delayed. But the route she followed was normal. There were, and indeed still are, two recommended transatlantic tracks, the northern and the southern, which are alternated according to the time of year. *Titanic* was on the southern, not the northern route. Immediately after the disaster, the recommended southern route was moved further south and then further south again, to avoid any risk of a second collision. But though the *Titanic*'s route turned out to be fatal, there was nothing unusual about it.

Trying to understand Captain Smith's state of mind before the disaster, one is tempted to take his own word for it, as expressed to the *New York Times*, and conclude that his errors stemmed from a belief that the dangers of the Atlantic had been neutralized by technology – that modern transatlantic travel had become safe and predictable. But there was too much daily evidence to the contrary for Captain Smith to have really believed anything of the sort. Newspapers reported shipping accidents then as faithfully as they report airline accidents or alarms today. The files of the *New York Times* in the months before the sinking are full of such reports. On the first day of the new year the White Star liner *Arabic* arrived in New York a day late because of a gale. During the next few weeks, three crewmen of an American ship were swept overboard during a storm off Key West, Florida; the US Atlantic Fleet lost two seamen when all its ships were struck, and some of them badly damaged, by an Atlantic gale; a British battleship at Portsmouth broke its moorings in a storm and crashed into a dreadnought; fifty-three out of a crew of fifty-seven were drowned when a British steamer sank off Aberdeenshire during a gale; the White Star liner *Adriatic* arrived in New York thirty hours late because of high seas; the

British steamer *Birchfield* arrived in New York having had a seven-day fire in its coal bunkers; the *Lusitania* was a day late because of bad weather and ice.

No doubt Captain Smith, after a lifetime at sea, regarded these incidents as regular, familiar hazards of seagoing. Can he have thought the same about icebergs and failed to take them seriously? If not, why on the fourth day of the maiden voyage did he take his ship at high speed into a region he knew to contain icebergs?

There does seem to have been general underestimation of the fact, fully accepted now, that icebergs are the most dangerous hazard of all, more dangerous than storms, collisions or fog. It is a pity that a long short story published in 1898 was not more widely read; it was written by a retired merchant navy officer and described how a ship called *Titan* collided with a huge iceberg. The correspondence with the *Titanic* disaster is so close that it was only when I had a first edition of the book in my hand that I could believe it was written before and not after 1912. The story was called *Futility* and the parallels are as follows:

	Titan (1898)	**Titanic** (1912)
Flag of registry	British	British
Time of sailing	April	April
Displacement (not gross) tons	70,000	60,000
Length	800 feet	882 feet
Propellers	Triple screw	Triple screw
Top speed	24–25 knots	24–25 knots
Capacity	About 3000	About 3000
Number aboard	2000	About 2227
Number of lifeboats	24	20

	Titan (1898)	**Titanic** (1912)
Capacity of lifeboats	500	1178
Watertight bulkheads	19	15
Engines	3 triple expansion	2 triple expansion and one steam turbine
Side of ship struck	Starboard hull pierced by spur of iceberg	Starboard hull pierced by spur of iceberg

Only after the *Titanic* went down was the story noticed and alleged to have a special significance as an example of second sight.

Unlike the *Titan*, the *Titanic* before she hit the iceberg had received by wireless telegraph no less than six ice warnings. Decades later, a member of the Titanic Historical Society read a newspaper item that led to a visit to the small German industrial town of Leisnig in Saxony, where an old gentleman suddenly fumbled in his desk, produced a crumpled scrap of paper, and exclaimed, 'If only they had heeded my warning!' The man's name was Otto Reuter; in April 1912 he had been first wireless officer aboard the German liner *Amerika*; and a scrawl on the piece of paper was the text of the radio telegram he sent via the Cape Race station to the US Hydrographic Office in Washington at 11.20 A.M. on Sunday, 14 April, the day the *Titanic* hit the iceberg. It read: '*Amerika* passed two large icebergs in 41 degrees 27 minutes N 50 degrees 8 minutes W on the 14 April Knuth.' Knuth was the captain. The message was intercepted by the *Titanic* and passed on to Washington.

But Herr Reuter was only one of the message senders. On Friday the 12th the French liner *Touraine* told the *Titanic* she had crossed a 'thick ice field'. Besides the

Amerika, on the fatal Sunday, the *Caronia* sent a message
reporting 'bergs, growlers and field ice'; the *Noordam*,
after congratulating Smith on his new command, reported
'much ice'; and the *Baltic* soon after midday passed on a
report from a Greek steamer which said she had passed
'icebergs and large quantities of field ice'. How many of
these wireless messages did Captain Smith see? One point
to remember about wireless telegraphy in 1912 is that
although not brand new, it was relatively new, and not
properly organized to meet a ship's needs. Wireless
operators aboard the liners were employed not by the
shipping company but, if they used the Marconi system,
by the Marconi Company. No iron routine had yet been
drilled into the operators about the treatment of wireless
messages, though they were under instructions to give
priority to any messages about navigation; still more
inefficient, Marconi operators thought of themselves in
competition with other wireless companies, and often
either declined to accept signals or treated them in a
cavalier fashion. Smith certainly saw four messages. It
came out in the inquiries that around lunchtime on the
Sunday he handed the *Baltic*'s message to Bruce Ismay,
the White Star chairman who was travelling on the ship's
maiden voyage, who put it in his pocket. The last warning
to come in, two hours before the collision, was from the
Mesaba; she reported 'much heavy pack ice and a great
number large icebergs'; but nobody saw it because the
Titanic operator put it under a paperweight and forgot it.
Even without this ominous final message, nobody could
deny – though some tried to – that the *Titanic* had been
warned. Captain Smith and his officers knew they were
heading into ice.

These days, the people in the world who know most
about icebergs are the members of the International Ice
Patrol. This indispensable organization was set up as a

direct result of the *Titanic* disaster; it is now based at Groton, Connecticut and, though responsible to the United States coastguard, it broadcasts regularly to all Atlantic shipping and is financed by the nations that make most use of the North Atlantic lanes, including Britain, France, Belgium, Canada, Denmark, Germany, Greece, Israel, Italy, Japan, Liberia, the Netherlands, Panama, Poland, the United States, Sweden, and Yugoslavia.

The Ice Patrol officers, who fly Hercules C.130 aircraft with side-looking airborne radar to monitor iceberg movements, take a keen interest in the *Titanic*, partly because she brought them into existence, and partly because the memory of the disaster keeps them on their toes. There have been one or two serious collisions since 1912 – the most serious being in 1959, when the *Hans Hedtoft*, on her maiden voyage, equipped with all the latest electronic equipment, struck an iceberg off Cape Farewell, Greenland, and sank without trace, taking with her ninety-five passengers and crew. But within the area monitored by the Ice Patrol, which encompasses only those regions of the North Atlantic through which the main transatlantic shipping tracks pass, not a single life has been lost because of icebergs since 1912, though a Canadian bulker smashed her bows to pieces on one not long ago. Nevertheless, even with all the advances in radar and satellite navigation and the Ice Patrol's computerized predictions about icebergs' whereabouts, there is still no reason why a ship today could not suffer exactly the same fate as the *Titanic*. The iceberg 'menace', says an official Ice Patrol publication, is a 'natural hazard which man, in all his ingenuity and resourcefulness, has not been able to control, regulate, or entirely avoid'.

With seventy years' study and records behind them, the Ice Patrol are familiar with the state of iceberg knowledge in 1912. Captain Smith, they say, would have known perfectly well that April is one of the worst months, because it is then that the rising spring temperatures melt the sea ice that has imprisoned the bergs, letting them float free. Icebergs start as the seaward tips of glaciers. Of the 10,000 to 15,000 icebergs that break off every year, some 85 per cent come from the west coast of Greenland, the largest island in the world, where the ice cap is nearly two miles thick. They are 'calved' by the hundred or so glaciers there (each glacier has a name, mainly Danish but sometimes Eskimo), head north along the Greenland coast, round the western side of Baffin Bay, and then drift south past Labrador and Newfoundland towards the Grand Banks. Most of them disintegrate, but on average about a thousand a year survive to reach the Grand Banks and the shipping lanes – the record is 1587 (the Ice Patrol count every iceberg) in 1972. The survivors by that time will have travelled some 1800 miles and taken anything from eleven months to three years for the journey, depending on whether or not they grounded for a time on some Arctic island or were sidetracked into a Labrador cove.

Icebergs come in all shapes and sizes, though not in all colours – which was a crucial point at issue in the *Titanic* inquiries. In an attempt to explain why the fatal iceberg had not been spotted earlier, it was said that it must have been black; but the Ice Patrol are sceptical, saying they have never seen a black iceberg.

One fact about icebergs that Captain Smith would not have known is that they are virtually indestructible. The US navy has conducted numerous experiments in the past twenty years to find a technique of breaking them up and rendering them harmless. Nothing has worked. Demolition of an average-size iceberg, the Ice Patrol conclude, would take 1900 tons of TNT. To melt an average-size iceberg would take the heat of combustion generated by 2.4 million tons of gasoline.

The Ice Patrol classify icebergs as small, medium, large and very large. The small ones go up to fifty feet above water, the medium size ones to a hundred feet, the large ones to two hundred feet, and the very large ones to anything over that. The Patrol's commanding officer told me that the biggest authenticated iceberg he had ever heard of would have weighed six million tons. If the iceberg that hit the *Titanic* was fifty feet high, which is perhaps the likeliest of many guesses, then – given that seven-eighths of any iceberg lies below water – its weight would have been something like 500,000 tons.

On the fatal night, the *Titanic* was steaming at 21 or 22 knots. However, she was not trying to break the transatlantic speed record. In the archives of the public library of Southampton is a letter written in the 1960s by an old surviving crew member in which he says categorically that Captain Smith, urged on by the owner, J. Bruce Ismay, was trying on White Star's behalf to capture from Cunard the Blue Riband, the record for the fastest transatlantic passage by a passenger liner. This notion is and always has been absurd. No ship can go faster than another ship that is lighter and has more power, which was the relation between the *Titanic* and the crack Cunarders. At both inquiries, Ismay was closely questioned about trying to break the record and categorically and repeatedly denied it. His indignant testimony was wholly plausible. It was simply not possible for the *Titanic* at full speed to go faster than the lighter and more powerful Cunard liners at full speed. Nor was it ever intended, either by the owners or by the builders, that the *Titanic* should be able to match them.

Many questions were asked at the inquiries about whether the *Titanic* was going flat out, or only nearly flat out, at the moment of impact. Ismay said she was not; a stoker discovered by Senator Smith, the chairman of the American inquiry, gave evidence to suggest that she was. The difference is unimportant. The point is that the ship was going very fast. Still more significant, both Smith and Ismay had it in mind that the ship would be tried at full speed the following day. The idea of slowing down was evidently far from their thoughts.

Experts were produced by counsel for White Star at the British inquiry who said there was nothing untoward about the *Titanic*'s speed. Other ships' captains said that Captain Smith was merely following the practice, established many years past, of maintaining course and speed in regions of ice provided that the weather was clear. But even if that was the practice, was it a safe practice? One man with experience of navigating among ice thought it dangerous and told the inquiry as much; this was Ernest Shackleton, recently returned from his first expedition to the Antarctic. He said his own custom in the vicinity of ice was to slow down to 3 or 4 knots. The lawyers defending White Star remarked that this might be so, but his own ship was very small, was it not? Naturally, Shackleton had to concede that by comparison with the *Titanic* his ship was indeed very small. But the difference in size was scarcely pertinent. The *Titanic* also was very small by comparison with the icebergs she was liable to meet, and indeed did meet: 46,000 tons compared with 500,000 tons.

The Ice Patrol say that hitting such a massive though largely hidden object would have been like hitting a small island, icebergs being not only virtually indestructible but unyielding. One member of the Patrol who spent three years in a US coastguard ship in northern waters says it was their custom, when ice was in the offing, to proceed at no more than 3 or 4 knots. The captain of a US

oceanographic vessel says the same; 4 knots is fast
enough. Even a 'growler', the smallest sort of iceberg –
defined by the Ice Patrol as being fifteen feet high or less,
and fifty feet long or less – should be, he says, treated
with extreme care.

At the American inquiry, great hilarity was caused
when Senator Smith asked Fifth Officer Harold Lowe of
the *Titanic* what an iceberg was made of, and Lowe
replied, 'Ice.' But the question was not quite so foolish,
nor the answer quite so witty, as might at first appear.
When more snow falls on a glacier, the pressure forces
ice out from between the snow particles and presses in air
instead. This process produces a very tight, very dense
crystalline structure. The commander of the Ice Patrol
said he had heard glacial ice described as 'metamorphic
rock', and he thought the description apt: 'You could call
it a mineral.' With time, it gets harder. The bottom layer
of the older glaciers has been estimated by carbon-dating
to be some 100,000 years old; the average age of icebergs
is some 3000 years old.

Asked why, in their opinion, Captain Smith was travelling at nearly full speed when he knew he was in an ice
region, the Ice Patrol say that in those days captains
seem to have thought of ice and icebergs simply as one
more natural hazard, like rough seas or fog. They did not
instinctively regard icebergs – as any ship's captain would
today – as uniquely menacing. This seems to approach
the heart of the mystery. The Ice Patrol are also inclined
to think that the flaw in Captain Smith's judgement was
compounded by arrogance. He must have believed that
the combination of his vast experience and the new
technology of his ship would surmount any conceivable
emergency. What he was doing on 14 April, in effect,
was to take his ship, at night, at speed, towards a
slow-moving archipelago of rock-hard islands without

–

the benefit even of a chart showing their approximate whereabouts.

From Southampton, the *Titanic* had called at Cherbourg and Queenstown, taking on mail and more passengers – more than a hundred Irish immigrants joined in Queenstown. Over the years, every *Titanic* relic has been carefully preserved, and a few postcards and letters posted in France or Ireland have survived. They are all humdrum, though in retrospect poignant. Mrs Straus, wife of one of the owners of Macy's store in New York, wrote to the owner of Harrods store in London to thank him for sending flowers to the ship. Mrs Thayer of Philadelphia wrote to a friend to say that her husband John had taken five photographs of the near-miss at Southampton (they were lost with her husband, alas). Sotheby's, the auctioneers, exhibited in January 1986 a letter on *Titanic* writing paper, posted in Queenstown four days before the sinking, from J. H. Loring giving instructions about the installation of a new motor-horn on his Daimler. 'This is a huge ship,' he added, 'and I think will be most comfortable.'

high proportion of the survivors has been exhaustively interviewed over the years, some of them many times. Every story of what happened after the collision is interesting; every account of life aboard the *Titanic* before the collision is unexceptional: the weather was fine and shipboard life at its most predictable. This couple met that couple; deck quoits were played; the ship's daily run guessed; the gymnasium, the swimming pool, and the squash court tried out and admired. Mr W. T. Stead, on his way to a peace rally in New York, talked politics. Mr Lawrence Beesley, a schoolmaster from Dulwich making his first trip outside England, discussed in the second class the comparative virtues of Oxford and Cambridge as character-forming institutions with a Church of England clergyman; and observed that the ship's lifts, operated by a smiling young lift-boy, were invaluable in helping the old ladies to get about. One or two trivial events were later magnified into omens; in Queenstown, a stoker for a joke climbed up inside one of the enormous funnels, a dummy, for ventilation, and stuck his head out of the top; for some reason his blackened face was subsequently seized on as a portent. Two nervous elderly ladies expected disaster; one of them refused to undress at night because she wanted to be ready for the crack of doom.

Four days out of Southampton, Sunday was properly observed. Smith presided over a service in first class at which two American ladies, Martha Stevenson and Elizabeth Eustis, were surprised that they did not sing the hymn 'For Those in Peril on the Sea'. In second class, the purser held a service. It was after the services, going on deck before lunch, that some passengers noticed that the weather had turned very cold. A second-class lunch menu survives: 'Consommé Fermier; Cockie Leekie; Fillets of Brill; Egg à l'Argenteuil; Chicken à la Maryland; Corned Beef; Vegetable Dumplings. From the grill: Grilled Mutton Chops; and mashed, fried, and baked jacket potatoes.' For pudding, a choice was offered between custard pudding, apple meringue, and pastry. Across the bottom of the menu was printed, 'Iced draught Munich Lager Beer 3d and 6d a Tankard.'

One routine that should have been followed before lunch was a boat drill, with all hands, passengers and crew assembling in lifejackets at their boat stations. In White Star ships, Sunday morning was always supposed to include a boat drill. Why on this occasion did Captain Smith skip it? There are two possible reasons: one is that he thought the chance of anyone having to take to the boats so remote that a boat drill would be a waste of time; the other is that, well aware of the gap between the capacity of the boats and the numbers on board, he considered that a boat drill would make the discrepancy too obvious, and perhaps disturb some of the passengers.

That Sunday evening, after dinner with his Philadelphian hosts, Captain Smith went up to the bridge shortly before 9 P.M. It was a clear, starry night and the sea was flat calm.

The officer on watch when the captain arrived, Herbert Lightoller, had already had an adventurous life. His family had originally been well-to-do, in Lancashire cotton, but their prosperity had suffered from the American Civil War, and the young Lightoller, to his own delight, had gone to sea at thirteen. Since then he had been wrecked four times, survived a fire at sea, and prospected for gold in the Yukon. He had also become a Christian Scientist. Besides possessing great physical courage and being a first-rate seaman, Lightoller was ambitious; he had been with White Star twelve years when he joined the *Titanic*, aged 38, and he was very put out when he was required to move down from First to Second Officer as a result of the captain's last-minute reshuffle in Southampton. The *Titanic* disaster determined the course of Lightoller's future, as of many others; he performed magnificently in the crisis, but during the subsequent inquiries found himself in the delicate position, as the senior surviving officer, of having to answer all the most awkward questions and to try to protect the reputations both of his employers and of Captain Smith. He got little thanks for his pains; White Star had no wish to remind potential customers about the *Titanic*, and Lightoller was never accorded the distinction he sought and deserved: a ship of his own. But he commanded a destroyer as a Royal Naval Reserve officer in World War One and rammed and sank a U-boat; and in World War Two he was one of the boldest of the old-timers – he was by then 67 – who took a private boat to join the makeshift armada of small ships that evacuated the British Expeditionary Force from Dunkirk.

The conversation on the bridge between Lightoller and Captain Smith at 9 P.M., two hours and forty minutes before the *Titanic* hit the iceberg, was subsequently described by Lightoller. He remarked on the cold and the calm. Both men were aware that ice was probably in the vicinity, though neither had seen the latest warning which would have told them that icebergs had been sighted no more than forty miles ahead. Captain Smith observed that it was an exceptionally clear night; and added that if it came over at all hazy they might have to slow down. Then he left the bridge, with the usual captain's reminder that he should be called if the weather changed.

At 10 P.M. Lightoller was relieved on the bridge by First Officer Murdoch, an experienced Scotsman. Lightoller told him, 'We might be up around the ice any time now.' They discussed the weather, and agreed that 'we seemed to be able to see a long distance'. Lightoller told Murdoch he had given the lookouts instructions to keep a sharp watch for ice, including growlers. Then Lightoller left the bridge to carry out his nightly rounds. Murdoch seems to have been the only officer who took any special action before the collision. At about a quarter past seven that evening, a 43-year-old lamp trimmer from Southampton, Samuel Hemming, whose job was to mix paint and trim lamps, had reported to Murdoch that all was in order with the lamps, and Murdoch said, according to Hemming's later testimony, 'Hemming, when you go forward see the fore scuttle is closed as we are in the vicinity of ice, and there is a glow coming from that, and I want everything dark before the bridge.' Hemming had closed the scuttle.

Lightoller finished his rounds and turned in; so did

most of the passengers. There was no dancing aboard White Star ships on Sundays; and the bars shut at half past eleven. During the evening Lawrence Beesley's new friend, Mr Carter the clergyman, had organized, by permission of the purser, Sunday night hymn-singing attended by a hundred people; Beesley had thereafter visited the library with its open fire before going to his cabin. Colonel Gracie of the USA had spent an energetic afternoon on the squash court with the resident professional and taken a swim. A few men were playing cards. Outside, it was freezing. Below, the men working in the engine department sweated in a temperature of about 100 degrees.

As the officers of the watch changed, so did the lookouts; and here we come to one of the cruxes of the *Titanic* story. Why, given that Captain Smith and Lightoller agreed that visibility was particularly good, even though there was no moon, and that they could even see the stars 'heading down towards the horizon' – proof that there was no haze – how was it that in these conditions nobody saw a fair-sized iceberg until it was too late to get out of the way?

The *Titanic* carried six specialist lookouts, more than any other ship afloat. They worked in pairs, two hours on and four hours off, and their place of work was the crow's nest, reached by a ladder inside the forward mast. Hogg and Evans had been on watch from six to eight; Symons and Jewell from eight to ten; Fleet and Lee had come on at ten. At the inquiries, Lightoller was asked whether, since ice was a possibility, extra lookouts had been posted. 'No, sir,' he said. It is hard to understand why not. One Ice Patrol officer told me that when ice is about at night (the Ice Patrol operates ships as well as aircraft), it is standard practice to post as many lookouts as possible, especially in the bows. Even today, with radar, the only reliable way to detect icebergs, the Ice Patrol says officially, is with the human eye. Still more cavalier, the *Titanic* lookouts were not supplied with binoculars.

This was one of the awkward facts that Lightoller had to explain and try to defend later on. 'We never had night glasses,' Hogg testified. 'Just the naked eye. I have always had night glasses in the White Star boats. I asked for the glasses and I did not see why I should not have them. I had them from Belfast to Southampton, but from Southampton to where the accident occurred we never had them . . . I asked for the glasses several times.' Symons said, 'It is always customary to have glasses in the crow's nest . . . I served three years and five months on the *Oceanic*, and they had glasses all the time . . . They have glasses in all the other ships.'

Where had the binoculars gone? The question was never resolved. Symons reported their disappearance to Lightoller in Southampton, and Lightoller said he had passed on the message to Murdoch. With the changed duties after the reshuffle, evidently the binoculars were overlooked. The lookouts were resentful, judging by their replies at the inquiries. They had been deprived of the tool of their trade; and they maintained that if they had had binoculars they might well have seen the iceberg earlier and the ship could have been saved. Fred Fleet, described as the man who 'discovered the iceberg' by one of the lawyers at the British inquiry, was insistent on the point and remained so for the rest of his life. The insistence might have been a form of self-protection; he might secretly have felt guilty that he had not seen the iceberg earlier. Lightoller on the other hand maintained that binoculars, though a useful aid, were not an essential piece of equipment. He himself relied first and foremost on the naked eye, using binoculars to survey what he had already seen. A captain from another ship supported him; he never supplied his lookouts with binoculars.

Still, whether the lack of binoculars was or was not decisive, the fact is that they were regarded as standard in White Star ships at the time, and have been so regarded ever since. In the British navy, lookouts are taught to sweep the horizon – each lookout having a defined sector of sea and horizon – first with the naked eye, then with binoculars, and so on. The Ice Patrol train their lookouts to scan with the naked eye, to cover the field, and to use binoculars for identification. 'You can get captivated by binoculars,' they say. To see things at night you must first concentrate on surveying a large visual field, and then you will be able to pick out any anomaly; when you do, you use the binoculars to narrow the field, enlarge the anomaly, and examine it. Exactly the same principle applies, they say, to side-looking airborne radar: big sweeps first with a wide field, searching for anomalies, then close-ups.

All this is pertinent to what happened in the *Titanic*'s crow's nest in the moments before impact. The crow's nest accommodated two lookouts standing up, Fleet and Lee; there was a locker for binoculars, empty; a telephone to the bridge; and a bell with a clapper, rung by hand. It was very cold, very calm, and the stars – everyone noticed – were very bright.

Now Fred Fleet was perhaps the most important man in the entire drama: the man who sighted the iceberg, the man who always insisted that if he had had binoculars he might have seen it earlier. If he had seen it, even a few seconds earlier, the action taken by Murdoch on the bridge might have been effective and the iceberg might have slid harmlessly by. In that case, probably nobody would ever have heard about it. Fleet and Lee would not have wanted it known that they as lookouts on a clear night had failed to see an iceberg until the ship nearly hit it; and Murdoch would not have wanted to be marked down in the White Star head office as the officer who nearly rammed an iceberg with their newest and largest liner. Not all near misses by aircraft are reported now; and the Ice Patrol wonder how many near collisions by ships were reported then.

But although Fleet was the key figure aboard the *Titanic* at 11.40 P.M. that Sunday night, he was scarcely cast for the role. The Philadelphia Maritime Museum possesses letters he wrote in 1964 and 1965 to Mr Edward Kamuda of the Titanic Historical Society in the United States, who had written to ask about his career. Fleet wrote back from Southampton, mentioning that he kept two framed photographs of survivors in his bedroom. A month later he wrote again, a sad letter:

I don't know who my parents where [sic], I have been an orphan all my life my Mother left when I was a baby she went to a place called Springfield Mass [oddly enough, Mr Kamuda's home town] I have been brought up in one of those homes Dr Barnadoes till I was twelve and then went to a training ship till I was sixteen then pushed out to look after myself. I started out as a deck boy worked up till I was an Able seaman, been all kinds of company's ships, finished up with the sea in 1936 the *Olympic* was my last ship, from the time I started deep sea, 1903 I was no better off, pay in those days was very poor, I was always without money always in debt.

On 8 January 1965 he wrote to Mr Kamuda again: 'My dear Friend, Just a few lines to let you know I am in deep trouble I have just lost my wife, also I am leaving my house the place where I have been living their [sic] is only my brother-in-law and myself we cannot agree. From yours sincerely, Fred Fleet.'

The letter was posted in Southampton at 1.30 P.M. on 9 January. It may well have been the last letter that

Fleet wrote. On 11 January the *Southern Evening Echo* reported that Mr Fleet the day before had been found hanged from a clothes post in the garden of his brother-in-law's house in Norman Road, Fremantle, a suburb of Southampton.

The paper recalled that in later life Fleet had worked as an occasional newspaper seller for the *Echo*. Every now and again, the paper had carried stories of the 'little do the people who buy papers from the seller at the corner of Market Street realize' variety. Interviewed for these stories, Fleet would always repeat that if he had had binoculars the *Titanic* might have been saved.

He was even more definite at the inquiries. Mr Scanlan, the lawyer representing the National Sailors' and Firemen's Union in London, asked him if with glasses he would have seen the iceberg sooner. 'Certainly,' he replied.

Q: How much sooner do you think you would have seen it?
A: In time for the ship to get out of the way.
Q: So that it is your view that if you had had glasses it would have made all the difference between safety and disaster?
A: Yes.
Q: After all, you are the man who discovered the iceberg?
A: Yes.
Q: Would you have used them constantly?
A: Yes.

Fleet, however, may have been a difficult character. After his death, his brother-in-law wrote to Mr Kamuda to say that he did not 'hold any pleasant memories of Mr Fleet'. He mentioned domestic differences to which, perhaps, little significance should be attached. But at the inquiries Fleet came out as truculent, even paranoid.

The Court was trying to establish whether or not there had been any haze. Lightoller said there was none; if

there had been, either he or Murdoch should have told
the captain. But Lee had testified that the haze was
serious: 'We had all our work cut out to pierce through it
just after we started' – that is, after he and Fleet went on
watch. He said Fleet had remarked to him, 'Well, if we
can see through this we will be lucky.' Fleet himself said
there was a 'slight haze'; but it was 'not difficult at all' to
see. A lawyer asked him to account for the conflict
between his 'slight haze' and his remark as reported by
Lee: 'Well, I never said that.'

Conducting the inquiry, Lord Mersey at that point
dismissed Lee's testimony altogether, saying it was incon-
sistent with everything else the Court had heard. 'This
man was trying to make excuses for not seeing the
iceberg,' he said, which was surely true.

But then Fleet was asked about Lightoller's testimony.
Lightoller had talked to Fleet after they were rescued,
and Fleet had not said anything about haze.

SIR ROBERT FINLAY, KC: Is that right?
A: Well, I'm not going to tell him my business. It is my place
in court to say that, not to him.
LORD MERSEY: You really do not understand. This gentleman
is not trying to get round you at all.
A: But some of them are, though.
MERSEY: They are not. I can see you think most of us are, but
we are not.

When another lawyer asked Fleet, not for the first time,
about the presence of women on the boat deck after the
collision, he declined to give any answer at all. The
verbatim transcript records 'No answer'. Fleet then said,
'Is there any more likes to have a go at me?'

A peculiarity of Fleet's emerged at the American
Senate inquiry. He could not judge distances. He refused
to give any estimate of how far away the iceberg had

been when he saw it, despite sympathetic questioning designed to help him. As Senator Smith remarked, an admitted inability to judge distances was a strange defect for a professional ship's lookout. Fleet drew a picture to show how the iceberg looked when he sighted it: the iceberg is on the horizon, which cannot have been accurate. Lookouts' eyesight was supposed to be regularly tested, and Fleet's had been tested five years earlier. In England, Board of Trade officials thought the Court should order a newer and more thorough test for all the *Titanic*'s lookouts, but their advice for some reason was not followed.

Fleet saw the iceberg, rang the bell three times, reached across Lee to the telephone, and called, 'Iceberg right ahead!' On the bridge, the Sixth Officer said, 'Thank you,' and repeated the warning to Murdoch who at once ordered, 'Hard-a-starboard!' – which meant, under the system of helm orders then in force, that the ship's head would go to port. Then Murdoch ordered, 'Stop. Full speed astern.' He pulled the switch that closed the watertight doors in the boiler and engine rooms. The ship's head swung slowly to port. In the crow's nest, Fleet thought they had missed the iceberg altogether; on the bridge they felt the impact.

Captain Smith came rushing out of his room.

'Mr Murdoch, what was that?'

'An iceberg, sir.'

It used to be thought that the iceberg tore a three-hundred-foot gash in the hull on the starboard side, above the double bottom. The Woods Hole underwater inspections have thrown doubt on this belief. At all events, within minutes, the water had reached fourteen feet above the keel. Six watertight compartments were breached. The transverse bulkheads, or upright partitions, had not been carried up to the deck-heads, so that as the ship's head went down adjoining compartments filled up too, like – as someone said later – the sections of an icecube tray. If only three of the *Titanic*'s compartments had been flooded, the ship could have stayed afloat, but with six gone she was doomed.

3

Survival of the Richest?

In all disasters, it is the fate of the rich and famous that attracts the most fascinated attention; and of this squalid but universal truth the *Titanic* is a glaring example. Like the poor on land, drowned steerage passengers have no history. Common humanity has little interest in knowing what happened to other common people like themselves; shocked by the sudden intervention of chance and chaos in human affairs, they draw reassurance from the knowledge that even the privileged can come to an untimely end.

Privilege has rarely, in modern times, been more blatantly on display than it was aboard the *Titanic*. Soon after the news of the disaster came through, newspapers and magazines such as the *Illustrated London News* published sectional drawings of the ship. Nothing could have exposed more starkly the social structure of the civilized western world. There on the top decks in the lavishly furnished and spacious cabins were the rich, 'the great merchants, the princes of trade, the controllers of the world's markets', as Sir Philip Gibbs called them in his pamphlet; next down were the second class, in more modest conditions; and there towards the bottom of the ship were the lower classes, four to a cabin. Finally, down below the waterline were the labouring class, in heat and noise and steam, shifting coal by shovel and barrow, stoking the fires in the boilers, tending the pumps, the electricity generators, the dynamos and the engines. The illustrations showed social inequality at its most extreme and at its most vertical, with the classes ranged one above the other, the richest visibly on top and the poorest visibly at the bottom. The drawings were almost caricatures of social stratification.

It was the rich that attracted most attention from the beginning. Sir Philip Gibbs went so far as to draw up a list of millionaires – 'men known to have represented a total capital of at least £120,000,000' – with the richest at its head. His list began:

Colonel J. J. Astor	£30,000,000
Mr B. Guggenheim	£20,000,000
Mr I. Straus	£10,000,000
Mr G. Widener	£10,000,000

He then, as in a league table, listed those thought to be worth between five million and a million.

But there was another circumstance that caught the public's attention besides the extreme wealth of some of the passengers. Soon after the disaster, the Board of Trade published tabulated statistics that showed the number of passengers, male and female, in each class. The same tables showed what proportion of passengers and crew had been saved. The figures were startling, and their implications inescapable. A far higher proportion of first-class passengers had survived than of any other class. 34 per cent of male first-class passengers had been saved, by comparison with 8 per cent of second-class males and 12 per cent in third class. There could be no arguing with these figures: the rich, defined as anyone in first class, must have had privileged treatment. Suddenly it looked as if death and disaster were not such great levellers after all.

It may have been for this reason that Colonel Astor's name became so closely identified with the name of the *Titanic*. Professor P. N. Furbank has shown with a wealth of scholarship that in Britain the idea of class and classes emerged during the first half of the nineteenth century. He has demonstrated the artificiality of the concept, and its subjectivity. But the class system aboard the *Titanic* was real, and seems particularly bleak and crude because it was based entirely on money. In the enclosed and temporary society of the great transatlantic liners it was logical that Colonel Astor, being the richest man on board, should be treated by everyone, not simply by the White Star Line servants, but by other passengers, by newspapers, and by newspaper readers as the most significant and important. But there was more to it than that. He was not only the richest, but he had been drowned. Looking back through the files, it is clear that 'Astor' was the evocative word that every newspaper wanted in its *Titanic* headlines.

The colonel, as it happens, was an interesting man. In a photograph taken at Waterloo station before he caught the boat train to Southampton he looks wholly conventional, equipped with bowler hat, perfectly rolled umbrella, and an overcoat with a velvet collar. He was 47; his moustache trim and military; his bearing upright; and his gaze at the camera direct. There is nothing American-looking about him. He could be one of a thousand similarly dressed Englishmen on his way to the City of London.

Behind the orthodox exterior, however, Colonel Astor, besides being fabulously wealthy, was enterprising and mildly eccentric. The Astors had (and still have) a confusing though understandable habit of naming sons after the founding father, John Jacob Astor, who emigrated to the United States from Waldorf in Germany in 1783 and made a fortune from the fur trade and subverting the Indians. The colonel, his great-grandson, was the fourth descendant to be named after him. He went to Harvard

and developed a keen interest in mechanical engineering
that came out in a passion for motor cars (he was once
fined by a British court for exceeding the speed limit in
Croydon). He invented a brake for bicycles, which was
successfully marketed, and a pneumatic device for flatten-
ing road surfaces that won a prize. He experimented with
a new sort of ship's turbine and waived the rights to its
patent. He wrote a novel that has been classified as
an early example of science fiction in which Colonel
Bearwarden, President of the Terrestrial Axis Straighten-
ing Company, pumps out the Arctic to put the globe on
an even keel.

He was also, in a mild way, a man of action. In the
Spanish-American war, he raised and financed his own
unit, called after himself, and attended in Cuba one of
the principal battles; hence the rank of colonel. He was
an intrepid yachtsman and once disappeared for sixteen
days aboard his private yacht *Nourmahal* in the Carib-
bean, affecting real estate markets in New York, causing
a United States revenue cutter to be sent to search for
him and provoking, after he appeared safe in San Juan,
an irritated leading article in the *New York Times* which
said crossly that national concern for the colonel's safety
had been unduly exaggerated. (The paper changed its
tune when he disappeared in the *Titanic*.)

In business, he maintained and extended the family's
vast real estate holdings in New York, showing a special
fascination with hotels. At the time of his death he owned
more hotels and skyscrapers in Manhattan than anyone
had ever owned; he had built the Knickerbocker, and the
St Regis. The old Astor family house had been at the
corner of Fifth Avenue and 34th Street; after the property
was divided between J.J. Astor and his cousin, the cousin
put up a hotel and called it the Waldorf, and J.J. Astor
put up an adjoining hotel and called it the Astoria; hence

the Waldorf Astoria which at once became, as it has remained, the best known hotel name in the city. (The Waldorf was given as a present to one of the English Astors, William Waldorf Astor, the MP and husband of Nancy Astor; he sold it to the Du Ponts in 1916.) Not long before Colonel Astor was drowned, he was assessed for tax on his Manhattan holdings; they were revealed to be an astounding accumulation of no less than 700 different lots.

The public were even more interested in his matrimonial affairs. In 1909, to the particular amazement of the residents of Dutchess County where the Colonel had an estate, it was abruptly announced that his wife was suing him for divorce. A month later, all legal proceedings having been kept secret, to the indignation of the New York press, and the papers in the case sealed, Mrs Astor was granted a divorce and discovered living under an assumed name in French Lick Springs, Indiana. Two years afterwards, the colonel allowed it to be known that he proposed to marry an 18-year-old New York girl named Madeleine Force. The announcement set off uproar among the churches. The judge who granted the divorce said that Astor could not remarry in New York State; but the Episcopalian bishops said he should not be remarried at all, and were supported by the president of the Federation of New York Churches. Astor thereupon offered a Baptist pastor a $1000 fee to perform the ceremony. He refused, Astor repeated the offer to a Methodist, who also declined. Volunteers came forward: a clergyman in Norwalk, and another in Providence, Rhode Island. Finally, the couple were married, on 9 September 1911, by the Reverend J. Lambert of the Elmwood Temple in Newport. The Berkshire, Mass., Ministers Club instantly condemned Lambert; so did the Chicago Congregational Ministers Union; the Rhode

Island Congregational Ministers Association passed a resolution deploring the marriage. Two months after he had performed the ceremony Lambert resigned – bowing, he said, to the criticism of his fellow clergymen. It was in the wake of these disputes that Colonel Astor, having spent most of the autumn of 1911 cruising up and down the east coast of the United States in his yacht, being assailed by newspaper reporters every time he put into harbour, decided to escape both the winter and the controversy by taking his young wife abroad on a trip to Egypt followed by a few days in Paris before catching the *Titanic* back to the United States. By this time, his wife was pregnant.

The second name on Sir Philip's list, Benjamin Guggenheim, was scarcely less interesting than Colonel Astor, though the £20,000,000 attached to his name turned out to be an exaggeration. He was born in 1865, the fifth of seven sons of Meyer Guggenheim, a Swiss emigrant, and the family had made their vast fortune principally in smelting, in Leadville, Colorado. Benjamin had moved from mining into mining machinery; he owned a plant in the United Kingdom. Then he went into the manufacture of pumps, some of them big enough to feed a city's main water supply with twenty million gallons a day. The story of how he met his death is well attested. When he heard the ship was doomed he went below and reappeared in full evening dress, saying that if he was going to die he wanted to die like a gentleman. Then he told a steward to tell his wife, if he was lost and the steward saved, that Ben Guggenheim had done his duty, a message the steward was able to deliver. The family went to the quayside to meet the *Carpathia* when the ship arrived in New York with the survivors, but down the gangplank came not Ben Guggenheim but the blonde singer reputed to be his mistress. Peggy Guggenheim, Ben's daughter who became a celebrated collector of modern art and patron of artists, always believed that the woman was paid by the family to return at once to Europe to avoid scandal. A further blow was in store for the young Peggy when her father's will was proved. He left one third of his money to his wife, and two thirds to his daughters; but the fortune had dwindled away, and Peggy inherited only $450,000, which was much less than she had been brought up to expect.

The third name on Sir Philip's list became, with his wife, one of the *Titanic*'s principal heroes. Isidor Straus arrived in the United States shortly before the American Civil War. Settled in Georgia, he and his family found themselves in what one descendant calls 'the world of *Gone with the Wind*' and became salesmen for Confederate bonds; Isidor travelled to Liverpool to sell them. After the war, when many Southerners defaulted, Straus Senior did not; having thus acquired a reputation for exceptional probity, he was able to raise credit in the North, and the family went into the glass and china business. In New York, the big new store of R. H. Macy was flourishing; Isidor and his brother asked if they could have a corner of the store to sell glass and chinaware; in return, they would give the store ten per cent of the takings. In ten years they owned the store, which is now the biggest in the world, with eighty-three branches nationwide.

Several eye-witnesses told substantially the same story about the Strauses' behaviour while the *Titanic* was sinking. Colonel Gracie described how Mrs Straus declined a seat in one of the lifeboats in order not to be separated from her husband, to whom she had been married for forty years; how he, Colonel Gracie, suggested that Mr Straus should be allowed to be an exception to the rule of women and children first, since he was old and infirm and

would have little hope of surviving by his own efforts;
how Mr Straus scotched the idea, refusing to accept
special treatment; and how the colonel last saw the couple
taking their seats in steamer chairs on the boat deck to
await their end.

Seventy-three years later a footnote was added to the
story. Iphigene Ochs Sulzberger, an elderly daughter of
Adolph Ochs, the founder of the *New York Times*, wrote
a brief article in the paper saying that the discovery of
the wreck was perhaps the time to make generally known
what she had known since 1912, when she was a student
at Barnard. Mrs Straus's maid survived. On the ship,
before the maid got into a lifeboat, Mrs Straus had taken
off her fur coat and said, 'Wear this, it will be cold in the
lifeboat, and I do not need it any more.' When the maid
arrived back in New York, she took the coat to Mrs
Straus's daughter, who told the maid to keep it, as it was
her mother's gift to her. Isidor Straus, a man of modest
tastes, had been a considerable philanthropist. A memorial service for him and his wife was attended by no less
than forty thousand New Yorkers, some of them from
the tenements of the lower east side. At Broadway and
107th Street a small park was dedicated to their memory
and presented to the city by the family; it was land that
had once formed part of Isidor Straus's dairy farm. Macy's
employees collected money for a plaque to be placed
over the 135 West 34th Street entrance, still known as the
Memorial Entrance.

As for the fourth name on the list, the sinking of
the *Titanic* resulted in Harvard University acquiring a
substantial library. The Wideners had made their money
as tramway kings; Harry Widener, aged 27 and a Harvard
graduate, was less interested in transport than in books
and was already respected on both sides of the Atlantic
as a bibliophile, a friend and customer of the two leading

antiquarian booksellers of the day, Bernard Quaritch in London and A. S. Rosenbach in Philadelphia. It was for Harry Widener that Rosenbach had recently bid a record £18,000 for a first folio Shakespeare. Before going to Europe with his mother and father, Harry Widener had attended in New York the first part of the Robert Hoe library sale, and had been the underbidder, at $49,000, for a Gutenberg Bible; Henry Huntington had bid a thousand more. Widener had also looked over the books due to form the next part of the sale, and had shown interest in one particular rarity, the Caxton edition of John Gower's *Confessio Amantis*. Both he and his father were drowned; and in Harry's memory his mother – the hostess at the last dinner party aboard the *Titanic* – gave Harvard the great library that bears his name. It is one of three American cultural institutions with a *Titanic* connection; the other two are the Guggenheim Museum in New York, and the New York Public Library, which inherited Colonel Astor's collection of rare books.

There were other well-off people aboard: a Washington banker, a telephone company widow, a yachtsman from Marblehead, Massachusetts, a cotton manufacturer, a Guernsey businessman going to Toledo to visit relations, and a 15-year-old heiress from St Louis with an allowance of $7500 a year (about £1300) for her education and clothes. Mr Clarence Moore was in first class; he was the Master of the Chevy Chase hunt, who had bought '25 brace of hounds', said the papers, in England. So was Charles M. Hays, the Canadian president of Grand Trunk Pacific Railroad Companies, who had built a new bridge over the Niagara River at Niagara Falls and was ranked second in North America as a railwayman to the late Edward H. Harriman. There may well have been some professional gamblers on the ship, too; and there was certainly a well-known man-about-town, Clinch Smith,

who had been present when Stanford White was shot.
One person who had planned but failed to take the trip
was the ultimate owner of the *Titanic*, J. P. Morgan
himself; it had been said that he was in poor health, but a
reporter found him, just after the ship went down, 'in
excellent health' at the Grand Hotel, Aix, where he was
undertaking the cure. The reporter was writing a seventy-
fifth birthday piece; but no one would think Mr Morgan
seventy-five, he said; he was hale, with 'the bright critical
eyes of the connoisseur'. He took no exercise, and at Aix
was concentrating on sulphur baths and massage, with
'occasional Naunheim treatment'. Apparently as an afterthought the reporter asked him about the *Titanic*, where-
upon, towards the end of the article, J. P. Morgan
indicated extreme distress.

It was to try to get a better understanding of this aspect
of the disaster – to see what lay behind the statistics
showing that the rich came off best, which might well be
thought the most scandalous part of the whole story –
that I went to Philadelphia to visit John Thayer, whose
grandfather, Vice-President of the Pennsylvania Railroad,
perished in the sinking, but whose grandmother and
father survived. On the telephone Mr Thayer had said he
had 'nothing much' to show me, and so I was taken aback
when he ushered me into the study of the comfortable
house well outside the city where he lives, having retired
from farming, with his wife. Mr Thayer – the fifth John
Borland Thayer – is in his sixties, trim and alert. His
study is a maritime museum. Paintings and photographs
of ships covered the walls; a glass case displayed ship
models, some of them made by Mr Thayer himself; here
were books about ships and relics of ships, and most of
the collection had to do with the transatlantic liners of
the past century. His lifelong absorption with his hobby
started at school, when he used to write to the captains of

the big liners asking for their autographs, and he has never stopped since, buying in London as well as in the United States.

After he had shown me some of his prize items, especially a group of framed representations of ships assembled by montage, partly using silk and velvet, to give a three-dimensional effect, he went to a corner and pulled open the drawer of a filing cabinet. Everything in the study is shipshape, and the drawer contained neat folders from which Mr Thayer carefully drew out an original first-class *Titanic* passenger list which he said his grandmother had happened to bring away from the ship in the pocket of her coat. Next he pulled out and handed to me a carbon copy of a typed document on good onionskin paper turned slightly yellow with age; four pages fastened by a rusty pin. The document was headed 'In the matter of an inquiry into the loss of the *Titanic*' and began as follows:

I, Marian Longstreth Morris Thayer, widow of John B. Thayer, of Haverford, Montgomery County, in the State of Pennsylvania, United States of America, hereby make oath and say:

I was a first-class passenger on the *Titanic*. My husband and I were guests at a dinner in the restaurant on Sunday evening, the 14th of April, given by Mr and Mrs Widener. Captain Smith was there, also Major Butt [President Taft's favourite aide] and others. We entered the restaurant at 7.35 P.M. I am sure that our party, including Captain Smith, left the restaurant, to have coffee, before 8.30 P.M., as the dinner was served very quickly. We went out into the hall by the companionway for that purpose. Captain Smith had left our party and gone towards his own quarters by a quarter of nine o'clock, at the latest.

My husband, my son and I were the only persons at the Captain's table in the Saloon. The Captain usually took his meals in the Saloon, but did not do so for about the first day and a half after sailing. I noticed that the Captain never took any alcoholic liquor of any kind at any meal.

I do not remember hearing, during the dinner on Sunday night, any mention made by any person of ice being in the neighbourhood, or that we might expect to see ice, as Mr Widener, Major Butt and I were deeply engrossed in conversation on other subjects during the entire time of the dinner.

The collision occurred at fourteen minutes before twelve o'clock, and at that time I was in my stateroom, No 68, on the port side of C deck, awake. I had just rung for the steward to open the porthole. He was in the middle of the room. The jar of the impact was slight, but prolonged. We threw on overcoats and went up to A Deck, on the starboard side. Upon looking over the side of the vessel I saw what looked like a number of long, black ribs, apparently floating nearly level with the surface of the water, parallel with each other but separated from each other by a few feet (two or three feet) of water. These long black objects were parallel with the side of the ship – the nearest one being probably twenty feet from the ship, and they extended from near the bow to about amidship. I saw no high iceberg at that time. We walked around to the port side of the deck. I then remarked to my husband and son that the ship was listing towards the starboard and bow.

I then went down to my cabin to dress. My son and husband told me the accident was serious and that we should put on life belts immediately. Our steward brought life belts to us and helped us to put them on. I saw other stewards helping passengers to put on the life belts. All the stewards were, I think, remarkably good, and quite self-possessed. There was no panic.

It was about five minutes past twelve when I left my cabin. I went up on A Deck with my husband and stayed probably for ten or fifteen minutes in the companionway. Then the women were ordered to go up to the boat deck. Mr Dodd, the Chief Dining Saloon Steward, told us to go there. I saw Captain Smith giving orders on the port side of the bridge, near where we were standing on the boat deck. I also saw Mr Wild [*sic*] and other officers. There seemed to be very few seamen about. A group of men – some of them with blackened faces, whom I supposed were stokers – came up on deck from below. At this time rockets were going up beside us, and the Morse signal light was begun. All the officers seemed to be very busy, and working hard. I saw only one man (who looked like a foreigner, and was evidently a steerage passenger) who had 'lost his head', and he was struggling and fighting, deliriously, near us. I think the steerage passengers had as good a chance as any of the rest of us to be saved. I saw many of them on the deck near us.

While still on the boat deck I saw, on the port side, what appeared to be the hull of a ship, headed in the opposite direction from our ship, and quite near us (perhaps a mile away) from which rockets were being sent up. I am certain of this, for later, on reaching the water, I was disappointed to find she had disappeared. The impression I had received was that the vessel was less than half the size of the *Cedric*, and higher out of the water at her bow than the *Carpathia*.

The order was now given 'All women to the boats', but it was found too difficult to get the women into the boats from the boat deck, as the boats swung out too far from the deck. We were then ordered to go to A Deck. Mr Wild [*sic*] took us there, and the boat was lowered there. Here again delay occurred on account of there being no means of getting from the ship into the boat – the boat being too far away from the ship. Ladders were called for, but there being none it was necessary to lash two steamer chairs to serve as a sort of gang plank to enable the women to get into the boat.

The lifeboat that I was in was No 4. As the boat was being lowered, when it was still about twelve feet above the water, we heard the order given above to 'Let her go', and only our shouts and protestations to those above prevented the letting go of the tackles while we were yet that distance above the water. As evidence of the danger we were in from this error, we passed an overturned boat shortly after reaching the water. There were two seamen at the oars of our boat, and one steering. There was also a man in the bow of our boat who said he was a Quartermaster. He was absolutely inefficient, and could give us no directions or aid whatever, and besides this was most disagreeable. I do not think he was a Quartermaster. There was no light in the boat – a search was made but nothing found but a bailer. There were forty-five women and some children in the boat when it was lowered, besides the seamen. Just as we reached the water and were about to cast off the boat at least two men from steerage slid down the davit ropes into the boat.

I think it was about 1.40 A.M. when our boat reached the water . . .

Here was one survivor, at least, who was saying – whatever the efficiency or lack of it with which the evacuation was handled – the first-class passengers were not given special treatment: that steerage passengers had as good a chance of escaping as anyone else.

Mr Thayer handed me another document, this time the copy of a letter that his father, then 17, wrote from Haverford to Judge Charles L. Long of Springfield, Mass. on 23 April 1912 – eight days after the disaster.

My dear Sir:

I received your letter this morning. Mother and I were very touched by it. Words cannot express how much we sympathise with you and Mrs Long.

The newspaper clipping is accurate as far as it goes, but it does not give any of the details relating to my short friendship with your son. These I will try to tell you now, giving our own words as I can recall them.

I was sitting in the room outside the main dining saloon, waiting for the music to begin. I had dined alone and was sitting alone, my father and mother having been invited out to dine in the restaurant. There was a box of matches on the small table at which I was sitting. Your son was sitting in front and to one side of us, with his back toward me. He took out a cigarette and, having no matches, came up to my table and asked if he might take a match. I said 'Yes'. In a few minutes he came back for another one. I told him he might take them back to his table if he wanted, as I didn't smoke. He looked lonely, sitting all alone, and I was lonely, so I pulled my chair up to his table and asked if I might join him. He smiled and said 'Yes, certainly.' I started the conversation by telling him that I had just been in Switzerland, Holland, Germany, Austria and England. He said he had just been in St Moritz, and he told me all about the winter sports. He said that he had been skiing mostly, and that he did not go on the 'Cresta' because he was your only son and you did not want him to run into any danger for nothing. He said that he expected to go back to England in a few months, to spend the summer and go to several house parties. We talked about cricket and baseball. He told me of his trip around the world and of getting shipwrecked near Alaska. He said he only got his feet wet, as he jumped from the boat to the shore. I asked him if he ever collected stamps, with his wonderful advantages for it while travelling. He said he did, but had lost interest in it. I told him it was my hobby. We talked about stamps for a while. Then we talked over different things we had seen, and he connected with some dates. I expressed some surprise, thinking he was about twenty-one or twenty-two. He laughed and asked me to guess his age. So as not to be too far out either way I guessed twenty-six. Then he told me he was thirty, but had been masquerading in Switzerland as twenty-two. We kept on talking about different things, which I do not remember. We talked for about two hours and a half together. Then I saw mother and father come downstairs, so I said goodnight to your son. He asked me to come and sit with him or walk with him on deck the next morning. He then went to walk on deck before going to bed. I went to bed with mother and father.

The *Titanic* struck the ice at fourteen minutes to twelve. There was only a slight shock and bumping – then all was still. It was about five minutes after twelve when I again saw your son. Father and mother and I were just going up the stairs, having dressed completely and tied on life preservers under our overcoats, when we met your son on A Deck. He had on an overcoat over his dress suit, and a life preserver on under his overcoat. I think he had just been sitting in the smoking room or had come in from his walk on deck. He came up to me and said 'Do you mind if I stick with you?' I replied 'No; come ahead; keep with us.' We all went up and walked around the boat deck for a while. Father and I said goodbye to mother at the top of the stairs on the boat deck, when they called all the women to the port side. Then your son and myself and father walked around to different boats, only to be directed to others. We then went to the port side. We met Dodd, the dining saloon steward. He took us to mother, as she had not yet gotten into a boat. We stayed with her for a few minutes when Mr Wild [*sic*], the Chief Officer, told us to go down onto A Deck and get into a boat that they were loading from there. Father and mother went ahead – your son and I followed. A crowd pushed ahead of us and we could not find my mother or father when we were able to pass on, so thinking they had managed to get off in a boat we went to the starboard side of the boat deck. There was an awful crowd around the last boat on the forward part of the starboard side, pushing and shoving wildly. We thought it best not to try to get in it, as we thought it would never reach the water right side up, but it did. We went and stood by the davits of a boat which had left. There was such a big list to port that it seemed as if she would turn over on her side as she sank. In such a case we would not have had the slightest chance, so I told him I was going to jump out and slide down the davit ropes into the water and try to swim to the boats in the distance. I started to do this three times, and each time he caught hold of me and asked me to wait awhile. In a few minutes she straightened up on an even keel. We hurried back and stood by the rail about even with the second funnel. She started to shoot down fast at an angle of about thirty degrees. We shook hands, said goodbye and wished each other luck. We did not give each other any messages for home, because neither of us thought we would ever get back. Then we jumped upon the rail. Your son put his legs over the rail, while I straddled it. Hanging over the side, holding onto the rail with his hands, he looked up at me and said, 'You're coming, boy, aren't you?' I replied, 'Go ahead, I'll be with you in a minute.' He let go and slid down the side and I never saw him again. Almost immediately after he jumped I jumped. All this last part took a very short time, and when we jumped we were about ten yards above the water.

Your son was perfectly calm all the time and kept his nerve, even to the very end. I wish I had more to tell you, but I hope this will be of some comfort to you.

I am sending you my picture, thinking you might like to see who was with him at the end. I would treasure it very much if you could spare me one of his.

Mother and I hope that if you and Mrs Long feel able to you will come and see us, and let us do what we can for you.

With our heartfelt sympathy, believe me,

Sincerely yours, John B. Thayer, Jr.

Next, Mr Thayer showed me a statement made by his father as soon as he got back to Philadelphia on 20 April; it was typed on foolscap headed 'The Pennsylvania Railroad' and went over some of the same ground as the letter to Judge Long, except that he explained in more detail how he tried and failed, because of the crowd, to find his parents: 'That was the last time I saw my father.' He also said, which shows the persistence of the idea that

the *Titanic* was unsinkable, that even after he had made
his three starts towards the davit ropes and had been held
back by Long, 'we thought she might possibly stay afloat'.

I asked Mr Thayer whether his father used to talk
about the *Titanic* and he said he did not; nor did his
grandmother. In 1940, however, his father suddenly wrote
an extended, reflective account of his experiences and
published it in a limited edition of 500 copies. Mr Thayer
said that unfortunately the family had failed to copyright
the little book, and it had since been published commer-
cially 'at four dollars'. The preface strongly suggests that
it was World War Two that stirred Thayer to think about
the *Titanic*'s significance. Evidently his long reticence had
not been due to any attempt to suppress the memory.
'The whole event passes before me now in nineteen
hundred and forty, as vividly and with the same clarity,
as twenty-eight years ago in nineteen hundred and
twelve.' The same seems to have been true of all survivors
able to talk about their experiences (some were not):
they remembered every detail as long as they lived.
Thayer in his preface went on to contrast the uncertainties
of 1940 with the certainties of his youth, saying that the
world had been moving at 'a rapidly accelerating pace
ever since, with less and less peace, satisfaction, and
happiness'. The *Titanic* disaster was to him the event that
left the old certainties in ruins.

He adds more details to his 1912 accounts. 'I have
spent much time on the ocean, yet I have never seen the
sea smoother than it was that night.' Blackish smoke
poured out of the three forward funnels (the fourth was
the ventilation dummy). After the impact – 'if I had had
a brimful glass of water in my hand not a drop would
have been spilled' – he told his parents that 'I was going
up on deck to see the fun'. He and his father learned of
the seriousness of the collision from Thomas Andrews of

Harland & Wolff, who told them 'he did not give the ship much over an hour to live'. The band was playing 'lively tunes' without being much attended to. Twenty-eight years on, Thayer was sharply critical of the organization; 'It seemed we were always waiting for orders and no orders ever came.' In the early stages the crowd, which included second- and steerage-class passengers as well as first, was 'fairly orderly', but he remembered one example of disorderly behaviour. He saw 'one man come through the door out onto the deck with a full bottle of Gordon Gin. He put it to his mouth and practically drained it. If I ever get out of this alive, I thought, there is one man I will never see again. He apparently fought his way into one of the two last boats, for he was one of the first men I recognized upon reaching the deck of the SS *Carpathia*. Someone told me afterwards that he was a State Senator or Congressman from Virginia or West Virginia.'

Thayer was one of the last to leave the ship voluntarily. He describes how, at around 2.15 A.M., as the ship went down by the head and water crept up the deck and right up to the bridge, the crowd gradually moved back towards the stern, keeping away from the rails – 'a mass of hopeless, dazed humanity'. He and Long kept near the rail, thinking their best chance was to stay clear of the crowd. The collision had been followed by the deafening hiss of steam escaping from the boilers, but now the noise had stopped, 'making a great quietness' occasionally interrupted by a thud or muffled explosion. Then, as without warning the ship seemed to start forward, moving into the water at an angle, the water no longer creeping but rushing towards the stern, a new clamour began: 'a rumbling roar mixed with more muffled explosions; it was like standing under a steel railway bridge while an express train passes overhead, mingled with the noise of a press steel factory and wholesale breakage of china'. Then he jumped.

His son next handed me another private document which, he said, like his grandmother's affidavit and his father's letter, had never been made public. From one point of view it was the most interesting of all, in its artless candour and detail, and it 'pretty well confirmed', as Mr Thayer remarked, his grandmother's account. It was headed 'The *Titanic* – Our Story' and was 'by M.E.S. and E.M.E.', two sisters, Martha Eustis Stevenson and Elizabeth Eustis, who were neighbours of the Thayers in Haverford.

The story, written by Martha, begins with the sisters thoroughly appreciating every moment of their trip. On the Sunday they had written letters before morning service, spent the afternoon reading, taken tea on deck, walked on the boat deck, and enjoyed 'a delicious dinner with souvenir menus'. After dinner they listened to 'a fine musical program in the reception room' and at about 9.30 went up to the lounge, 'a most beautiful room with an open fire'. Because she had finished all her own books, Martha borrowed Shackleton's book about the South Pole from the library steward, and spent half an hour looking at pictures of icebergs and ice fields.

Before turning in, she remarked to Elizabeth that they only had two more nights to go and 'neither of us had had one bit of discomfort from seasickness'. Their friend John Thayer, I thought, would have considered their orderly day an excellent example of how life was lived by persons of his circle in the pre-*Titanic* era when 'the world had an even tenor to its ways . . . It seems to me,' Thayer wrote, 'that the disaster about to occur was the event which not only made the world rub its eyes and awake, but woke it with a start.'

Martha's account of this seminal event is as follows:

I was sound asleep when at a quarter before twelve I was awakened by a terrible jar with ripping and cutting noises which lasted a few moments. [The sisters were among the very few who were alarmed by the impact.] We were both much frightened, sitting up in bed and turning on the electricity. Our door was on the hook and we soon heard voices in the hall so that Elizabeth put on her wrapper, slippers and cap and ran out. I was bitterly cold, and shivering from fright and cold, sat undecided as to what to do. Our steward came down to close the port and I asked him if the order had been given to close all the ports, but he said 'No, it's only cold, go to bed; it's nothing at all.' Before Elizabeth returned I decided to get dressed as I had seen a gentleman in one of the rooms opposite pull his shoes in from the passageway. When she came in she told of many people outside half-dressed, one woman having a thin white pigtail down her back and a feather hat; also that some man was fastened in his inside room unable to open his door. He was much worried, calling for help, and young Williams, a well-known amateur tennis-player and a friend of young Thayer's put his shoulder to the panels and broke it in. The steward was most indignant and threatened to have him arrested for defacing the beautiful ship.

I had my shoes nearly buttoned, and she said, 'Why, Martha, are you dressing?' And I said I should feel much safer with my clothes on and could go to bed later if it all was right. She then decided to dress also. We did not hurry, and dressed fully as if for breakfast, putting on our burglar pockets containing our letters of credit and money. I determined also to do my hair and put on a lined waist and old winter suit as it was so cold. While Elizabeth was doing her hair the ship suddenly settled, frightening me very much, and I urged her not to take pains but to hurry.

Just as I was wholly dressed and she hooking her waist Mr Thayer [Mr Thayer Senior] appeared at the door, which we had opened, and said he was very glad that we had dressed. He thought there was no danger, but we had struck ice and there was much on deck and he urged us to come up and see it, saying we would find him and Mrs Thayer on the deck. I put on my fur coat over everything and Elizabeth said she thought she would wear her watch, which reminded me that mine was hanging by the bureau and I quickly put it on. I took my glasses and small change purse, also a clean handkerchief. We then left our room, leaving the electric lights on, also the electric heater so it would be warm on our return. We closed the door and started down the long passageway and up the stairs.

On the next deck we met the Thayer family, who seemed to be waiting for us, and started up to go on the deck when a steward called 'All back to staterooms for life preservers.' We turned around and I cannot remember that we ran but we walked quickly to our rooms and Elizabeth climbed up, pulling down two life preservers from off the top of her closet. We said then we felt it must be serious if they had ordered the life belts, and we were much frightened though very quiet. We again went up the stairs, with our life preservers in our hands and once more joined the Thayer family. We quietly read the notices of 'inside front' and 'inside back' and put them on over our heads, Elizabeth tying mine and I tying hers. We put ours on over our heavy coats. After our life preservers were on, Mrs Thayer suggested getting Jack's coat, and Elizabeth and I followed to the steward's room, and when Mrs Thayer took the coat we each took our steamer rugs, not knowing why, but simply that we were there.

My mind is a blank as to the trip we took to the boat deck, when I distinctly remember being beside the gymnasium on the starboard side and seeing Mr Ismay come out, noting the fact that he had dressed hurriedly, as his pyjamas were below his trousers. After getting our rugs we were in the companionway of A Deck when orders came for women and children to boat deck and men to starboard side. Elizabeth and I took each other's hands, not to be separated in the crowd, and all went on deck, we following close to Mrs Thayer and her maid and going up narrow iron stairs to the forward boat deck which, on the *Titanic*, was the captain's bridge.

At the top of the stairs we found Captain Smith looking much worried, and anxiously waiting to get down after we got up. The ship listed heavily to port just then. As we leaned against the walls of the officers' quarters, rockets were being fired over our heads, which was most alarming, as we fully realized that if the *Titanic* had used her wireless to ill effect and was sending rockets it must be serious. Shortly after that the order came from the head dining saloon steward to go down to the A deck, when Mrs Thayer remarked, 'Tell us where to go and we will follow. You ordered us up here and now you are taking us back,' and he said 'Follow me.'

On reaching the A deck we could see, for the decks were

lighted by electricity, that a boat was lowered parallel to the windows; these were opened, and a steamer chair put under the rail for us to step on. The ship had listed badly by that time and the boat hung far out from the side so that some of the men said, 'No woman could step across that space.' A call was made for a ladder on one of the lower decks, but before it ever got there we were all in the boat. Whether they had drawn the boat over with boathooks nearer the side I do not know, but the space was easily jumped with the help of two men in the boat. The only gentleman I remember seeing at all was Colonel Astor, who was stepping through the window just in front of me when the crew said, 'Step back, sir; no men in this boat.' He remarked that he wanted to take care of his wife [who was pregnant], but on being told again that no men could go, he called 'Goodbye' and said he would follow in another boat, asking the number of our boat, which they said was 'No 4'. In going through the window I was obliged to throw back the steamer rug, for, with my fur coat and huge cork life preserver, I was very clumsy. Later we found the stewards or crew had thrown the steamer rugs into the boat, and they did good service, Elizabeth's round a baby thinly clad, and mine for a poor member of the crew pulled in from the sea.

Our boat I think took off every woman on the deck at that time, and was the last on the port side to be lowered. Only one man went down with us; the boat was lowered slowly, first at the bow, then at the stern, and very carefully. When near the water the man gave the order to 'Let her go,' but we all called 'Not yet, it's a long way to the water.' On reaching the water they called from the deck to know who was in command and a man answered, 'The quartermaster.' They then said, 'Who else?' and he said, 'I am alone.' Then they said 'We will send you two more men,' and shortly a boatswain and common sailor came down over the davit ropes and into the boat . . .

Of the scores of survivors who told their stories at the time or left private accounts for posterity, John Thayer, his mother, and the two sisters are among the most persuasive. They had no axe to grind; they knew one another; they produced the accounts themselves, at home. They had nothing to hide. None of them had cause to feel guilty about surviving: the head of the Thayer family had been lost; the women had done as they were told; and John Thayer Jr had survived by luck. Martha Stevenson's story about Colonel Astor must be true. Mrs Astor went to stay with the Thayers in Haverford when they all returned to the United States, and if Martha's memory had been at fault, or if she had confused Astor with another passenger, the Thayers would have known it. Besides, her account is confirmed by Lightoller, who said he was the officer who prevented Astor from leaving.

Colonel Gracie, an amateur military historian, wrote the longest and best researched account by any first-class passenger. During the crisis he was indispensable, rounding up, with his friend Clinch Smith, women and children for the boats. (Smith, after the collision, picked up a flat piece of ice and told Gracie he could take it home as a souvenir.) One of the surprises in Gracie's book, which he put together with Lightoller's help, was his eye-witness evidence about the number of women among the dazed crowd huddled on the *Titanic*'s stern when she went down. Gracie was washed overboard at the last moment; he saw the women, to his astonishment, in the final minutes; he had thought all women had been got away.

Gracie made the point that because of the size of the *Titanic* no one could know what was happening except in his or her immediate vicinity, any more than someone standing on a street corner can know what is happening a block away. Nevertheless, from the Thayers, Gracie, and others a reasonably clear picture does emerge of what happened in first class.

The best witness from second class is the young schoolmaster Lawrence Beesley, though his general comments on the cause of the disaster and his recommendations about the steps that ought to be taken for the prevention

of similar disasters are over-confident for someone whose
entire seatime consisted of four days aboard the *Titanic*.
But his account of his own experiences is level-headed
and especially illuminating about the time it took for
passengers to realize that something was seriously wrong.
He himself left his cabin and went on deck not because
he was startled by the collision – he felt 'nothing more
than an extra heave of the engines and a more than
usually obvious dancing motion of the mattress' – but
because he was curious to find out why the ship had
stopped; he guessed she had dropped a propeller blade.
He went up on deck, which was deserted, and then into
the smoking room where a game of cards was in progress,
with several onlookers. One man had seen an iceberg go
by, 'towering above the decks', and had told the others:
'They all watched it disappear but then at once resumed
their game'. None of them – incredibly – had been
surprised or interested enough to go out on deck and
take a closer look. Their estimates of its height varied
from sixty to a hundred feet. 'One of the players, pointing
to his glass of whisky standing at his elbow and turning to
an onlooker, said "Just run along the deck and see if any
ice has come aboard: I would like some for this."' The
roar and hiss of the steam escaping from the boilers
surprised nobody in the smoking room; a steam train
blew off steam when it stopped, so why not an ocean
liner? It was only when the rockets started going up that
people realized that matters were serious; but even then
they scarcely understood that the ship was sinking. They
felt 'a wonderful sense' of security, Beesley said, as if
standing on 'a large rock'. On the boat deck, about an
hour after the collision, he saw one of the bandsmen
running down the starboard side, 'his cello trailing behind
him, the spike dragging along the floor'. It was soon

afterwards that the band started playing on the promenade deck and went on playing until the ship went down.

Beesley remembered one incident that helps to explain the statistics. He was on the boat deck when two women walked towards the rail separating the second-class from the first-class part of the deck. They asked an officer, who stood barring the way, if they could pass through to the boats. No, the officer politely told them, their boats were down on their own deck. Beesley concludes: 'If the second-class ladies were not expected to enter a boat from the first-class deck, while steerage passengers were allowed access to the second-class deck, it would seem to press rather hardly on the second-class men, and this is rather supported by the low percentage saved.' Beesley himself got away because, when he was looking down from the top deck at a boat swinging level with B deck, a member of the crew told him he had better jump, which he did, having first thrown in his dressing gown.

Beesley jumped some two hours after the *Titanic* was struck. The starboard side of the boat deck was then deserted; and Beesley was advised to take his chance only after the crew on B deck had searched for and failed to find any more women. Yet more than a hundred women died. Where had they been? And where – at the time that Beesley jumped from a deserted boat deck – was the rest of the 'mass of humanity' that Colonel Gracie, half an hour later, suddenly saw flooding up from below just before the ship foundered?

The British inquiry was not interested in these questions; Lord Mersey did not call a single steerage passenger. But they worried the politician from Michigan in charge of the American investigation, William Alder Smith. After the Senate inquiry officially closed in Washington, Senator Smith went to New York to pursue some independent research. He told a reporter he was deeply troubled by the thought of what had happened to the third-class passengers and wanted to find out whether they had been under any restraint. Evidently, he had reservations about the evidence of the *Titanic* officers, since both Lightoller and Lowe had told him categorically that there had been no restraint and that all classes had been given equal treatment. However, it turned out that Lightoller and Lowe had not been precisely accurate. In New York, Smith found a migrant who had seen a member of the crew locking a gate between steerage and the upper decks. But the incident seemed to be isolated and inconclusive, since the migrant went on to say that the passengers had broken the gate down and were thereafter treated the same as other passengers. Elsewhere in the records are reports by third-class survivors about being herded behind ropes by crew members. How many were thus restrained, or for how long, or why, is obscure. There is no evidence that it was general ship's policy to keep the steerage passengers back while the rest escaped.

One enterprising third-class passenger told an innocent tale of how he had found his way on to the boat deck and quietly stepped aboard a lifeboat, evidently entirely unaware, even at the time he was making his statement, that he had done anything in the least deplorable.

Clearly, there was much more confusion and even more bewilderment in steerage than in other classes. By 1912, the balance of migrants heading for the United States had shifted away from northern Europe towards southern Europe, Russia and the Middle East. There were Syrians and Armenians aboard the *Titanic* and many of the migrants spoke no English. Unlike the first- and second-class passengers, whose immediate instinct was to put on warm clothes, the migrants' instinct was to try to save their belongings, appearing in the passageways laden with parcels and suitcases, or carrying bundles on their backs. Fewer crew members were on hand to tell them what to do. Those who were ignorant of their true plight thought they would be safer on board than in a lifeboat; others were so alarmed that they despaired too early. The American psychologist Wynn C. Wade not long ago was allowed to publish the recollections of a Swedish survivor, the late August E. Wennerstrom. The protestant Swede had been irritated by the pious and supine Catholicism shown by fellow passengers: 'Hundreds were in a circle with a preacher in the middle, praying, crying, asking God and Mary to help them. They lay there still crying till the water was over their heads. They just prayed and yelled, never lifting a hand to help themselves. They had lost their own will power and expected God to do all the work for them.' Besides, the geography of the ship was against them. The route from steerage to the upper decks was long and complicated; the *Titanic*'s designers had not envisaged circumstances in which easy access would be crucial.

Senator Smith told a crowded Senate of his conclusions about the steerage passengers in a speech on 28 May.

The occupants of the forward steerage were the first of the passengers to realize the danger – one or two witnesses said they stepped out of their berths into water probably an inch or two inches deep. Those in the forward steerage knew directly of the impact and of the presence of water which came up from the lower part of the ship into the mail room and the forward steerage. Those steerage passengers went on deck, and as fast as they were able took places in the lifeboats. While the after steerage, more than an eighth of a mile away, was by the operation of the added weight raised out of the water . . . so that these steerage passengers got their first warning of real danger as the angle of the deck became very great. I feel that the small number of steerage survivors was thus due to the fact that they got no definite warning before the ship was really doomed – when most of the lifeboats had departed.

This analysis begged the question of why 'no definite warning' reached them. Captain Smith's policy can only be guessed at. Glimpses of him after the collision have come down to us: exclaiming 'My God!' when he saw the degrees of list registered on the commutator on the bridge; giving Lightoller permission to take the covers off the lifeboats; telling the wireless operators to call for help; being handed a gun by the first officer; shouting through a megaphone. At the end, he told the wireless operators that they had done their duty and should now look out for themselves; the evidence that he was seen on deck calling, 'Every man for himself' is strong; that he urged others to 'Be British' is less strong. Why did he not issue a general alarm as soon as he himself knew the seriousness of what had occurred, which was within a very short time of the collision? He had then ordered the carpenter to sound the ship; he had toured her himself with Thomas Andrews, the head of the Harland & Wolff team (none of whom survived); and he conveyed a sense of urgency to those passengers he happened to encounter. He talked to Chief Engineer Bell, who would have agreed that he and his men would do all they could to keep the pumps and power supply working for as long as possible. But neither Lightoller nor Lowe nor Boxhall of the surviving officers seem to have been given any general orders by the captain. When Lightoller was asked whether he was obeying his captain's orders in sending away women and children first, he said he was obeying 'the rule of human nature'. The presumption must be that Smith thought a general alarm would cause panic below decks and chaos above.

At all events, no general strategy was applied to the emergency. This was true even of the lifeboats, where a definite plan was vital – given the lifeboat shortage – if as many lives as possible were to be saved. The government department responsible for lifeboat requirements was the Board of Trade. Its regulations called for ships of 10,000 tons and over to carry a minimum of sixteen boats, with a total minimum cubic capacity of 5500 feet. It further laid down that 'If the boats placed under the davits do not furnish sufficient accommodation for all persons on board, then additional wood, metal, collapsible, or other boats of approved design (whether placed on davits or otherwise), or approved life-rafts shall be carried.' But the regulations included a fatal concession. Provided a ship was efficiently divided into watertight compartments – as seemed indubitably true of the *Titanic* – then the total cubic capacity of all lifesaving boats could be reduced. Thus the law, in the *Titanic*'s case, only called for 8250 cubic feet, which, given the Board of Trade estimate that 10 cubic feet was enough for one person, meant that legally there needed to be enough space for only 825 people. American regulations were much stricter. They would have required the *Titanic* to provide enough lifeboat space for 2142 people – still not enough places for a full complement.

The builders and owners of the *Titanic* changed their minds about the lifeboats late in the day. An article in *Engineering*, published while the ship was being built, described a new and improved device for lowering boats on board ship, the quadrant davit for double-banked boats. The article explained the success of the standard Welin quadrant davit, of which 3000 had recently come into use. Its popularity was due not merely to its mechanical superiority but to the fact that it took up less deck space.

To all familiar with the conditions of modern ocean travel [said the journal] it will be patent what this really means. Nowadays the success of a line of passenger-carrying steamers depends (at least on certain routes) largely upon its popularity among the travelling public. Competition has in many instances afforded a wide choice of routes, and passenger lines must provide, at the present day, vessels not only as safe and well found as possible in all respects, but also boats which are attractive and offer special facilities for the pleasurable occupation of the long hours of enforced leisure. For these and other reasons, saving in deck space is a distinct advantage, and it may be taken that any gear which renders this possible has much to recommend it.

The new and improved davits made it possible to double-bank boats in a way that satisfied Board of Trade regulations. Hitherto, the Board of Trade had said that all boats must be 'under davits', which meant that inboard boats did not count. So lifeboats had to be in a long straight line, which took up space and spoiled the view. Now ships could have twice as many boats in much less than twice the space, because one pair of davits could be swung through an arc wide enough to raise and lower two or even, if required, three boats.

This was the system originally planned for the *Titanic*. *Engineering* published a drawing showing how double-banked boats would provide lifesaving space for 1700 people. Triple-banking would have provided space for 2500. But the plans were revised. Owners and builders decided that, to give the *Titanic* a competitive advantage, more deck space was more desirable than more boats. So the *Titanic* was equipped with sixteen lifeboats and four emergency rafts, enough for some 1200 people. It should have been possible to get away all these boats fully laden during the two hours or more before the ship sank; the ship took on an increasingly awkward list, but the sea was calm.

All boats were got away, but with only some 700 people on board, and of those a sizeable number were crew, not passengers. The operation got off to a slow start. The collision was immediately followed by the order, 'All hands on deck.' At that point Lightoller, according to his own account, used his initiative to tell the bosun's mate of his watch to strip the covers off the boats and clear them away. Then he asked Chief Officer Wilde if he should swing the boats out, but Wilde told him to wait. Next, Lightoller saw Captain Smith leaving the wireless room, 'his face stern but haggard.' In one Lightoller version he cupped his hand to the captain's ear (because of the noise of escaping steam) and asked if he should swing the boats out; in the other, if he should get the women and children away. Captain Smith in both versions agreed. But Smith did not tell Lightoller that he had just ordered the wireless operators to send out the international distress call. Thus Lightoller did not know the damage was serious until the first few boats had been loaded and lowered the 75 feet from davit to sea level, and even then did not believe the ship would sink. He only came to realize she was doomed after making a series of brief visits to the head of a long narrow stairway, constructed for the use of the crew, that led down from the boat deck to some four decks below; it was the sight of the water creeping further and further up the stairway that gave him a sense of urgency. The form it took was to make him sharply conscious of the 'unutterable disgrace of going down with boats still hanging on the davits.' He was frustrated and briefly delayed in his work by the refusal of some people, including Mr and Mrs Straus, to get into the boats, and he ran out of experienced help, since few of the crew were all-round seamen and those that were competent were needed to accompany the women and children in the boats. Instead of organizing and supervising the efforts of others, he himself had to throw off his overcoat and set to work – lifting women, who stood in a row with their arms held out, bodily across the gap between the boats' gunwales and the ship's deck.

Very soon after the disaster there was a public outcry, especially in the United States, from newspapers and others wanting to know why the *Titanic* had carried so few lifeboats, and why they had not all been filled. The first question was soon answered: the *Titanic* had adhered to British regulations which were disgracefully out of date. The second question was less rapidly answered, but it eventually emerged at the American inquiry that both Lightoller and Lowe, on the port and starboard sides respectively, assumed it would be hazardous to fill up the boats when still suspended from the davits; either the boats might 'buckle up', as Lowe put it, or the davits might give way. They did not know that Harland & Wolff had tested the davits and established that they would carry the weight of lifeboats filled to capacity.

Lightoller's idea was to get the boats into the water safely, though only partly full, and then send them to an open hatch at the bottom of a gangway to fill up with more passengers. But the bosun's mate and team he sent below for this purpose were never seen again. One mystery remains, however. Even if Lightoller and Lowe did not know about the strength of the davits, what about Captain Smith? Supposing that Smith did not know either, what about all the Harland & Wolff representatives on board? They included Thomas Andrews, the Harland & Wolff director, Lord Pirrie's nephew, who had been trained by the firm and had taken a deep interest in all practical details of the ship's design from the initial stages. They also included the chief shipyard draughtsman, Mr R. Chisholm, than whom, said *Engineering*, 'no one was more conversant with modern practice in the building of large merchant ships'. They must have seen what was happening. Yet it was only the last boats, after pushing and shoving, that were filled up.

One gets the impression from Lightoller and Lowe that they were fearful of being rushed by panic-stricken passengers. As soon as he heard that the ship had struck, Lowe equipped himself with a revolver. When about half the boats on the port side had been got away, Chief Officer Wilde came over to Lightoller from the starboard side and asked him where the small arms were. It had been one of Lightoller's jobs in Belfast to receive and take charge of revolvers and ammunition, so he led Wilde and the captain to his cabin and gave them a revolver each. Lightoller deduced that 'there had been some trouble' with the starboard side boats. Lowe told the Senate inquiry he had fired to deter 'a lot of Italians' who were 'glaring more or less like wild beasts ready to spring' into a boat. Later he issued a statement saying he had not meant that the 'wild beasts' were Italian; he meant only that they were 'of the types of the Latin races'. Lightoller also found his revolver useful. After getting the last lifeboat away he went forward to fill and lower the much smaller No 2 emergency boat. 'I climbed aboard to find three or four men hidden under the thwarts.' Nearly a quarter of a century later, Lightoller wrote of this incident: 'Let me say at once they were neither British nor American; in fact, never in my life have I been so unspeakably proud of the English-speaking race as I was during that night. The cool, calm unselfish courage exemplified throughout has never been excelled.' The 'would-be stowaways', he continued, were rapidly dealt with. 'A few threats, accompanied by the flourish of an empty revolver, soon cleared the boat which was quickly filled and in the water.'

The *Titanic*'s officers knew from the beginning that there were not enough boats to accommodate all those on board; they soon realized that there was also a shortage of trained crew. It is hard to resist the conclusion that, consciously or unconsciously, their aim in these desperate circumstances was to get away as many first- and second-class passengers as possible – who were in any case the nearest to the boats – before the whole operation was swamped by uncontrollable hordes from steerage.

To that extent, it is fair to say the rich were favoured over the poor. But one should remember that of the men in first class only 58 out of 173 were saved: 34 per cent is not a high percentage, even though it is strikingly higher than that in the other classes. Money was not enough; many of the richest and best known drowned. Wilfred Scawen Blunt, the writer and adventurer, wrote in his diary that if anyone had to drown, it was best that it should be the Anglo-American millionaires. It was a foolish sentiment, and no doubt widely shared. But it was, and is, incompatible with the notion that all the rich received favoured treatment.

4

In the Lifeboats

Leaving the ship was a fearful experience even for those who found a place in the boats. It was unimaginably terrifying for those who jumped or were swept overboard. For most survivors, though, the hours still ahead were to bring the most horrific moments of all. During that time, some of them faced character tests they failed to pass.

Few of the lifeboats got away smoothly. Falls jammed; the lights required by Board of Trade regulations in all boats were found in some cases to be missing; so were plugs. As Lowe blithely explained to the American inquiry, not every seaman member of a liner's crew was competent to handle a large 30-foot lifeboat, or had even set foot in one. True all-round seamen were rare aboard the *Titanic*. 'Many of the sailors could not row,' said Lowe. Mrs Thayer concluded that the man in charge of her lifeboat could not be a quartermaster, as he claimed, because he was so 'absolutely inefficient'. She was mistaken, however; he was Quartermaster Perkis.

Besides Mrs Thayer and the quartermaster, No 4 lifeboat contained Martha Stevenson and her sister; Mrs Astor and her trained nurse and maid; Mrs Thayer's maid; Mrs Widener and her maid; Mrs Carter, her two children and maid; Mrs Arthur Ryerson, her boy, two daughters, governess and maid; and many women and children from second and third class; some forty-five in all.

Martha Stevenson described what happened after the boat was in the water.

When we reached the sea we found the ship badly listed, her nose well in so that there was water to the D deck, which we could plainly see as the ship was lighted and the ports on D deck were square instead of round. No lights could be found in our boat and the men had great difficulty in casting off the blocks as they did not know how they worked. My fear here was great, as she [the *Titanic*] seemed to be going faster and faster and I dreaded lest we be drawn in before we could cast off.

When we were finally ready to move on, the order was called from the deck to go to the stern hatch and take off some men [this was the Lightoller plan that failed because the bosun's mate and the party sent to execute it disappeared]. There was no hatch open and we could see no men but our crew obeyed orders, much to our alarm, for they were throwing wreckage over and we could hear a noise resembling china breaking, which we learned later was the cracking of the boiler plates. We implored the men to pull away from the ship but they refused, and we pulled three men into the boat who had dropped off the ship and were swimming towards us. One man was drunk and had a bottle of brandy in his pocket which the quartermaster promptly threw overboard and the drunk was thrown into the bottom of the boat and a blanket thrown over him. After getting in these three men they told how fast she was going and we all implored them to pull for our lives to get out from the suction when she should go down.

The drunk was a fireman from Belfast, Paddy Dillon, and he was the luckiest man of the night. He found the brandy somewhere, rapidly became drunk, toppled over the *Titanic*'s side, and was immediately picked up. Beesley was also lucky. He was young and wide-eyed enough to experience the lowering of himself and sixty others down the liner's black hull as 'a great adventure'. If anyone wanted to know what the sensation was like, he recommended them to measure seventy-five feet from a tall house or block of flats, look down on the ground, and then imagine themselves being crammed into a boat and descending in a continuous series of jerks. When his

boat was in the water no one knew how to release the
falls. It was carried parallel to the ship until it was directly
underneath another boat being lowered. The crew on the
boat deck could not hear the shouts from the Beesley
boat, nor the subsequent shouts from the boat being
lowered, and Beesley and his sixty companions were
about to be crushed when at the last moment a sailor
found a knife and cut the falls. The crew members in
Beesley's boat were useless:

> I do not think they can have had any practice in rowing, for
> all night long their oars crossed and clashed; if our safety had
> depended on speed or accuracy in keeping time it would have
> gone hard with us. Shouting began from one end of the boat to
> the other as to what we should do, where we should go, and no
> one seemed to have any knowledge how to act. At last we
> asked, 'Who is in charge of this boat?' but there was no reply.

Beesley could not be sure exactly who was in the boat,
because in the darkness he could see only a few feet, but
he thought the list was as follows; no first class; three
women, one baby, and two men from second class; and
the other passengers steerage – mostly women; a total of
about thirty-five passengers. The rest, about twenty-five
or possibly more, were crew, including stokers. A stoker,
by common consent, was appointed captain. How such a
comparatively large number of crew got away is obscure.
Of the 900 odd crew carried nearly a quarter were
saved, by comparison with the 16 per cent saved of male
passengers.

Beesley's boat was launched, he reckoned, about an
hour and a half before the *Titanic* sank; yet it contained
almost as many crew as passengers. One stoker told him
he had been at work in the stokehole when the collision
occurred. The whole side of a compartment had caved in
and the inrushing sea had thrown him off his feet. He

went on deck, but was ordered down again with others to draw the fires from under the boilers; that done, they were allowed back on deck. He must thus have been one of the first to know the extent of the damage, and one of the first to get away; perhaps the facts were linked. The stoker got away because he knew early on that the ship was doomed; many steerage passengers died because they did not know until too late.

The stoker had been safely in his lifeboat for at least an hour, possibly much longer, when John Thayer jumped. Thayer thought later that pure chance, a matter of five seconds, saved him from the same fate as Long, his new friend. Long did not jump but let go of the rail and slid down the side of the ship. Thayer jumped outwards, feet first. 'I am afraid that the few seconds elapsing between our going, meant the difference between being sucked into the deck below, as I believe he was, or pushed out by the backwash. I was pushed out and then sucked down.'

The shock of the cold water, he said, took the breath out of his lungs. Down and down he went, spinning. Fortunately he was a good swimmer. Under water, he swam as hard as he could in the direction he thought to be away from the ship, and finally came up with his lungs bursting, but not having swallowed any water. Facing him, about forty yards distant, was the *Titanic*. 'I don't know why I didn't keep swimming away. Fascinated, I seemed tied to the spot.' The ship appeared to be surrounded by a glare, the water was over the base of the first funnel, and the people massed on the stern were still edging backwards. As the ship rumbled and roared, a funnel lifted off among a cloud of sparks and fell, missing Thayer by thirty or forty feet. Again he was sucked down, struggling and trying to swim, but 'spent'. As he came up for the second time he felt some obstruction near his head and, putting up his hand to push it away, found it to be the cork fender of a canvas collapsible lifeboat, floating beside him bottom up. Four or five men pulled him aboard. Although it seemed like hours, he had probably been in the water for no more than four minutes, if that. His watch stopped at 2.22 A.M.

Lightoller spent his last moments on board freeing this same collapsible, borrowing Colonel Gracie's pocket knife to cut the lashings. That was the last boat on the port side. Lightoller then made sure that all boats on the starboard side had also been got away and, with nothing further to be done that could be of the slightest help to those remaining, took a header into the sea from the top of the wheelhouse. First he was sucked up against the wire grating over the immense airshaft at the base of the forward funnel, and glued there by the force of water rushing down to the decks below. He began to sink with the ship. Blown away from what he thought was certain death by a sudden blast of hot air at his back, he surfaced briefly among floating bodies before he was again dragged down by water pouring into a second grating. He could not remember afterwards how he escaped from there. When he recovered his wits he realized he was alongside the collapsible he had just freed. He was clinging to a length of rope attached to it when the *Titanic*'s forward funnel went. As it crashed into the sea nearby, the 'terrific wash' picked up both the boat and Lightoller and flung them clear.

Gracie's experience was comparable. By the time his useful pocket knife had done its work, Gracie was trapped between the massed crowds astern and the advancing water forward. He tried to climb on to the roof of the officers' quarters, but as he did so the ship took the sudden dive that everyone noticed and a wall of water came at him. He had been hanging on to a rail, but soon let go. He found himself in a whirlpool, under water, terrified that he might be boiled in the hot water coming up from the boilers. However, swimming with what seemed to him to be 'unusual strength', he surfaced, got clear, and clambered on to the same upturned boat as the stalwart officer whose conduct in the crisis he had much admired, Lightoller.

The time now, two hours and forty minutes after the iceberg had struck, was about twenty past two in the morning. In the immediate vicinity of the *Titanic*, this was the situation. The ship herself was rapidly foundering. Nobody except the most ignorant or the most credulous can have believed at this stage in the possibility of her survival as a floating hulk and haven. It is probable that the engineers were dead. Almost fifteen hundred people, mainly men but some women, crowded the stern. Many wore lifejackets. An English priest, Father Byles, moved among them, hearing confessions. The last well-attested glimpses of Captain Smith describe him using his megaphone to hurry people into the last boats, telling the crew in the final minutes that it was every man for himself, and then taking up a stand on the bridge to await the end.

Near the ship, the sea was strewn with steamer chairs and other wooden debris, thrown down in the desperate hope that it might give someone something to cling on to. Further off floated sixteen lifeboats, some full, some half empty. A few of the boats had pulled away from the *Titanic* under the impression, given them by Captain Smith himself, that they would be transferred immediately to another ship that had been seen – many thought – no more than a few miles away. That expectation had proved false. None of the boats, even those under competent leadership, had a clear idea of what should be done next. There seemed no reason to try to head in any particular direction. In many of the boats, the oars were manned not by crew but by women. The night continued to be spectacular; stars of a brilliance that nobody had seen before, the visibility so clear that when a star sank below the horizon, the horizon bisected the star, with half of it shining above and half of it below the water. The sea was still as calm as a backwater of the Thames, but it was bitterly cold, and the temperature of the water 4 degrees below freezing.

'It was Sad when the Great Ship Went Down' is the first line of a ballad still sung at American summer camps. The line scarcely does the moment justice.

Lightoller was standing on the upturned collapsible:

I could now see the massive outline of the *Titanic* silhouetted against the starlit sky, her blackness emphasized by row upon row of lights still burning. But only for a matter of minutes. With her attaining an angle of about 60 degrees all the lights suddenly went out, and, with a roar, every one of the gigantic boilers left their beds and went crashing down through bulkheads and everything that stood in their way.

Crowds of people were still on the after deck and at the stern, but the end was near. Slowly and almost majestically, the immense stern reared itself up, with propellers and rudder clear of the water, till at last she assumed the exact perpendicular. Then with an ever-quickening glide, she slid beneath the water of the cold Atlantic.

Despite our own danger, every one of us had been held spellbound by the sight, and like a prayer as she disappeared, the words were breathed, 'She's gone.'

John Thayer wrote:

Her deck was turned slightly towards us. We could see groups of the almost fifteen hundred people still aboard, clinging in clusters or bunches, like swarming bees; only to fall in masses, pairs or singly, as the great after part of the ship, two hundred and fifty feet of it, rose into the sky, till it reached a sixty-five or seventy-degree angle. Here it seemed to pause, and just hung, for what felt like minutes. Gradually she turned her deck away from us, as though to hide from our sight the awful spectacle.

We had an oar on our upturned boat. In spite of several men working on it, amid our cries and prayers, we were being gradually sucked in towards the great pivoting mass. I looked upwards – we were right underneath the three enormous propellers. For an instant, I thought they were sure to come right down on top of us. Then, with the deadening noise of the bursting of her last few gallant bulkheads, she slid quietly away from us into the sea.

There was no final apparent suction, and practically no wreckage that we could see.

I don't remember all the wild talk and calls that were going on in our boat, but there was one concerted sigh or sob as she went from view.

The description by John Thayer's mother was a formal statement, made under oath:

All the lights were burning up to the very time the ship sank, as I saw tier upon tier of lights disappear beneath the water as the forward part of the ship slid down as though being launched – at the same time there was a sound as of drawing a boat over a pebbly beach. Then there was a rumbling noise, and a red glare of cinders in the air, and the forward part of the ship sank out of view. The after part of the ship then reared in the air, with the stern upwards, until it assumed an almost vertical position. It seemed to remain stationary in this position for many seconds (perhaps twenty), then suddenly dove straight down out of sight.

The time was 2.20 A.M., according to a wrist watch worn by one of the passengers in Mrs Thayer's boat.

Martha Stevenson tried not to look. 'When the call came that she was going I covered my face and then heard someone call, "She's broken." After what seemed a long time I turned my head only to see the stern almost perpendicular in the air so that the full outline of the blades of the propeller showed above the water. She then gave her final plunge.'

As the ship went down, Mr Wennerstrom, in the same collapsible as Lightoller, Gracie and Thayer, saw a man lowering himself down the logline beside the enormous rudder.

'At the last,' said one onlooker, 'the end of the world. A smooth, slow chute.' 'She tilted slowly up, revolving apparently about a centre of gravity just astern of midship,' Beesley wrote, 'until she attained a vertically upright position; and there she remained – motionless! As she swung up, her lights, which had shone without a flicker all night, went out suddenly, came on again for a single flash, then went out altogether.'

Then came the noise, described as partly a groan, and partly a smash, that some thought was an explosion, and some, including Lightoller and Beesley, the sound of engines and machinery and boilers coming adrift and crashing their way through the bulkheads. No one, said Beesley, had ever heard anything like it before, and no one wanted to hear anything like it again. 'When the noise was over the *Titanic* was still upright like a column: we could see her only as the stern and some 150 feet of her stood outlined against the star-specked sky, looming black in the darkness, and in this position she continued for some minutes – I think as much as five minutes, but it may have been less. Then, first sinking back a little at the stern, I thought, she slid slowly forwards through the water and dived slantingly down; the sea closed over her . . .'

Many survivors long remembered the sequence of sounds that night: the 'tearing calico' when the iceberg struck; the hiss of the boilers that made speech impossible when they were shut down by the engineers; the detonation of the rockets; the stupendous noise from inside the ship as she tipped on end. The silences were remembered, too: the silence after the hiss of the boilers ceased; the silence as the survivors climbed aboard the *Carpathia*. Nobody forgot the most terrible sound of all, the cries of hundreds that came from the *Titanic* after she sank; nor did anyone forget the unearthly silence that eventually followed. Beesley, for one, was taken unawares. He did not know how many boats the *Titanic* carried, nor how many people were still on board. He would not have been surprised to learn that everyone was safe. 'Unprepared as we were for such a thing, the cries of the drowning floating across the quiet sea filled us with stupefaction.' John Thayer remembered 'one continuous wailing chant – It sounded like locusts on a mid-summer night, in the woods of Pennsylvania. This terrible continuing cry lasted for twenty or thirty minutes, gradually dying away, as one after another could no longer withstand the cold and exposure. Practically no one was drowned, as no water was found in the lungs of those later recovered. Everyone had on a life preserver.'

Then Thayer posed the question that had troubled him for twenty-eight years.

The partially filled lifeboats standing by, only a few hundred yards away, never came back. Why on earth they did not come back is a mystery. How could any human being fail to heed those cries?
The most heart-rending part of the whole tragedy was the failure, right after the *Titanic* sank, of those boats which were only partially loaded, to pick up the poor souls in the water. There they were, only four or five hundred yards away, listening to the cries, and still they did not come back. If they had turned back several more hundred would have been saved. No one can explain it. It was not satisfactorily explained in any investigation.

Some boats did their best. On Thayer's overturned boat, people were helped aboard 'until we were packed like sardines. Then out of self-preservation we had to turn some away.' No 4 boat went back. 'We rowed back and pulled in five more men from the sea,' wrote Martha Stevenson. 'Their suffering from the icy water was intense and two men who had been pulled into the stern afterwards died, but we kept their bodies with us.' Mrs Thayer, despite her disapproval of the 'disagreeable' and allegedly incompetent Quartermaster Perkis, helped to row No 4; and it was Perkis who decided to go back. They rescued another fifteen or so who were standing up on a second capsized boat, until they were so full that there was nowhere to sit except on the gunwales and they were taking in water.

Fifth Officer Lowe made a valiant attempt to organize a rescue in a seamanlike manner. His lifeboat, No 14, was virtually full. Assembling four emptier boats, he redistributed the passengers among them, picked a crew of seamen to join him in No 14, and took it back among the wreckage, turning over bodies for signs of life. Many were dead, apparently frozen rather than drowned. Lowe and his men rescued three people alive, including one 'Japanese or Chinese young fellow'.

One officer who did not go back was the Third Officer, Herbert John Pitman. He was 34, from Castle Cary in Somerset, and appears in contemporary photographs wearing a walrus moustache. He had served a four-year apprenticeship, then spent three years with James Nourse Ltd, a year with Blue Anchor running to Australia, six months running to Japan, and five years with White Star.

After the collision, he had worked on the starboard side under First Officer Murdoch, uncovering and swinging out No 5 lifeboat, and helping women climb aboard. He had been impressed by the modern davits, a great improvement on the old-fashioned kind. 'I thought what a jolly fine idea they were, because with the old-fashioned davits it would require about a dozen men to lift her, a dozen men at each end.' With five or six men, he swung out

No 5 in two or three minutes. When there were 'no more ladies', he allowed a few male passengers aboard, and then five male crew. (On the port side, Lightoller was adopting a more rigorous policy; no male passengers, and only two crew to each boat.) When the boat was, as he thought, reasonably full, with forty-five people aboard, Pitman jumped back on deck, whereat Murdoch told him, 'You go in charge.' He obeyed with some reluctance, thinking he would be better off on the ship. Once in the water, he told the crew to row to the north and then to lie on their oars, 'awaiting further developments'. An hour and a half later the *Titanic* went down.

Nine days later he was in Washington before the Senate committee of inquiry, where Senator Smith, like John Thayer twenty-eight years later, was wondering why some lifeboats, though not full, had failed to go to the help of the drowning. There followed this verbatim exchange between Smith and Pitman, as set down in the official Senate record.

SENATOR SMITH: Did you hear any cries of distress?

A: Oh, yes.

Q: What were they, cries for help?

A: Crying, shouting, moaning.

Q: From the ship, or from the water?

A: From the water, after the ship disappeared; no noises before.

Q: There were no noises from the ship's crew, or officers, or passengers, just preceding the sinking?

A: None.

Q: Immediately following the sinking of the ship you heard these cries of distress?

A: Yes.

Q: But, as I understand you, you were not in close proximity to those uttering the cries?

A: I may have been three or four hundred yards away; four or five hundred yards away.

Q: Did you attempt to get near them?

A: As soon as she disappeared I said, 'Now, men, we will pull towards the wreck.' Everyone in my boat said it was a mad idea, because we had far better save what few we had in my boat than go back to the scene of the wreck and be swamped by the crowds that were there.

Q: As a matter of fact, do you now know your boat would have accommodated twenty or twenty-five more people?

A: My boat would have accommodated a few more, yes; certainly.

Q: According to the testimony of your fellow officers –

A: My boat would have held more.

Q: Your boat would have held about sixty or sixty-five people.

A: About sixty.

Q: Tell us about your fellow passengers on that lifeboat. You say they discouraged you from returning or going in the direction of these cries?

A: They did. I told my men to get their oars out, and pull towards the wreck – the scene of the wreck.

Q: Yes.

A: I said, 'We may be able to pick up a few more.'

Q: Who demurred to that?

A: The whole crowd in my boat. A great number of them did.

Q: Women?

A: I could not discriminate whether women or men. They said it was rather a mad idea.

Q: I ask you if any woman in your boat appealed to you to return to the direction from which the cries came?

A: No one.

Q: You say that no woman passenger in your boat urged you to return?

A: None.

MR BURLINGHAM (appearing for White Star): It would have capsized the boat, Senator.

SENATOR SMITH: Pardon me, I am not drawing any unfair conclusion from this. One of the officers told us that a woman in his boat urged him to return to the site of the ship. I want to be very sure that this officer heard no woman asking the same thing. (*To the witness*) Who demurred, now, that you can specifically recall?

A: I could not name any one in particular.

Q: The men with the oars?

A: No. They did not; no. They started to obey my orders.

Q: You were in command. They ought to have obeyed your orders?

A: So they did.

Q: They did not, if you told them to pull toward the ship.

A: They commenced pulling towards the ship, and the passengers in my boat said it was a mad idea on my part to pull back to the ship, because if I did, we should be swamped with the crowd that was in the water, and it would add another forty to the list of drowned, and I decided I would not pull back.

Q: Officer, you really turned this No 5 boat around to go in the direction from which these cries came?

A: I did.

Q: And were dissuaded from your purpose by your crew –

A: No, not crew; passengers.

Q: One moment; by your crew and by the passengers in your boat?

A: Certainly.

Q: Then did you turn the boat toward the sea again?

A: No; just simply took our oars in and lay quiet.

Q: You mean you drifted?

A: We may have gone a little bit.

Q: Drifted on your oars?

A: We may have drifted along. We just simply lay there doing nothing.

Q: How many of these cries were there? Was it a chorus, or was it –

A: I would rather you did not speak about that.

Q: I would like to know how you were impressed by it.

A: Well, I can not very well describe it. I would rather you would not speak of it.

Q: I realize that it is not a pleasant theme, and yet I would like to know whether these cries were general and in chorus, or desultory and occasional?

A: There was a continual moan for about an hour.

Q: And you lay in the vicinity of that scene for about an hour?

A: Oh, yes; we were in the vicinity of the wreck the whole time.

Q: And drifted or lay on your oars during that time?

A: We drifted towards daylight, as a little breeze sprang up.

Q: Did this anguish or these cries of distress die away?

A: Yes; they died away gradually.

–

Q: Did they continue during most of the hour?

A: Oh, yes; I think so. It may have been a shorter time. Of course I did not watch every five minutes –

Q: I understand that and I am not trying to ask about a question of five minutes. Is that all you care to say?

A: I would rather that you would have left that out altogether.

Q: I know you would; but I must know what efforts you made to save the lives of passengers and crew under your charge. If that is all the effort you made, say so –

A: That is all, sir.

Q: And I will stop that branch of my questioning.

A: That is all, sir; that is all the effort I made.

Pitman's conduct did not concern the British inquiry. On the whole, Lord Mersey and his commissioners avoided matters of individual behaviour except when they bore on the reasons for the wreck. Rather against the will of Lord Mersey, however, the British court was inadvertently driven to look into the actions of one first-class passenger and his wife after they had been described in an unfavourable light by a member of the crew.

Sir Cosmo Duff Gordon, Bart., was of Scottish descent. One of his ancestors, James Duff, was British consul in Cadiz during the Peninsular War, and kept Wellington's armies so efficiently supplied that at the end of the campaign he was given a baronetcy. As consul, he had a finger in every pie; he went into the sherry business, which remained in the family for much of the nineteenth century. He never married, however; and at his death the title passed to his nephew William Gordon, a grandson of an earl of Aberdeen (and a cousin of Lord Aberdeen the Prime Minister of the 1850s) who added 'Duff' by special licence to his surname of Gordon. Sir Cosmo, the fifth baronet, was a tall, fine-looking man remembered in the family circle as someone who could be difficult. He was a good bridge player, and had fenced for England in the 1908 Olympics.

His wife Lucy was better known than he was: a sister of Elinor Glyn, the novelist and mistress of Lord Curzon, and a brilliant and sought-after dress designer with a very successful salon, Madame Lucile, in Hanover Square, where she was the first dress designer to require her models to move about. She taught Molyneux. She owned other establishments in Paris and New York, and the purpose of the trip to the United States was for Lady Duff Gordon, travelling with her secretary, Miss Laura Mabel Francatelli, to conduct business in Chicago. Sir Cosmo was her second husband.

The Duff Gordons' name came up in the British inquiry as a result of a decision to question one person from each lifeboat. For No 1 emergency boat the choice fell on a leading fireman, Charles Hendrickson of Southampton.

Hendrickson's story was that after finishing his duties below he had gone on deck and, without particularly being ordered to do so, had started to help clear away and lower lifeboats on the starboard side.

He had spent an hour or an hour and a half at this work when he was told to get into No 1 emergency boat. Two emergency boats were kept swung out and ready to be lowered at all times; they were smaller than the other lifeboats, with a capacity of thirty-five as against sixty-five. The No 1 boat went away, however, with one of the lookout men, Symons, in charge as coxswain and only eleven others: six crew (five firemen and trimmers, and one seaman) and five passengers, of whom only two were women. The women were Lady Duff Gordon and her secretary; one of the three male passengers was Sir Cosmo.

The arresting point about Hendrickson's story was that 'there was plenty of room for another dozen in the boat', despite the space taken up by four oars and a mast, yet no one except himself had proposed going back after the

Titanic sank to pick up other people. Once in the water, with members of the crew at the oars, the boat had pulled away about two hundred yards from the ship, and had been at that distance when she went down. When they heard the cries, Hendrickson had made a general appeal, he said, not addressed to anyone in particular, that they should look for survivors. 'I proposed in the boat that we should go back, and they would not listen to me,' he said. He never heard anyone else propose going back. But who was it, he was asked, who objected? 'Well, the passengers,' he said. 'I think it was the women objected.' There were only two women in the boat: Lady Duff Gordon and her secretary.

The force of Hendrickson's allegations came out most sharply when he was questioned by Harbinson, the counsel representing the third-class passengers. Hendrickson had said that the coxswain had not paid any attention to his proposal to go back.

Q: You say that that attitude of his [the coxswain's] was due to the protests of the Duff Gordons?
A: Yes.
Q: You say you heard cries?
A: Yes.
Q: Agonising cries?
A: Yes, terrible cries.
Q: At what distance?
A: About two hundred yards.

And later:

Q: They said it would be too dangerous to go back, we might get swamped. Who said that?
A: Sir Duff Gordon.

The original objection to going back had been made by Lady Duff Gordon, Hendrickson said, and her husband had backed her up. Hendrickson had been sitting close to them. 'Duff Gordon asked me if I wanted a smoke, and he gave me a cigar.'

That was not the only thing Duff Gordon had given him. 'In the early hours of the morning before we were picked up he said he would do something for us' – 'us' being the members of the crew. After they had been picked up by the *Carpathia*, Duff Gordon gave them all 'an order for £5', (Lady Duff Gordon had asked them to sign their names on her life preserver). Here was a sensational piece of news. Had Duff Gordon bribed the crew not to go back?

Hendrickson did not shift his position under cross-examination, though he was caught out on one minor point. He said there had been no sea-anchor in the boat, but admitted under questioning that he had never looked for one and nor had anyone else.

The burden of his story, however, was supported by another member of the crew, Taylor, also a fireman, who said he had been sitting on a thwart next to a man he later found out to be Sir Cosmo. He had heard Hendrickson's proposal about going back; he had also heard a woman whom he later found out to be Lady Duff Gordon say that the boat would be swamped if it did.

The coxswain, Symons, denied hearing any proposal or any protests. Symons in the witness box sounded extremely self-important, constantly using two phrases about being 'master of the situation' and 'using my discretion'. He was not in a very easy position himself. For one thing he had told the US inquiry that there had been between fourteen and twenty people in the boat, whereas in London he was forced to admit that there had only been twelve. Why had he given a wrong figure to the Senate, the Attorney-General asked him. 'I think

out that?
ut a doubt.
hat with the room in your boat, if you
you could save some?
what occurred to me. Again, I was
were rather in an abnormal condition,
many things to think about, but of
urred to one that people in the water
, yes.
s room in your boat; that they could
and been saved?

no suggestion that the boat should
the cries were coming from. The
w again immediately after the cries;
s to stop the sound.' He was asked
me he had thought about whether or
have been able to save any of the
'I do not know; it might have been
uld have been very difficult to get
ve were, and in the darkness, to find
ot thinking about it; he was attending
d had rather a serious evening, you
d nothing about the danger of being
e was taken in the boat of the cries
eople, and there had been no conver-
t.
neral kept probing the failure of the

om what you said, and correct me if it is
ht entered into your mind that you ought
save some of these people?
ot.
last witness [Hendrickson] told us that in

myself, sir, that the mistake I made then was through the way they muddle you about there.'

Symons claimed that the boat was much further than 200 yards away from the *Titanic* when she went down, and that he had in fact started to head in the direction of the cries; but they had stopped and so had he.

From the Duff Gordons' standpoint, Symons's most damaging assertion concerned the way they got into the boat in the first place. According to him, the two women had come running down the deck and jumped in, and were rapidly followed by Duff Gordon and two Americans.

A further allegation damaging to Sir Cosmo came from one of these Americans, a Mr C. E. H. Stengel. He had been asked at the American inquiry whether he knew who was giving directions in the boat. 'I think between Sir Duff Gordon and myself we decided which way to go.' ('Duff' was widely supposed to be Sir Cosmo's first name, not part of his surname.)

There was one more awkwardness. Lady Duff Gordon, as part of her professional life, had written articles for a Hearst newspaper, the *Sunday American*. The morning after the *Carpathia* arrived in New York, the paper's stable-mate, the *New York American*, had printed an article about the disaster signed by her. Immediately syndicated to England, as elsewhere, it said, among other things: 'We watched her – we were 200 yards away – go slowly down, almost peacefully.' It also said: 'Women and men were clinging to bits of wreckage in the icy water . . . And it was at least an hour before the awful chorus of shrieks ceased, gradually dying in a moan of despair.'

Thus the behaviour of the Duff Gordons – together with the conduct of J. Bruce Ismay, which we shall come to later – became the focus of rumour and scandal: all the

more so since it appeared to contrast shamefully with
the courage and self-sacrifice displayed by others – the
musicians, playing on as the ship went down; the engineers, who had given their lives to keep the ship afloat and
the lights burning as long as possible; Captain Smith,
who had gone down with his ship; the Strauses, who had
refused special treatment; the bravery of the Marconi
operator Phillips; the stoicism and sang-froid of the American millionaires. The list of heroes was long. Had a
British baronet let down the side?

On 20 May, the Duff Gordons appeared before the
British inquiry at their own request. Fashionable London
turned out for the occasion. Sir Cosmo, represented by
Henry Duke, KC, MP, faced three troublesome questions. How had he, as a man of honour, found a place in
a lifeboat when women were still on board? Why had the
lifeboat he was in not gone back to rescue others? What
inspired him, alone of all the passenger survivors, to hand
out money to the crew?

Sir Cosmo was first examined by the Attorney-General,
Sir Rufus Isaacs. Sir Cosmo explained that his wife had
awakened him just after the impact with the iceberg; he
had not at first got up, but when he did so he went to the
top deck, where the noise was 'perfectly indescribable',
and spoke to Colonel Astor. 'Who went down with the
vessel?' 'Yes.' The Attorney-General had made a point.

Sir Cosmo next described how he had watched men
stripping down a lifeboat, had gone below again to fetch
his wife and her secretary, and how they had all watched
three further lifeboats being filled, almost entirely with
women, and lowered. His wife and Miss Francatelli had
been asked two or three times to go, but had refused.
Once 'some men got hold of her [Lady Duff Gordon] and
tried to pull her away', but she still would not go. Then,
after the three lifeboats they had all been watching had

left, whe
started g
do someth
orders.' T
the emerg
"May we
wish you v
expression
helped Sir
up, and the
firemen tha
– Symons –

The Atto
concede that
In that case,
slightly, how
lifeboats, wh
could possibl
Cosmo; no o
there were pe
all the women

And where
went down? Si
been ordered b
the first two hu
fits and starts,
ship went down
yards away. He
to be a judge of
the figure was ab

Had he heard
first, and I heard,
confused sound.'

SIR RUFUS ISAACS:
the discussion of it,
drowning?

A: Yes.
Q: There is no doubt ab
A: Yes, I think so witho
Q: Did it occur to you
could get to these people
A: It is difficult to say
minding my wife, and we
you know. There were
course it quite well occ
could be saved by a boat
Q: And that there wa
have got into your boat
A: Yes, it is possible.

Sir Cosmo had heard
go back to the place
men had begun to ro
'In my opinion it wa
once more if at the ti
not his boat would
people in the water.
possible; but it wo
back, the distance v
anything.' He was n
to his wife; 'we ha
know.' He had said
swamped. No notic
from the drowning
sation on the subje

The Attorney-G
boat to go back.

Q: I understand fr
wrong, that no thou
to go back and try to
A: No, I suppose
LORD MERSEY: The

his opinion it would have been quite safe to have gone back. What do you say to that?

A: I do not know, my lord, whether it would have been safe. I do not know. I think it would have been hardly possible.

ATTORNEY-GENERAL: Why not possible?

A: I do not know which way we should have gone.

LORD MERSEY: When I say 'gone back' I mean towards where the cries came from.

A: I do not know about that. I could not speculate.

It was put to Sir Cosmo that two witnesses had said that a suggestion was made that the boat should go back. Sir Cosmo replied that he could only say that he himself had not heard any such suggestion.

The Attorney-General asked his final questions on this theme.

Q: You know now, do you not, that you might have saved a good many if you had gone back?

A: I do not know that.

Q: You know that your boat would have carried a good many more?

A: Yes, I know that is so, but it is not a lifeboat, you must remember; there are no air-tanks.

Later, Sir Cosmo was asked about Symons's evidence. Symons had said they did not go back when they heard the cries, but did go back later; however, he had strained his ears and heard nothing. Had Sir Cosmo heard Symons give that order to the men rowing in the boat? No, he had not.

Next came the money.

There was a man sitting next to me [Sir Cosmo said] and of course in the dark I could see nothing of him. I never did see him, and I do not know who he is. I suppose it would be some time when they rested on their oars, 20 minutes or half an hour after the *Titanic* had sunk, a man said to me, 'I suppose you have lost everything,' and I said, 'Of course.' He said, 'But you can get some more,' and I said 'Yes.' 'Well,' he said, 'we have lost all our kit and the company won't give us any more, and what is more our pay stops from tonight. All they will do is to send us back to London.' So I said to them, 'You fellows need not worry about that; I will give you a fiver each to start a new kit.' That is the whole of that £5-note story.

Aboard the *Carpathia*, he asked Hendrickson to give him a list of the men's names, which he did. It was Sir Cosmo's usual practice to draw cheques on his bankers, Coutts, on notepaper, and he told Miss Francatelli to make out cheques in this way to all the men. He saw Hendrickson, asked him to assemble the men, 'and just gave them each their cheque, asking each fellow what his name was . . . I said, "I am sorry I cannot give you money; but if you had it you would probably spend it all in New York, so it is just as well it should be in a cheque which will enable you to start your kit again."'

Lady Duff Gordon followed her husband to the witness box, after her counsel had told the Court that she insisted on doing so. She took the Court from the moment of impact and into the boats in a single answer.

I had quite made up my mind that I was going to be drowned, and then suddenly we saw this little boat in front of us – this little thing – (*pointing to a model*) and we saw some sailors and an officer apparently giving them orders and I said to my husband, 'Ought we not to be doing something?' and he said, 'Oh, we must wait for orders,' and we stood there for quite some time while these men were fixing up things and then my husband went forward and said, 'Might we get into this boat?' and the officer said in a very polite way indeed, 'Oh certainly; do; I will be very pleased' . . . They hitched us up in *this* sort of way into the boat and after we had been in a little while the boat was started to be lowered and one American gentleman got pitched in and one American gentleman was pitched in while the boat was being lowered down.

She was 'awfully sick' and very hazy about what happened thereafter, but she saw the *Titanic* sink.. She heard 'terrible cries' before the ship sank, and afterwards her impression was that there had been 'absolute silence'. She certainly had never said it would be dangerous to go back.

As for the article in the *New York American*, what happened was that the night they reached New York and the Ritz-Carlton hotel she and Sir Cosmo had had dinner with six ladies and a 'great friend of ours', Mr Merrett, the editor of the *Sunday American*. 'After he had left us about half an hour he telephoned to me and he said, "Mr Hearst has just rung me up, and must have your story of the *Titanic* wreck for tomorrow's newspaper." He said, "May I tell your story as I have heard it?" . . . I said "Yes," and he tells me afterwards he telephoned to their head office all he knew about it, and then a clever reporter put all that into words and it appeared next morning in the *New York American*.' It had been, she said, 'rather inventive', and much of it 'quite untrue', including the statements about being only 200 yards away when the ship went down and the shrieks lasting an hour.

Mr Harbinson had no questions for her.

What is one to make of the Duff Gordon episode? The lawyer Harbinson asked Sir Cosmo whether he would be stating the position accurately if he summed it up by saying that 'You considered when you were safe yourselves that all the others might perish.' Harbinson did his best to make it sound as if Sir Cosmo had promised the crew five-pound notes in order to induce them to row away from the drowning people. A whiff of class antagonism was in the air; Lord Mersey thought so, at any rate. He told Harbinson it was his duty to assist him, Lord Mersey, in arriving at the truth, 'not to try to make out a case for this class or that class or another class', or to make out a case against one person or another. Harbinson, before this intervention, had been suggesting to Sir Cosmo that his promise of financial help to the crew had coincided with the audible 'harrowing cries' of the drowning.

One interesting point about Lady Duff Gordon's testimony is that she denied telling the *New York American* that the lifeboat had been only 200 yards away when the *Titanic* sank – a figure that would have been in sharp contrast to her husband's, and Symons's, estimate of 1000 yards. But whatever else the 'clever reporter' invented, would he have invented 200 yards? It was at the least a strange coincidence that his invention agreed with Hendrickson's estimate.

Seventy-two years later, I learned from Sotheby's the auctioneers, a remarkable and apparently unrecorded letter came up for sale. It was written in pencil by Miss Francatelli on Ritz-Carlton hotel writing paper and dated 28 April 1912, thirteen days after the sinking. Miss Francatelli was writing to a Miss Marion Taylor in London, and the salient points, interspersed in the original with emotional comment on her ordeal, are as follows:

I was just getting into bed. Madame, & Sir Cosmo . . . were up on A deck the top, and I on E, the bottom deck for saloon Passengers . . . two Gentlemen came up . . . and told me . . . we had run into an iceberg, but we were quite safe . . . I still stood there quite 20 minutes . . . the water was on my deck, coming along the corridor . . . I found all the people, running up, & down the stairs . . . Oh Marion that was a sickening moment, I felt myself go like Marble . . . Sir Cosmo then took us up on top deck. Crowds were up there . . . several life boats had been lowered, they were preparing the last two, on that side of the ship, the Starboard side, they cried out, Any more women, saw us, & came to try & drag Madame & I away from Sir Cosmo, but Madame clung to Sir Cosmo . . . after all the lifeboats had gone, everybody seemed to rush to the other side of the boat, & leave ours vacant, but we still stood there, as Sir Cosmo said, we must wait for orders, presently. An officer started to swing off a little boat called the 'Emergency' boat . . . he saw us, & ordered us in, they were then firing the last rockets beside us . . . two other American gentlemen jumped in, & seven stokers . . . The dear officer gave orders to row away from the sinking boat at least two hundred yards . . . We saw the whole thing, and watched that tremendous thing quickly sink, there was then terrible, *terrible*, explosions, and all *darkness*, then followed the Awful cries & screams of the 1600 dear souls, fighting for their lives in the water. *Oh never shall I forget that awful night . . .*

The letter in general bears out the Duff Gordons' statements that they got into the boat under an officer's auspices and did not come running down the deck as alleged by Symons. But it tends to weaken the assertions that the boat was a thousand yards away from the sinking *Titanic*; it sounds as if Miss Francatelli was nearer than that to the explosions and the cries.

Lord Mersey in his report found any suggestion of bribery by Sir Cosmo 'unfounded'. But he added: 'I think, that if he had encouraged the men to return to the position where the *Titanic* had foundered they would probably have made an effort to do so and could have saved some lives.'

The verdict sounds just. Other boats went back and did their best.

Sir Cosmo died in 1931. He was deeply distressed by the aftermath of the sinking, and spent much of his time abroad, some of it in Cairo. Otherwise, he stayed in Scotland.

The present, eighth baronet, Sir Andrew Cosmo Lewis Duff Gordon, said not long ago in defence of his great uncle that any man who survived that nightmare ordeal by getting away in a lifeboat, when so many others perished, was likely to be regarded with suspicion. The slur on the fifth baronet's name notwithstanding, the ninth baronet will be another Sir Cosmo Duff Gordon.

5

The Conundrum of Captain Lord

The *Titanic* disaster had many sub-plots, but the most dramatic and mysterious concerns the stony-faced Captain Lord of the *Californian*. But for Captain Lord, there would not have been a disaster, because nobody aboard the *Titanic* would have been drowned.

At least, that is the official view. The American inquiry pronounced an unqualified and damning verdict. 'There is a very strong possibility that every human life that was sacrificed through this disaster could have been saved,' Senator Smith told the Senate. The senator did not spare the captain. His failure on the night the *Titanic* sank, said Smith, 'places a tremendous responsibility upon this officer from which it will be very difficult for him to escape'. The Senator was right. The British inquiry condemned him also. 'She [the *Californian*] might have saved many if not all of the lives that were lost,' the inquiry stated. Since then, the Board of Trade and its successors have resisted repeated attempts to get the case of Captain Lord reopened, so that the verdict of 1912 may still be said to stand.

In Britain, the fight to clear Captain Lord's name has been led by the Mercantile Marine Service Association, supported by Captain Lord's son. After I read the evidence given both in the United States and in London, I agreed with the official view. It appeared incontrovertible. On a subsequent visit to the United States, however, I met two people, Mr Kamuda of the Titanic Historical Society in Springfield, Mass., and Mr Russ Lowndes, late of the Maritime Museum in Halifax, Nova Scotia, who both called themselves 'Lordites', as supporters of Captain Lord have come to be known in *Titanic* circles. Both men are convinced that the official inquiries, partly because they were looking for a scapegoat, arrived at too hasty and definite a conclusion about Captain Lord, and compelled me to wonder whether I had not done the same.

As in an old-fashioned detective story, I shall first set out the complicated circumstances of the mystery. Then I shall summarize the case against the captain and the case for him.

Stanley Lord (no relation of Walter Lord, the author of *A Night to Remember*, whom the captain thought of suing for libel in 1958, when the book came out) was born in Bolton in 1877. He went to sea in 1891, serving first in sailing ships. Aged 23, he obtained an extra master's certificate, which is the highest voluntary qualification open to an officer in the British Mercantile Marine. At the early age of 29 he was appointed by the Leyland Line, which he had joined nine years before, to captain their passenger cargo liners.

On 14 April 1912 the 6000-ton *Californian* – which had a passenger certificate but was not carrying passengers at the time – was bound from London to Boston under Captain Lord's command when she ran into field ice. Prudently, Lord stopped, telling the wireless operator to send out a general ice report. That was at 10.20 P.M. The *Californian* did not move again under her own steam until 5.15 the next morning. While the *Californian* was hove to, some 1500 people from the *Titanic* drowned.

The *Titanic* hit the iceberg at 11.40 P.M., and some time after that Fourth Officer Boxhall, as he was helping to lower lifeboats, heard that someone had reported a light ahead. He went to the bridge to see what it was.

Through glasses, he saw the two masthead lights of a steamer.

Meanwhile he had sent for some distress rockets. He told Captain Smith he had seen the light, and asked permission to send off the rockets. Captain Smith told him to carry on. As he sent off the rockets – 'between half a dozen and a dozen' – he was 'watching the steamer approach'. The rockets – larger than ordinary firework rockets – were a distress signal, with a luminous tail behind them; they exploded loudly in the air and burst into white stars. They were sent off at intervals of 'probably five minutes'. At one stage, 'the vessel got close enough, as I thought, to read our electric Morse signal, and I signalled to her. I told her to "Come at once, we are sinking." The captain was standing . . . with me most of the time when we were signalling.' The captain also saw the vessel. There was no answer to the Morse signal.

After Boxhall left the *Titanic* in No 2 lifeboat – perhaps at about 1.45 A.M. – he continued to see the vessel 'for a little while, but then lost it'. He judged she had headed away in a westerly direction; her distance from the *Titanic* had been about five miles.

Second Officer Lightoller also saw the lights of a ship five or six miles away.

So much for what was seen and done on the *Titanic*. A ship was sighted by the *Titanic*'s officers; she was judged to be five or six miles away; she was signalled by lamp, and failed to respond; rockets were fired – these facts are not and never have been in dispute.

But was the ship the *Californian*?

At 11 P.M. on the stationary *Californian* the officer of the watch, Third Officer Groves, saw a steamer's lights approaching from the east. Captain Lord told him to call her with the Morse lamp. No answer. Lord then went into the wireless cabin and asked the inexperienced young operator, Evans, whether he had been in communication with any ships. Evans said he had had the *Titanic* and judging by the strength of her signals she was about a hundred miles away. Lord told Evans to call up the *Titanic* and let her know that the *Californian* was surrounded by ice and stopped. Evans started to send a cheery informal message beginning, 'Say old man we are surrounded by ice and stopped', but was told by the *Titanic*'s chief operator, Phillips, to shut up as he was busy talking to the wireless relay station on Cape Race.

11.30 P.M. Evans heard the *Titanic* sending passengers' telegrams.

11.35 P.M. Evans turned in.

11.40 P.M. Groves, the officer of the watch, observed that the unknown vessel had stopped, and thought he saw the steamer's lights go out. Captain Lord said he didn't believe she was a passenger steamer. Groves said she was.

Just before midnight, on his way to the bridge to relieve Groves, Second Officer Herbert Stone met Captain Lord at the door of the wheelhouse. Lord pointed to the steamer, and said she was stopped. Lord told Stone to let him know if the ship came any nearer, and added that he was going to lie down on the chart-room settee. On the bridge, Stone observed that the other steamer was showing one mast-head light, her red side light, and one or two small indistinct lights round the deck that looked like port-holes or open doors. Stone judged her to be a tramp steamer, and about five miles distant.

Stone tried and failed to raise the steamer by Morse lamp.

12.15 A.M. approximately. The apprentice on watch with Stone, James Gibson, came up to the bridge with coffee. He too tried the 'tapper' and got no answer.

Gibson left the bridge to attend to the log line. While he was away, the Captain called up Stone and asked if the steamer had moved. Stone said no.

12.45 A.M. approximately. Stone saw a flash of white in the sky just above the steamer which he thought was a shooting star. Soon afterwards he saw what this time he identified as a white rocket. In the next half-hour or so he saw three more rockets, all of them white. He saw no flash on the steamer's deck or any indication that the rockets were coming from her, and had the impression that they came from a good way beyond her.

In 1912, each shipping company had its own private recognition signals which were often shown when passing other ships at night. They might be Roman candles, flares, or rockets of different colours – and white was sometimes one of the colours. Distress signals were white, and usually bigger and noisier.

1.15 A.M. approximately. Stone whistled down the speaking-tube to Captain Lord, who went from the chart room into his own room to answer. Stone told Lord about the rockets. Lord told Stone to call the steamer on the Morse lamp and try to get some information from her. Lord also asked if the rockets were 'private signals', to which Stone replied that he didn't know, but they were all white. Lord then said: 'When you get an answer let me know by Gibson.'

Gibson and Stone next observed three more rockets going off at intervals. They also noted that the ship, which had not replied to their continual signalling, was apparently steaming away to the south-west.

2 A.M. Stone observed that the ship was steaming away fast, by now showing only her stern light and a glow at the mast-head. Gibson went down to wake the captain. He told the captain that, in all, he and Stone had sighted eight rockets, and that the steamer was moving out of

sight. The captain said (according to Gibson), 'All right. Are you sure there were no colours in them?' Gibson replied, 'No, they were all white.'

2.45 A.M. Stone again whistled down and told the captain that they had seen no more lights and that the ship was out of sight.

4.00 A.M. Chief Officer Stewart came on to the bridge to relieve Stone. Stone told him of the events of the past four hours. Stewart woke up first Captain Lord and then Evans the wireless operator and told him to find out what was going on and what was wrong. Evans picked up a message from the Canadian Pacific liner *Mount Temple*; the message said the *Titanic* had struck an iceberg and was sinking.

Meanwhile, the *Carpathia*, a Cunarder commanded by Captain Arthur Rostron, sailing from New York to Gibraltar, had picked up the *Titanic*'s distress calls. At once, she went at full speed, past scores of icebergs, to the rescue. As dawn broke she began to pick up survivors.

5.15 A.M. approximately. The *Californian* got under way and made for the last radioed position of the *Titanic*.

Soon after 8.00 A.M., the *Californian* was within semaphore distance of the *Carpathia* and learned that the *Titanic* had gone down. Captain Rostron signalled Captain Lord to tell him that he had taken aboard all lifeboat survivors, and was setting course for New York. He asked Lord to stay in the area and pick up bodies.

Between 9.00 A.M. and 10.00 A.M. the *Californian*, having failed to sight any bodies, resumed its voyage to Boston.

Ashore, by this time, the horrified attention of much of the world was focused on the *Titanic* disaster, though not at this stage on the *Californian*. Brief reports on the day after the sinking noted that the ship was on the scene picking up bodies, but when she found none she was forgotten. On Thursday, 18 April, the *Carpathia* and the survivors arrived in New York among mourning and chaotic crowds. That night, the *Californian* docked at a freight pier in Boston, met only by a pilot boat.

The ship and her captain remained in obscurity over the weekend while newspapers and public concentrated on the Senate hearings already starting in the Waldorf Astoria hotel. During the hearings, however, it was mentioned that, after the iceberg struck, a ship had been sighted five miles from the *Titanic* and had not answered signals. Someone on the *New York Times* remembered the *Californian*. A reporter went to interview Captain Lord.

On Tuesday morning the *New York Times* carried the interview on the front page, datelined Boston. It was not much of a story, but the reporter gave it the strongest lead he could. 'The Leyland steamer *Californian* was less than 20 miles from the *Titanic* when the latter foundered,' the story began. 'Captain Lord of the *Californian* said tonight that had he only known of the *Titanic*'s plight, all the passengers could have been saved. That his ship was the steamer reported to have passed within five miles of the sinking, Captain Lord denied emphatically.' The reporter next had him saying, 'I figure that we were from 17 to 19 miles distant from the *Titanic* that night,' which is unlikely to have been an accurate quote but accurately represented Lord's stance. If the reporter had then asked whether Captain Lord or any of the crew had seen any rockets, he would have had a better story, as he no doubt realized next day when he picked up the *Boston American*.

'From *Californian* I saw *Titanic* signals,' said the banner headline. 'Man of *Californian* crew says was near the *Titanic*' read a headline underneath. A picture showed a man in a cloth cap looking to his left, with dark eyebrows and luxuriant handlebar moustache. The paper was so pleased with the scoop that it encircled its head and shoulders shot with a sinuous art nouveau capital 'G'. Over the picture a line read, 'Ernest Gill, who says he saw *Titanic* rockets' ('rockets' was the word that should have been in the main headline). The caption read: 'Gill was donkeyman on the Leyland liner *Californian* and says his captain paid no attention to signals from the doomed vessel.'

The main text of the story consisted of an affidavit sworn by Gill in the presence of a named notary public and, said the paper, four members of the crew, who were not named. It was a lengthy statement. Gill said he had been on duty in the *Californian*'s engine room during the first watch on 14 April and had come up on deck at four minutes to midnight. He looked over the starboard rail and 'saw the lights of a very large steamer about 10 miles away'. A few minutes later he went to his cabin and woke his mate William Thomas. Thomas heard the ice crunching on the side of the ship and asked, 'Are we in ice?' Gill said, 'Yes, but we must be clear off to the starboard for I saw a big vessel going along at full speed. She looked as if she might be a big German.' Gill then turned in.

Half an hour later, unable to sleep, he went back on deck for a smoke. After ten minutes he saw rockets going up about ten miles away, saying to himself, 'That must be a vessel in distress.' It was not his business to notify the bridge or lookouts, but he was certain that they must have seen the rockets, he stated, as they must earlier have seen the very large steamer. He turned in again, and knew nothing more until the chief engineer woke him at 6.40 A.M. with the news that the *Titanic* had gone down and that he was needed to lend a land; the *Californian* by this time was under way.

In the engine room, Gill overheard the second and fourth engineers talking about rockets seen during the night, and about the captain being notified by the apprentice, Gibson. The captain had given orders for Morse signals to be sent, but there had been no reply. Then Gill had heard the second engineer exclaiming, 'Why the devil didn't they wake up the wireless man?'

Gill ended his statement by saying he was quite sure the *Titanic* was closer than the twenty miles claimed by his officers, since he could not have seen her at twenty miles and he had seen her plainly. He had no ill will towards Captain Lord or any other officer, and he was losing a profitable berth by making his statement; but he was 'actuated by the desire that no captain who refuses or neglects to give aid to a vessel in distress should be able to hush up the men'.

The story caused a sensation. Captain Lord issued a strong denial. Gill, it soon came out, had been paid $500 by the *Boston American*: more than a year's wages at his rate of £6 a month. Thomas, named in Gill's affidavit, said Gill had not consulted him before swearing it. He was evidently not one of the four unnamed crew members present, according to the *Boston American*, at the signing. Thomas told a rival paper, the *Boston Herald*, that he remembered asking about the ice, but was positive Gill said nothing about any steamer; nor had Gill mentioned rockets. The *Herald* quoted Thomas as saying that Gill was engaged to a girl in England, and 'I could see where the offer of a sum as large as reported in the forecastle would greatly tempt him.' Thomas thought Gill could buy a small shop with that amount of money.

Gill returned to England and faded from sight, but only after he had repeated his story to the American and British inquiries. He was not cross-examined with any rigour. He claimed in his affidavit to have seen 'a big vessel going along at full speed'; and was very precise about the time – 11.56 P.M. But even if the clocks on the *Californian* and the *Titanic* were keeping the same time, Gill's alleged sighting occurred sixteen minutes after the time the *Titanic* hit the iceberg. He was not pressed on this point. Nor was he required to explain how he had been able to see so clearly a vessel ten miles away.

It scarcely mattered. What mattered was that Gill said he had seen rockets, which compelled Captain Lord, appearing before the Senate inquiry the day after Gill's revelations, to admit for the first time that 'flashes or rockets' had been seen from the *Californian*. Lord had not said anything about rockets when talking to reporters. He told the senators that he had been informed about the first rocket, but had not taken in Gibson's message about the other rockets because he was half asleep. He admitted that 'flashes or rockets' had been seen from his ship, that these 'flashes or rockets' might have been distress signals, and that the ship he captained had done nothing – except to try to raise the other vessel with a Morse lamp.

These admissions formed the bedrock of the case against Lord. It was central to his defence that the ship seen from the *Californian* was not the *Titanic*, and that the ship seen from the *Titanic* was not the *Californian*. But no other ship could be found. The Senate inquiry called for an expert opinion from the United States Hydrographics Office as to whether a third vessel might have been between the two; the expert thought not. The British Board of Trade tried to find a third vessel and failed.

The written verdict of the Senate committee was harsh, especially since it condemned, and could be expected to ruin, a foreign national. It censured Captain Lord's failure to respond to distress signals 'in accordance with the dictates of humanity, international usage, and with the requirements of the law'.

Lord Mersey's verdict was harsher still, and forcefully argued. After setting out the reasons why the *Californian* had stopped, he turned to the problem of where she had stopped. The master (Captain Lord) had told the court that he made her position to be 42 degrees 5 minutes N., 50 degrees 7 minutes West. This position – reached by dead reckoning and verified by observation – was recorded in the log; it was about nineteen miles north by east away from that of the *Titanic* when she foundered. But, Lord Mersey wrote, 'I am satisfied that this position is not accurate.'

He then rehearsed the evidence about the steamer first sighted from the *Californian* at about 11 P.M. The master himself stated that he had seen the steamer approaching, that he saw more lights as she got nearer, and that she was about five miles off when she hove to. In deciding what sort of steamer had been seen, Lord Mersey laid emphasis on the evidence of Third Officer Groves. 'Mr Groves never appears to have had any doubt on this subject; in answer to a question during his examination, "Had she much light?" he said, "Yes, a lot of light. There was absolutely no doubt of her being a passenger steamer, at least in my mind."' Lord Mersey also quoted Gill, who had said, 'It could not have been anything but a passenger boat, she was too large.'

Lord Mersey then drew attention to a conflict of evidence between Groves and Lord. Groves had said that he had made a remark to the captain about the way the steamer's deck lights seemed to go out when she stopped. Captain Lord stated that Groves made no observation to him about the steamer's deck lights going out.

Lord Mersey next quoted an exchange between himself and Groves.

LORD MERSEY: Speaking as an experienced seaman and knowing what you do know now, do you think that steamer that you know was throwing up rockets, and that you say was a passenger steamer, was the *Titanic*?

A: Do I think it? Yes. From what I have heard subsequently? Yes. Most decidedly I do, but I do not put myself as being an experienced man.

Q: But it is your opinion as far as your experience goes?

A: Yes, it is, my lord.

Lord Mersey moved on to the rockets. Gill had stated that at some time after 12.30 A.M. he had seen two rockets fired from the ship he had been observing. At about 1.10 A.M. Stone (who relieved Groves on watch) reported to the captain by voice pipe that he had seen five rockets coming from the direction of the steamer. Stone said that the master had asked him, 'Are they company's signals?' and he replied, 'I do not know, but they appear to me to be white rockets.' Stone and the apprentice Gibson then saw the vessel firing three more rockets.

'Between one o'clock and 1.40 A.M. some conversation passed between them. Mr Stone remarked to Gibson, "Look at her now, she looks very queer out of the water, her lights look queer." He also is said by Gibson to have remarked, "A ship is not going to fire rockets at sea for nothing," and admits himself that he may possibly have used that expression.'

Next Lord Mersey described the episode of Gibson's visit to the chart room at five past two to tell the Master, on Stone's instructions – 'and be sure and wake him' – that the pair of them had now seen altogether eight 'white lights like white rockets' and that the steamer was disappearing. At about 2.40 A.M. Stone had again called up the Master by voice pipe and told him that the ship from which he had seen the rockets come had disappeared bearing south-west. Stone again assured the Master that the rockets 'were all white, just white rockets'.

Lord Mersey wrote:

There is considerable discrepancy between the evidence of Mr Stone and that of the Master. The latter states that he went to the voice pipe at about 1.15 but was told then of a white rocket (not five white rockets). Moreover between 1.30 and 4.30 when she was called by the chief officer, he had no recollection of anything being reported to him at all, although he remembered Gibson opening and closing the chart room door.

He concluded:

There are contradictions and inconsistencies in the story as told by the different witnesses. But the truth of the matter is plain. The *Titanic* collided with the berg at 11.40. The vessel seen by the *Californian* stopped at this time. The rockets sent up from the *Titanic* were distress signals. The *Californian* saw distress signals. The number sent up by the *Titanic* was about eight. The *Californian* saw eight. The time over which the rockets from the *Titanic* were sent up was from about 12.45 to 1.45 o'clock. It was about this time that the *Californian* saw the rockets. At 2.40 Mr Stone called to the Master that the ship from which he had seen the rockets had disappeared. At 2.20 A.M. the *Titanic* had foundered. It was suggested that the rockets seen by the *Californian* were from some other ship not the *Titanic*. But no other ship to fit this theory has ever been heard of.

These circumstances convince me that the ship seen by the *Californian* was the *Titanic* and if so, according to Captain Lord, the two vessels were about five miles apart at the time of the disaster. The evidence from the *Titanic* corroborates this estimate but I am advised that the distance was probably greater though not more than eight to ten miles. The ice by which the *Californian* was surrounded was loose ice extending for a distance of not more than two or three miles in the direction of the *Titanic*. The night was clear and the sea was smooth. When she first saw the rockets the *Californian* could have pushed through the ice to the open water without any serious risk and

so have come to the assistance of the *Titanic*. Had she done so
she might have saved many if not all of the lives that were lost.

Odd circumstances surrounded the case, though Lord
Mersey either omitted or did not stress them. The *Californian*'s scrap log had vanished. This was the rough log in
which (following the practice of all ships) the officer of
the watch noted wind and weather, speed, changes of
course, and any events or sightings occurring during his
watch. Later, the entries in the scrap log were copied
neatly into a fair log. But the *Californian*'s scrap log had
disappeared and, equally curious, the fair log that survived contained no mention of any of the rockets that
had preoccupied Stone and Gibson during the middle
watch. The log had been written up from the scrap log by
the chief officer. He had, he said, noticed early on
Monday morning that there was nothing in the scrap log
about what had happened between midnight and four
o'clock; he conceded that there should have been; but
nevertheless he had not spoken to anyone, not to Stone
and not to the captain, about the gaps.

Another unusual circumstance was that on the voyage
to Boston, after abandoning the search for bodies,
Captain Lord asked both Stone and Gibson to make
written statements about what they had seen and done
between midnight and 4 A.M. Perhaps pointedly, both
statements make it plain that they have been asked for by
Captain Lord. 'At your request . . .', Stone's letter
begins. Gibson's begins, 'In compliance with your wishes
. . .' There are no discrepancies between these statements, made three days after the night in question, and
their evidence to the British inquiry a month later. Why
did Lord take the unusual step of asking for them? It can
only have been because he thought he might at some
stage be required to account for his own actions, or lack

of action. If he had not found out from questioning Stone and Gibson, he would have found out from their statements that he was highly vulnerable; and the most damaging testimony was that of Gibson, who reported telling him face to face that he and Stone between them had seen eight white rockets, and that he, Lord, had questioned him and asked him the time.

Lord had a month to think about this episode and to rehearse the explanation he would offer the British court of inquiry to account for his inactivity. Yet his answers to the Attorney-General's questions were bafflingly inadequate.

ATTORNEY-GENERAL: Gibson did come down?
A: So I understand.
Q: But you know perfectly well that he came?
A: I know now.
Q: Did you know then?
A: I did not.
Q: I think you told us you heard Gibson open and close the door?
A: Yes.
Q: And you said, 'What is it?'
A: Yes.
Q: And he said nothing?
A: He did not say anything.
Q: And you were expecting him to come down and tell you what the meaning of the rocket was?
A: But in the meantime I was asleep.
LORD MERSEY: Yes, but you were not asleep – at least I suppose not – when you said to the boy, 'What is it'?
A: I was wakened up by the opening of the door – the banging of the door.

Later Lord said he had also asked Gibson the time; and he thought he asked him whether there were any colours in the light. But he continued to maintain that he had 'no recollection of this apprentice saying anything to me at all that morning'. When examined as to why he had asked about the colours in the signals if not in order to know whether they were distress signals, he said, 'I really do not know what was the object of my question.' Of all the ninety-four appearances before the court, Captain Lord's was the most contradictory and inept.

What happened next to Captain Lord is surprising. One might expect that having been roundly condemned for incompetence, inhumanity, and law-breaking – both in the United States and Britain there were demands that he should face criminal prosecution – Lord would never again have found employment. Shortly after Lord Mersey handed down his verdict he was indeed forced to resign from the Leyland Line. But he was soon re-employed. He was taken on by a Scottish shipowner named John Latta, a partner in Lowther, Latta & Co., and chairman of the Nitrate Producers Steamship Company. Latta was a man of some reputation. He had been received by Edward VII for the help his ships had given during the Boer War; and he was later to be made a baronet, though at a period when baronetcies were not hard to come by for a man of means. According to Captain Lord's son, Mr S. T. Lord, Latta told his father that if he had been employed by a Latta enterprise, instead of Leyland, he would not have been so ill-treated. Captain Lord evidently acquired and retained the confidence of his new employers, who took a risk in hiring him, since before long he was appointed captain of the newest and largest ship in the Nitrate Producers Steamship Company fleet. He retired with an immaculate record – apart from the *Californian* incident – in 1927.

It is difficult to imagine that Lord could have served a further fifteen years at sea, much of the time as a ship's captain, if he had himself believed that while in command of the *Californian* he had failed, through negligence or cowardice, to save 1500 men and women from a terrible death. At all events, he behaved after 1912 like a man who thinks he has been badly done by, not like a criminal.

Ten days after the report of the British inquiry was published, he wrote from his home in Liscard, Cheshire, to the assistant secretary of the Marine Department at the Board of Trade. The letter was handwritten, with no corrections, and dated 10 August.

Dear Sir,

With reference to Lord Mersey's report on the *Titanic* disaster, he states the *Californian* was 8 to 10 miles from the scene of the disaster. I respectfully request you will allow me as Master of the *Californian* to give you a few facts which prove she was the distance away that I gave viz 17 to 19 miles. [On] ·Apl. 14th [at] 6.30 P.M. I sent my position to the *Antillian* and *Titanic*, this gives me 17 miles away, and you see it was sent some hours before the disaster. Apl. 15th about 5.30 P.M. gave my position to SS *Virginian* before I heard where the *Titanic* sunk, that also gave me 17 miles away. I understand the original Marconigrams were in Court.

The evidence of Mr Boxhall of the *Titanic* who was watching the steamer they had in view, states she *approached* them between ·one and two A.M., the *Californian* was stopped from 10.30 P.M. to 5.15 A.M. next day.

The steamer seen from the *Californian* was plainly in view from 11.30 P.M., the one seen by the *Titanic* was not, according to the lookout men seen until 0.30 A.M.

Capt Rostron of the *Carpathia* states 'When at the scene of the disaster, it was daylight at 4.30 A.M. I could see all around the horizon, about 8 miles North of me' [this was the direction the *Californian* was] 'there were two steamers, neither of these was the *Californian*.' Had the *Californian* been within 10 miles from the *Titanic* she would have been in sight at this time from the *Carpathia*, as she was in the same position as when stopped at 10.30 P.M. the previous evening.

With regard to my own conduct on the night in question. I should like to add a little more. I had taken every precaution for the safety of my own ship, and left her in charge of a responsible officer at 0.40 A.M., with instructions to call me if he wanted anything, and I lay down fully dressed. At 1.15 A.M., (25 minutes after he had seen the first signal) the officer on watch reported the steamer we had in sight was altering her bearing, in other words was steaming away, and had fired a rocket. I did not anticipate any disaster to a vessel that had been stopped nearly for an hour, and had ignored my Morse signals, and was then steaming away, I asked him was it a Co's [company's] signal, and to signal her and let me know the result. It is a matter of great regret to me that I did not go on deck myself at this time, but I didn't think it possible for any seaman to mistake a Co's signal for a distress signal, so I relied on the officer on watch.

Altho further signals were seen between 1.15 A.M. and 2.00 A.M. I was not notified until 2.00 A.M., and then I had fallen into a sound sleep, and whatever message was sent to me then, I was not sufficiently awake to understand, and it was sufficient indication to anyone that I had not realized the message, by the fact that I still remained below, curiosity to see a vessel pushing through the ice would have taken me on deck. The message sent to me at 2.00 A.M. was I heard later, to the effect that the steamer we had in sight at 11.30 P.M. had altered her bearing from SSE. to SW ½W. (to do this she must have steamed at least 8 miles, the *Titanic* did not move after midnight) and had fired 8 rockets, and was then out of sight.

The question of 'drink' has been raised as the reason I could not be roused, I don't drink, and never have done.

Further signals were seen after 2.00 A.M. but the officer was so little concerned about them, that he did not think it necessary to notify me. I was called by the Chief Officer at 4.30 A.M., and in conversation he referred to the rockets seen by the second officer. I immediately had the wireless operator called, heard of the disaster, and proceeded at once, pushing through field ice to the scene, and I would have done the same had I understood, as I had everything to gain and nothing to lose.

There is the conversation between the second officer and the apprentice whilst watching the vessel, that they thought she was a tramp steamer, this is their opinion at the time, which is most likely the correct one.

My employers, the Leyland Line, altho their nautical advisers are convinced we did not see the *Titanic*, or the *Titanic* see the *Californian*, say they have the utmost confidence in me, and do not blame me in any way, but owing to Lord Mersey's decision and public opinion caused by this report, they are reluctantly compelled to ask for my resignation, after 14½ years service without a hitch of any description, and if I could clear myself of this charge, would willingly reconsider their decision.

If you consider there was any laxity aboard the *Californian* the night in question, I respectfully draw your attention to the information given here, which was given in evidence, which also proves [it] was not on my part.

I am told that at the inquiry I was a very poor witness, this I don't dispute, but I fail to see why I should have to put up with all this public odium, through no fault or neglect on my part; and I respectfully request you will be able to do something to put my conduct on the night in question in a more favourable light to my employers and the general public.

> I am Sir
> Your Obedient Servant
> Stanley Lord.

At the British inquiry, the Attorney-General told Lord with exasperation, as he stumbled over his replies, that he was not doing himself justice. His letter did not do him justice either. Clearly he had not asked a lawyer to help him make a case. But the ill-expressed arguments and poor punctuation at least show that the letter was all Lord's own work and, to that extent, is more revealing than a legal document. No matter how cogently Lord had stated his arguments the Board of Trade would have been deeply reluctant to order the case to be reheard. To do so would have been to repudiate Lord Mersey, for Lord had no new evidence to produce. He asked the Board to 'do something'; but even had the Board been willing, what could it do? It could scarcely have been expected to issue a public statement saying that Lord's conduct should be seen in a more favourable light by the public than it had been by Lord Mersey, even if the Board believed any such thing. The Board declined to take action, and there the matter rested until 1958.

In that year, when he was over 80, Lord was gravely

concerned to find that he was, as he thought, libelled in the successful book about the *Titanic* written by his American namesake Walter Lord, *A Night to Remember*. The book had also been made into a film. He at once approached the Mercantile Marine Service Association, the British shipmasters' professional organization, of which he had been a member for sixty-one years. The Association took up his case, but the idea of suing for libel, which they thought the best way of resolving the matter, was ruled out by Captain Lord's age and indifferent health. Instead, the Association attempted to awaken public interest in his cause by issuing statements in his support, but with little effect. Lord died in 1962, on the eve of the fiftieth anniversary of the disaster. Three years later, the Association submitted a petition to the President of the Board of Trade, Mr Douglas Jay, MP, asking for the 1912 inquiry to be re-opened and detailing what were claimed to be 'gross technical inconsistencies' in the case against the *Californian*. The Board, however, declined to answer these points and rejected the petition.

In 1968, refusing to give up, the Association presented another petition to the Board. 'New evidence of the utmost importance supporting Captain Lord's case' was in their possession, the Association said. The new evidence was a statutory declaration by the Dulwich schoolmaster, Lawrence Beesley, who had died aged 89 the year before. Once again, however, the Board of Trade was unmoved.

What, then, are the main arguments of the Lordites?

1. The *Californian*'s position, worked out by dead reckoning and later by observation, was seventeen or nineteen miles away from the position of the *Titanic*. This argument, which was the first point in Lord's letter of 1912, has been eroded by time. Lord thought that he

and his officers knew exactly where the *Californian* was stopped. Lord Mersey, supported by experts, concluded that the *Californian*'s position was not what Lord said it was. But the exact whereabouts of the *Californian* is of significance only if it can be related with confidence to the position of the *Titanic*. From 1912 until 1985 almost everyone accepted the accuracy of the *Titanic*'s amended position as worked out by Fourth Officer Boxhall and broadcast in the wireless distress call, of 12.25 A.M. Captain Rostron of the *Carpathia* congratulated Boxhall on the 'splendid' position he provided, which enabled Rostron to take the *Carpathia* at full speed for fifty-eight miles and at once find the *Titanic*'s lifeboats. Boxhall never had any doubts about it: he asked towards the end of his life for his ashes to be scattered on the Atlantic over the *Titanic*'s wreck, at 41 degrees 46 minutes N. 50 degrees 14 minutes W.; and on a fine June morning in 1967 the master and crew of the Cunard liner *Scotia* duly carried out his request. But Dr Robert Ballard, who discovered the wreck in 1985 only after a long search, and after others had failed to find it, has revealed that the *Titanic* was a long way from where she was supposed to be – as much as ten miles. If the *Titanic*'s calculations were inaccurate – despite Rostron's tribute, and despite Boxhall's reputation as an outstanding navigator – why should those of the *Californian* have been accurate?

2. The ship seen from the *Titanic* cannot have been the *Californian* because that ship was moving whereas the *Californian* was stopped. Boxhall indeed testified that the ship he and his fellow officers saw was approaching. He told the British inquiry that he was 'watching this steamer . . . and watching this steamer approach us'. At that time the *Californian* was, undeniably, stopped.

3. The ship seen by the *Titanic* cannot have been the *Californian* because the *Titanic*'s lifeboats could not find

her. Captain Smith told more than one lifeboat to row towards the lights and then return to the *Titanic* to pick up more people. But if the ship was the stationary *Californian*, why did the lifeboats that rowed towards her lights fail to find her? Where had she gone? She might have drifted, but not far enough to have put her out of reach and out of sight of the lifeboats.

The reliable and level-headed Boxhall – after he got into his lifeboat – thought the lights of the ship he had been watching moved away to the west.

SENATOR FLETCHER: Apparently that ship came within four or five miles of the *Titanic*, and then turned and went away in what direction, westward or southward?

A: I do not know whether it was southwestward. I should say it was westerly.

Q: In a westerly direction; almost in the direction in which she had come?

A: Yes, sir.

If Boxhall was right, then the ship cannot have been the *Californian*.

4. If the ship sighted by the *Titanic* was the *Californian*, and vice versa, then the times of the sightings should more or less coincide. But they do not.

The *Californian* saw the lights of another ship at about 11.00 P.M. Boxhall's evidence, however, was that the *Titanic* only made her sighting after he had handed in his Marconigram to the wireless room at 12.25 A.M. Throughout this period lookouts were on duty in the *Titanic*'s crow's nest; they were the first to sight the other ship and alerted the bridge by ringing the look-out bell. How is this long interval between mutual sightings to be explained?

5. If the *Californian* was as close to the *Titanic* as Lord Mersey said she was, why did nobody on board hear the rockets exploding?

6. The times that the rockets were being fired from the *Titanic* do not match the times that rockets were seen from the *Californian*.

This is where the Beesley evidence comes in. To explain its importance, the Mercantile Marine Service Association gives the times of lifeboat launchings and rocket firings the paramount role in the mystery that Freeman Wills Croft, the old detective story writer, used to give railway timetables.

When were the *Titanic*'s distress rockets fired? The first rocket (the Association maintains) was fired before 12.35 A.M. By that time, the *Carpathia*, another ship called the *Ypiranga*, and the shore station at Cape Race had all received the *Titanic*'s amended position, as worked out by Boxhall. But Boxhall gave the wireless room the amended position after he had started to send off rockets.

This timing is confirmed by others. Third Officer Pitman saw rockets fired 'shortly after' he left the *Titanic* in No 5 boat 'at about 12.30'. Fifth Officer Lowe heard the first rocket go off as he turned from filling No 5 boat to No 3. Quartermaster Rowe said he was ordered to bring 'detonators, which are used in firing distress signals' to the bridge at 12.25 A.M.; he gave them to Boxhall.

When was the last rocket fired? The evidence about the rate of firing is conflicting. Lightoller thought 'somewhere about eight rockets' were fired 'at intervals of a few minutes – five or six minutes, or something like that'. Boxhall thought the interval was 'probably five minutes'. Quartermaster Bright thought only six rockets were fired 'at intervals'. Symons the lookout thought they were fired 'every minute, minute intervals'.

The significance of Beesley's evidence is that it can be taken to resolve the question of when the last rocket was fired. He says in his statutory declaration, 'While still on board the *Titanic* I saw about eight distress rockets fired from her. I left the ship in Number Thirteen lifeboat and I am quite confident that the last of these rockets had been fired *before* this lifeboat cleared the *Titanic*'s side after being lowered into the water.'

Beesley in his book of 1912 set out to record the history of the disaster 'as correctly as possible'. He made a point of stating the time of events. He was on the top deck 'at about 12.20 A.M.' He saw the musician running down the deck with the spike of his cello dragging on the floor at 'about 12.40 A.M.' He was in No 13 lifeboat being lowered down the *Titanic*'s side at 12.45 A.M.

If the *Californian* was the ship seen from the *Titanic*, then the times the rockets were fired and the times they were seen from the *Californian* must coincide. But in comparing events, it is essential – the Association says – to do what both the American and British courts failed to do: to take into account the fact that the times indicated by the clocks in the *Californian* were twelve minutes behind those in the *Titanic*. Here is a masterstroke worthy of Freeman Wills Croft himself. 'The reason for this important difference is that the *Californian*'s clocks had been adjusted at noon on Sunday, 14 April, to conform to the apparent time of her then calculated longitude of 47 degrees 30 minutes West, or one hour and fifty minutes in advance of New York Time. Similarly, the *Titanic*'s clocks had been set to an apparent time based on her noon longitude of 44½ West, or two hours and two minutes ahead of New York Time.' It is consequently necessary to add twelve minutes to all times noted in the *Californian* before they can be accurately compared with times observed by those in the *Titanic*.

The first rocket seen by the *Californian* was at about 12.45 A.M., which was 12.57 A.M. *Titanic* time. But the first rocket was fired before 12.23 A.M. (12.35 A.M. *Titanic* time).

Stone and Gibson saw the last of the eight rockets shortly before 2 A.M. Gibson then went down to the chart room to report these eight rockets to Captain Lord. When the captain asked him the time, he said it was five past two. But no rocket was fired, according to Beesley, after 12.45 A.M. *Titanic* time (12.33 A.M. *Californian* time): a discrepancy of at least an hour.

Half asleep, Captain Lord had no reason to suppose that the rockets or flares were necessarily distress rockets. Even if they were white, they could have been part of a private recognition signal.

These are the bare bones of the Association's case. They and other Lordites also expound a complex argument about the direction the *Titanic* faced while sinking, and the way the *Californian*'s head swung to starboard during the night; these relative movements do not fit the starboard and port lights seen, it is claimed.

The Lordites complain, besides, about the inquiries' procedures. The senators questioned Lord only briefly, because he said he was due to sail back to England. In London, Lord and the other *Californian*s who gave evidence were in court merely as witnesses; thus the counsel representing them and the Leyland Line had no opportunity to expose the weak links in the deceptively strong-looking chain of arguments subsequently deployed by Lord Mersey in his report.

How is one to reach a conclusion about such a controversial matter? Those who condemn Captain Lord have one especially powerful argument on their side. Quite apart from the complex dispute about whether or not the rockets came from the *Titanic*, the simple fact remains that signals that could only have been distress signals were seen coming from somewhere. Yet the *Californian* did nothing; and the captain remained in his cabin from 12.40 A.M. until 4.30 A.M. The point affects officers of the

Californian besides the captain. Suppose that every word that Captain Lord said in his own defence was true. Suppose he understood nothing of what he was told because he was only half awake. This still does not explain or excuse the apathy of the officer of the watch. If he was in awe of Captain Lord, as has been suggested, he could have shaken the first officer. He could have aroused the wireless operator. But there is no evidence that he even discussed what should be done; he seems to have regarded himself purely as a spectator.

If Captain Lord did indeed understand what the apprentice was telling him, his behaviour seems inexplicable. As he said in his letter, he had everything to gain and nothing to lose by action. Captain Rostron thereby won international renown. It has been proposed, as a general, though cynical, explanation of Lord's failure to act, that he might have been afraid that if he took the distress signals seriously he would be required to risk the safety of his ship; he therefore pretended not to realize what they were, both at the time and later. But he at once got moving through the ice next morning when news of the sinking finally reached him.

However, he did not behave immediately afterwards like a man with an entirely clear conscience. It can have been only from motives of self-protection that he told Stone and Gibson to write down their version of what happened. After he reached Boston and was questioned about the voyage, he dissembled – presumably because he hoped nothing further would be heard of the matter. This was not merely unadmirable but foolish, since, as he should have been aware, the entire ship's company as well as the donkeyman Gill knew roughly what had happened.

Even if the Lordites are correct in maintaining that the *Californian* never saw the *Titanic*, and no convincing candidate for the 'third ship' has ever been found, it is thus not wholly unjust that Lord should have been one of the disaster's scapegoats. The disaster was a shocking event; and the public, and perhaps not only the public, was looking for someone to blame. The balance of probability is still against Lord, though he had the right to feel aggrieved that his case never received a thorough hearing.

The other scapegoat, who suffered even more 'public odium' than Captain Lord, was J. Bruce Ismay.

6

J. 'Brute' Ismay

The *Titanic* disaster changed the lives of many of the survivors, and one man was broken by it: J. Bruce Ismay. During the night of 14–15 April 1912 he took a step that transformed – indeed blighted – his whole life; the reasons why it had such a profound, permanent effect on his self-esteem may lie in the familiar problem of a son finding himself unable to follow in the footsteps of a self-made and dominating father. His fall was all the more dramatic because until the crisis came, on the eve of his fiftieth birthday, he had seemed his father's apt successor.

At the time J. Bruce Ismay was born, in 1862 – the J. stood for Joseph, after his grandfather the Cumberland boatbuilder – his father was at the beginning of his outstanding career as one of the great Victorian figures of Liverpool, and therefore British, shipbuilding. Thomas Ismay started work in the shipyards at the age of 16. His son was given a very different upbringing. Moving up a step in the social ladder, Bruce Ismay was educated not in the north of England at all, but first at a leading boys' private school at Elstree run by a celebrated headmaster, the Revd Lancelot Sanderson MA, known to the boys as the 'Guv', and then at Harrow, with which Elstree was closely connected. Both schools in that era produced a succession of fine games players. Ismay was one of them; he had an outstanding physique, excelling at all forms of sports. He was a good soccer player at school, and won prizes for lawn tennis. Later he took to field sports, becoming one of the finest shots in the country, especially at high pheasants, and a first-class fisherman. He was six foot four: a man with an imposing presence.

On leaving school, he was sent for a year with a tutor to Dinard in France, and then round the world. At home his father, by now a rich man, was building a vast new house eleven miles outside Liverpool on the banks of the River Dee. The architect was the fashionable Norman Shaw; the style was that of an Elizabethan mansion; the cost was a prodigious £50,000; all nails were of brass; the indoor servants numbered twenty-two. The choice of Norman Shaw was important. The new mansion had one of the imposing high entrance halls that were a Shaw speciality. When Ismay came to build the *Oceanic*, he was dissatisfied by the original decor and brought in Norman Shaw to re-do it. The ideas of the *Oceanic* were developed and enlarged for the *Olympic* and *Titanic*; but the amphitheatres of the new leviathans were recognizably the entrance hall of Dorwell, the new Ismay Elizabethan mansion, on a larger scale.

On his world tour, Bruce Ismay played tennis in Australia and umpired tournaments. On his return, he went into his father's shipping office to learn the business. A revealing story is told of his introduction there. He left his hat and coat in his father's private room. When his father arrived, he told a subordinate, in the hearing of the whole staff, including Bruce Ismay, to instruct the new office boy to leave his hat and coat somewhere else. Having served a brief apprenticeship in Liverpool, he was appointed the firm's representative in New York. In 1888 he married an American, Julia Schieffelin, who was herself the heiress to a pharmaceutical fortune. Their prospects were brilliant and assured. Bruce Ismay returned to England as a director and in 1899, aged 37, when his father died, inherited control of the White Star Line.

Even his father would have had difficulties in beating off the American pressure that soon developed. Certainly Bruce Ismay was not capable of doing so, especially as he was dependent on advice and support from his father's old associate, Pirrie of Harland & Wolff, and Pirrie favoured the sale of White Star to the J. P. Morgan combine. Besides, Morgan's terms to the shareholders were generous, and based on White Star's earnings in 1900 – a particularly profitable year because of the Boer War. In December 1902, Ismay gave in. His mother saw it as the end of an era.

Outwardly, his dignity was preserved. He remained chairman of White Star. Within a year, after prolonged negotiations, Morgan persuaded him to become president and managing director of the new combine, International Mercantile Marine. At first, Ismay was reluctant. Morgan wanted him to live in New York, which Ismay was not inclined to do. But Morgan was a persuasive man; he told Ismay he would give him 'entire control' over everything to do with all the shipping lines in the combine, except finance; and if Ismay took the job, Morgan in person would make available a substantial private line of cash, which would be greatly to the advantage of both White Star and Harland & Wolff. Ismay asked his mother's advice. The new post gave him real power; but there was no disguising the fact that, only three years after he took over White Star, he had been unable to prevent the great firm built by his father from passing into the hands of American financiers and railroad magnates, and that he had become one of J. P. Morgan's salaried employees.

It was Ismay and Pirrie – more Pirrie than Ismay, one suspects – who conceived the grandiose idea of the *Olympic* and the *Titanic*, but the idea had to be approved by Morgan. Ismay's relatively subordinate role became plain when he sailed on the *Olympic*'s maiden voyage. He made a number of detailed observations and enthusiastic suggestions for improvements, but all were trivial by comparison with the scale of the enterprise: the reception room was the most popular space in the first class; the after-companionway was not used; the deck space was excessive; a potato peeler was needed in the crew's galley; steam ovens were wanted in the bakehouse; holders for cigarettes and cigars should be supplied to the WCs; the springs in the beds were too springy. More important defects, such as the inadequate access from steerage to the upper decks – a defect that Lightoller spotted as soon as he joined and explored the *Titanic* – escaped him, unfortunately; nor was he enough of a shipbuilder to be able to form his own opinion about the structural merits of the two new giants. He relied instead on the unrivalled experience of Pirrie and Harland & Wolff which, admittedly, neither he nor anyone else at that stage had any reason to doubt.

A photograph exists of Ismay walking with Pirrie beside the towering hull of the *Titanic*: Ismay in his bowler hat, the picture of a confident shipowner, and Pirrie in a peaked cap, the picture of a shrewd shipbuilder. Ismay's reputation in shipping circles at that time was high; he had started the cadet ship *Mersey* for training mercantile marine officers, helped to make Southampton the main port for transatlantic travel, and had shown his public spirit by supporting a scheme for exchange visits between British and American teachers. But as a man he was regarded as taciturn and austere. After his death, an anonymous correspondent wrote an appreciation in *The Times* saying that his outward appearance had been misleading. 'Of a reserved and extremely sensitive nature,' the correspondent wrote, 'he shrank from exposing to the world the kindness and sympathy which were in him, and no one but those very close to him was permitted to be aware of his innumerable kindly and generous actions.' He was also a man who detested personal publicity. These characteristics had a bearing on his fate.

He attended the launch of the *Titanic*, but was evidently not excited enough by the mechanics of the biggest and most luxurious liner afloat to go on her trials. He joined her instead in Southampton, accompanied by a secretary and a valet. From the accounts of first-class passengers, we learn that he chatted to them on the first few days about the progress of the voyage, and we learn from his answers to questions put to him at the inquiries – though he did not express it like this – that he was still so incurious about the way the ship worked that he never once visited the bridge.

On the 'very fateful night', as the Attorney-General called it, he invited the ship's doctor, Dr O'Loughlin, to dine with him in the restaurant at half past seven; he had lunched alone. The meal was not prolonged, and Ismay soon turned in. He was awakened, he supposed later, by the collision. For a few moments he remained in bed, speculating that the ship had perhaps lost the blade off a propeller, but then he stirred himself and went out into the passageway. There he saw a steward and asked if he knew what was wrong. The steward could not tell him, so he returned to his stateroom, donned a coat over his pyjamas, and paid his first visit to the bridge, where he found Captain Smith. 'We have struck ice,' said Smith. Ismay said, 'Do you think the ship is seriously damaged?' Smith answered, 'I am afraid so.' Ismay then started to go back to his cabin to get dressed but met on the way Chief Engineer Bell. Like Captain Smith, Bell told Ismay that the damage was serious, but was 'quite satisfied' – or 'hoped' or 'thought', Ismay was not sure of Bell's exact words – that the pumps would keep her afloat. Ismay dressed and returned to the bridge, where he was in time to hear Smith give the order to prepare the lifeboats for lowering. He then went to the starboard boat deck, and for the next hour and a half, or 'perhaps longer', helped to put women and children into the boats.

The ship was sinking fast when Ismay took the step that caused his ruin. He had been putting women aboard what he believed to be the last boat. He told the Senate inquiry: 'The boat was there. There was a certain number of men in the boat, and the officer called out asking if there were any more women, and there were no passengers on the deck.' He was asked, 'There were no passengers on the deck?' and he replied, 'No, sir; and as the boat was in the act of being lowered away, I got into it.'

The ship's barber said he had seen Mr Ismay getting into the boat 'because there were no women in the vicinity of the boat . . . The boat was the last to leave to my knowledge.' (The barber himself was washed overboard very shortly afterwards and climbed on a bundle of floating deck chairs; he was only a hundred feet from the ship when she sank.) Lightoller said he had been told aboard the *Carpathia* after the rescue, he could not remember by whom, that Chief Officer Wilde, a physically powerful man, 'simply bundled him [Ismay] into the boat'. Ismay made no attempt to hide behind these alibis. No passengers were on deck; the boat he had been helping to fill was, he thought, the last one (it was in fact the penultimate); it was 'practically' full; men were in it already; it was being lowered; he got into it.

It is clear that in the hour and a half after the collision Ismay did his best to be helpful. However, glimpses of him and his curious conduct subsequently reported by passengers and crew indicate that some kind of mental breakdown – which has been surprisingly little commented on – began immediately after the impact. Martha Stevenson, who herself had dressed carefully and, like her sister, done her hair, noticed when she came up on deck that Ismay must have dressed very hurriedly 'as his pyjamas were below his trousers'. Colonel Gracie saw him soon after the accident. 'He wore a day suit' – Gracie was not as observant as Martha Stevenson – 'and, as usual, was hatless. He seemed too much preoccupied to notice anyone.' Accounts by other people do not contradict Ismay, but show his behaviour, after the impact, as ineffectual and, in one account, hysterical. Fifth Officer Lowe was loading one of the boats when an unknown man suddenly appeared shouting, 'Lower away! Lower away! Lower away! Lower away!' Lowe thought this person was 'over-anxious' and 'getting a trifle over-excited', since he (Lowe) was already 'on the floor' lowering away. 'If you will get the hell out of that,' Lowe shouted back, 'I shall be able to do something.' The man made no reply. Lowe said, 'Do you want me to lower away quickly? You'll have me drown the whole lot of them!' The man still did not explain why he was shouting or who he was. Indeed Lowe only realized that he had been swearing at the owner when a steward identified him to Lowe at the Senate hearings. Ismay was present when Lowe described the incident from the witness stand and did not contradict him; on the contrary, he urged Lowe to tell the senators the rough words ('get the hell out of that') he had used.

Boxhall told a similar story. He too was busy getting boats away when a stranger approached and started telling him what to do. Boxhall took no notice, and the stranger, who turned out later to have been Ismay, made no attempt to press his point or to identify himself. Still more strange, although he was the titular owner of the ship, Ismay at no point, during the hour and a half that elapsed after he learned that the damage was serious, made any attempt to speak to the principal authorities on board: the captain, the chief engineer, and the leader of the team from Harland & Wolff.

The lifeboat containing Ismay got away only with difficulty. The *Titanic* by this time had developed a pronounced list, so that the boat's rubbing strake kept catching on the rivets, and everyone, women included, had to help fend the boat from the ship's side. Once the boat was in the water, Ismay took one of the oars, but because he had been rowing with his back to the *Titanic* – the oars were manned by more than one person, and the rowers were not all facing the same way – he had not seen her go down and had not looked over his shoulder. 'I am glad I did not,' he said later. At the London inquiry, Ismay caused some confusion when he explained that they had for some considerable time rowed in the direction of a light, until the sea got up and they felt they were making no progress, adding that he was sure the light did not belong to the *Californian*. The Attorney-General and Lord Mersey thought Ismay was denying that the ship's lights seen from the *Titanic* were those of the *Californian*, but Ismay eventually explained that he was talking about a quite different light coming from another quarter; this light belonged, he thought, to a sailing ship. The Attorney-General and Lord Mersey were glad to have cleared up the confusion, but did not then or later address themselves to the mystery of the sailing ship's identity. If she existed – and Quartermaster Rowe saw the light also – those on board must have been close enough to have watched the *Titanic* go down. Perhaps the light was an illusion; a star.

When rescue arrived with the dawn, Ismay was in good enough shape to climb aboard the *Carpathia* by Jacob's ladder. Two weeks later, at the Senate inquiry in Washington, he gave a rambling, inconsequential account of what happened next. Senator Smith asked a straight-forward question about the *Carpathia*; Ismay replied with his longest statement of the whole inquiry:

I understand that my behaviour on board the *Titanic* and subsequently on board the *Carpathia* has been severely criticized [a woman had complained that he appropriated one of the best cabins]. I want to court the fullest inquiry, and I place myself unreservedly in the hands of yourself and of your colleagues, to ask any questions in regard to my conduct; so please do not hesitate to do so, and I will answer to the best of my ability. So far as the *Carpathia* is concerned, sir, when I got on board the ship I stood with my back against the bulkhead, and somebody came up and said, 'Will you not go into the saloon and get some soup or something to drink?' 'No' I said, 'I really do not want anything at all.' He said, 'Do go and get something.' I said, 'No. If you will leave me alone I will be very much happier here.' I said, 'If you will get me in some room where I can be quiet, I wish you would.' He said, 'Please go into the saloon and get something hot.' I said, 'I would rather not.' Then he took me and put me into a room. I did not know whose the room was, at all. This man proved to be the doctor of the *Carpathia*. I was in that room until I left the ship. I was never outside the door of that room. During the whole of the time I was in this room, I never had anything of a solid nature. I lived on soup. I did not want very much of anything. The room was constantly being entered by people asking for the doctor. The doctor slept in the room the other nights that I was on board that ship. Mr Jack Thayer was brought into the room the morning we got on board the *Carpathia*. He stayed in the room some little time, and the doctor came in after he had been in, I should think, about a quarter of an hour, and he said to this young boy, 'Would you not like something to eat?' He said, 'I would like some bacon and eggs,' which he had. The doctor did not have a suite of rooms on the ship. He simply had this small room, which he himself occupied and dressed in every night and morning.

It was the doctor who asked John Thayer to visit Ismay, hoping it might relieve his 'terribly nervous condition' if he could be persuaded to talk to someone he knew. Thayer wrote later:

> I immediately went down and as there was no answer to my knock, I went right in. He was seated, in his pyjamas, on his bunk, staring straight ahead, shaking all over like a leaf.
>
> My entrance apparently did not dawn on his consciousness. Even when I spoke to him and tried to engage him in conversation, telling him he had a perfect right to take the last boat, he paid absolutely no attention and continued to look ahead with his fixed stare.
>
> I am almost certain that on the *Titanic* his hair had been black with slight tinges of gray, but now his hair was virtually snow white.
>
> I have never seen a man so completely wrecked. Nothing I could do or say brought any response.
>
> As I closed the door, he was still looking fixedly ahead.

Immobilized by guilt or shame in the doctor's cabin, Ismay did nothing for three days except scribble Marconigrams. It was Captain Rostron who persuaded him to send the first of the series, all of which were addressed to P. A. S. Franklin, vice-president of the International Mercantile Marine Company, at the White Star offices on Broadway, New York. It read: 'Deeply regret advise you *Titanic* sank this morning after collision iceberg, resulting serious loss life. Full particulars later. Bruce Ismay.' The full particulars, however, were not sent, possibly because Ismay's mind became preoccupied with the problem of getting himself and his employees back home as quickly as possible. It was Lightoller who persuaded him that he must give orders for the immediate return to England of the surviving crew. Lightoller's explanation of his motives, as given to the American inquiry, is confused. He said he thought it desirable to keep the crew together. Left to their own devices, he said, they would not have hung round New York, but would have quickly found new jobs, particularly with the owners of private yachts, with the result that 'we would have lost a number of them, probably very important witnesses.' The pronoun cannot have embraced the senators. Had Lightoller's plan succeeded, they would have had no crew to examine, since they would all, including Lightoller, have been on their way back to England before the Senate inquiry opened; and so would Ismay.

Lightoller explained with candour why he had felt it necessary to tell Ismay what to do. Another White Star liner, the *Cedric*, was in New York and preparing to sail. Lightoller told Ismay, 'You ought to telegraph and insist on their holding her.' Lightoller added, 'I may say that at that time Mr Ismay did not seem to me to be in a mental condition to finally decide anything . . . He was obsessed with the idea, and kept repeating, that he ought to have gone down with the ship because he found that some women had gone down. I told him there was no such reason; I told him a very great deal; I tried to get the idea out of his head, but he was taken with it.'

So, instructed by Lightoller, Ismay sent a message to Franklin signed with the transparently disguised name he used for confidential communications: 'Very important you should hold *Cedric* daylight Friday for *Titanic* crew. Answer. Yamsi.'

Franklin did not at once reply to this demand. Instead, he forwarded Ismay a message from his wife in England. 'So thankful you are saved but grieving with you over terrible calamity. Shall sail Saturday to return with you.' Franklin added: 'Accept my deepest sympathy horrible catastrophe. Will meet you aboard *Carpathia* after docking. Is Widener aboard? Franklin.'

Ismay tried again: 'Most desirable *Titanic* crew aboard *Carpathia* should be sent home earliest moment possible. Suggest you hold *Cedric*, sailing her daylight Friday unless you see any reason contrary. Propose returning in her myself. Please send outfit of clothes, including shoes, for me to *Cedric*. Have nothing of my own. Please reply. Yamsi.'

Franklin received this message at 5.20 P.M. on the Wednesday and sent a reply within three hours rejecting Ismay's request: 'Have arranged forward crew *Lapland* sailing Saturday, calling Plymouth. We all consider most unwise delay *Cedric* considering all circumstances. Franklin.'

The next Marconigram from Ismay was sent on behalf of Rostron, who wanted the *Titanic*'s lifeboats removed from the deck of the *Carpathia* before he docked. 'Send responsible ship's officer and fourteen White Star sailors in two tugboats to take charge of thirteen *Titanic* lifeboats, at quarantine. Yamsi.' Ismay added on his own behalf: 'Please join *Carpathia* at quarantine if possible.' Then he sent two more Marconigrams about the *Cedric*. 'Very important you should hold *Cedric* daylight Friday for *Titanic* crew. Reply. Yamsi.' Franklin received this injunction at 8.23 A.M. on 18 April, the Thursday. Eleven minutes later he got a second: 'Unless you have good and sufficient reason for not holding *Cedric*, please arrange do so. Most undesirable have crew New York so long. Yamsi.'

Ismay's final message shows him still clinging to the hope of returning home at once in the *Cedric*: 'Widener not aboard. Hope see you quarantine. Please cable wife am returning *Cedric*. Yamsi.' Franklin's last message to Ismay was delivered only after the *Carpathia* was alongside in New York: 'Concise Marconigram account of actual accident greatly needed for enlightenment public and ourselves. This most important. Franklin.'

Given the scale of the event, it was an unimpressive exchange. Ismay, although he had had three days in which to do so, failed to supply even his own office, let alone the waiting world, with more than the barest facts about the disaster. He provided no news about the morale or physical condition of the survivors aboard the *Carpathia*. He gave no instructions about what arrangements should be made for them. The notion that some *ex gratia* payment should be made to the crew of the *Titanic*, whose wages had automatically ceased as soon as the ship went down, did not occur to him. He sent no message of condolence. Yet he worried about his shoes.

After the *Carpathia* docked, Franklin was quickly aboard, to be followed in a few minutes by Senator Smith, who told Ismay that the Senate proposed to conduct an inquiry into the disaster and that he, Ismay, would be required to appear before it. Meanwhile, none of the *Titanic*'s crew must leave the United States. The senators suspected that Ismay might be planning to remove himself from American soil as rapidly as possible in order to avoid awkward questions; and their suspicions were increased when they learned the contents of the messages that Ismay had sent from the ship. Ismay protested that the senators were mistaken. He had 'not the faintest idea' there would be an inquiry until Senator Smith had told him so. Still, however pure his motives in trying to arrange an immediate passage to Liverpool, the head of the White Star Line might have been expected to think it seemly, at the very least, to stay in New York in order to ensure that everything possible was done for the relief and comfort of the survivors and their relations, and to supervise the recovery of the many hundreds of bodies – White Star passengers and White Star employees – still floating in the north Atlantic.

Perhaps the mounting urgency of his Marconigrams to Franklin reflected Ismay's apprehension about the

The *Titanic* leaving Southampton

A section through the *Titanic* from the *Illustrated London News*,
April 1912

Above left: Artist's impression of Quartermaster Hitchins giving evidence to the British inquiry

Above right: Lord Mersey *(right)* and his son, the Hon. Clive Bigham, arriving at the British inquiry

Right: Embalming a corpse aboard the *Mackay-Bennett*

Below right: Undertakers and coffins on the jetty in Halifax, Nova Scotia, awaiting bodies picked up by the *Mackay-Bennett*

(Popperfoto)   *(Popperfoto)*

Above left: Dr Robert G Ballard

Above right: Members of the Franco-American team that found the *Titanic.* Standing in front of *Argo,* from left to right: Jean-Louis Michel, Lieutenant George Rey, US Navy, Jean Jarry, Dr Robert Ballard, and Bernard Pillaud

The research vessel *Knorr* returning to Woods Hole in September 1985

(Popperfoto)

the
The

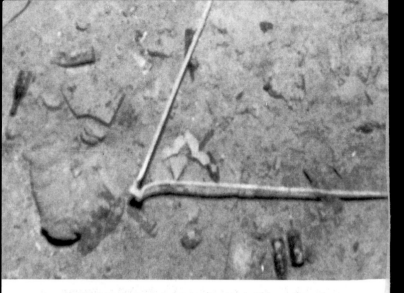

Bottles of wine, including French Bordeaux, are scattered over the ocean floor around the wreck. A photograph taken by the Woods Hole expedition of 1985

Two cranes still locked into position on the deck of the *Titanic* on the sea bed

opprobrium awaiting him. From the beginning, the sinking was a huge newspaper story, filling the front pages. The papers carried drawings, tables of other disasters, photographs of the *Titanic*'s lavish interiors, imaginary reconstructions of the collision and, as lists of those drowned filtered through, columns of obituaries. Ismay was a prominent part of the story from the time it broke. On the morning after the news of the sinking was confirmed, he was the first person named in the *New York Times* seven-column headline: 'Titanic Sinks Four Hours After Hitting Iceberg; 866 Rescued by *Carpathia*; Probably 1250 Perish; Ismay Safe, Mrs Astor Maybe, Noted Names Missing.'

For the next three days, the newspapers had little hard news to go on, as rumours about rescue missions by ships other than the *Carpathia* flickered and died. The arrival of the *Carpathia* in New York was a news editors' field day. She docked at 9.35 P.M. Next morning, in the best organized piece of mass reporting in journalistic history, the *New York Times* achieved what one of its historians has called, with reason, 'the ultimate in disaster news coverage': fifteen out of twenty-four pages were given to the disaster, mainly to stories told by the survivors. Other papers trailed, but not for want of trying. One survivor told her story to the Associated Press, the wire service, which distributed it nationwide. It was published in one of Senator Smith's hometown papers, the *Evening Press* of Grand Rapids, Michigan, under the headline, which was not in quotation marks: 'Ismay Took Care To Save Own Life.' The supporting headlines read: 'Stories of Survivors Severe on White Star Managing Director; Helped into a Boat; and Selected Men Who Were to Row it; On Board the *Carpathia* He Shut Himself Up, a Sign on Door that He Was Not to be Disturbed.' neath, Mrs W. J. Cardeza of Philadelphia was

reported as saying, after she had arrived at the Ritz-Carlton (one of the city's best hotels), that Ismay was not only seated safely in the lifeboat before it was filled, but also selected the crew that rowed the boat. 'According to Mrs Cardeza, Mr Ismay knew that Mr Cardeza was an expert oarsman and he beckoned him into the boat. Mr Cardeza manned an oar until Mr Ismay's boat was picked up about two hours later.' Mrs William Bucknell, who had rowed 'until her hands were blistered', said that aboard the *Carpathia* Ismay had refused to come out of his cabin until a committee of survivors had demanded that he saw them. They wanted to know what White Star would do for them in the way of reparations, but Ismay had said merely that it would do all in its power to make 'a partial repayment for their suffering', and had then retired back into his cabin.

Afternoon papers the same day carried a story from Washington reporting a statement by Senator Rayner of Maryland. It was headlined by the *Arkansas Democrat* 'Senator Rayner says Ismay is Responsible for the Disaster.' Underneath, the senator was quoted as saying, 'The captain of the *Titanic* undoubtedly acted under the orders of Mr Ismay who risked the life of the entire ship to make a speedy passage across the sea.' The senator added that Mr Ismay should be held responsible for the disaster, and that the civilized nations would applaud criminal prosecution of the management of the White Star Line.

Neither the newspapers nor the senator were prepared to wait for evidence before putting a noose round Ismay's neck. Very soon after the *Carpathia* docked it was announced that Ismay and the surviving officers of the *Titanic* had agreed to appear before a Senate subcommittee hastily appointed to investigate the disaster, and that the hearings would start at once in New York. But newspapers' verdict was already being delivere

heroes were nominated overnight – Captain Smith, Mr and Mrs Straus, the musicians – and so was the villain. He was 'J. Brute Ismay'.

The allegations were uninhibited, and so were the cartoons. Ismay was reported by the Associated Press to be worth $40,000,000; one cartoon portrayed an overweight capitalist in a top hat, smoking a cigar, alone in a lifeboat while the *Titanic* went down in the background. But the most telling shaft was fired by Ben Hecht, later a co-author of *The Front Page*. He contributed the following poisoned dart to the *Chicago Journal*:

News Item – Mr Bruce Ismay's name appears among those of the 'women and children saved'. Mr Ismay is one of the owners of the White Star Line.

> The Captain stood where a Captain should,
>   For the law of the sea is grim;
> The Owner romped ere his ship was swamped
>   And no law bothers him.
>
> The Captain stood where the Captain should,
>   When a captain's boat goes down;
> But the Owner led when the women fled,
>   For an Owner must not drown.
>
> The Captain sank as a man of Rank,
>   While his Owner turned away,
> The Captain's grave was his bridge and, brave,
>   He earned his seaman's pay.
>
> To hold your place in the ghastly face
>   Of death on the sea at night,
> Is a seaman's job, but to flee with the mob
>   Is an Owner's noble right.

Nor was it only newspapers and politicians who were damning. Rear Admiral A. T. Mahan, the great naval historian, wrote to the New York *Evening Post* saying, 'I hold that, under these conditions, so long as there was a soul that could be saved, the obligation lay upon Mr Ismay that that one person and not he should be on the boat.' Currents of private opinion were running in the same direction. Brooks Adams, the brother of Henry Adams and not much less distinguished, wrote a private letter along the same lines to a senator, urging Ismay's condemnation.

In this atmosphere of intense hostility and curiosity, Ismay's public ordeal began. He was the first witness put on the stand before the Senate inquiry the morning after the *Carpathia* docked. By then, he had acquired some clothes; and he arrived at the Waldorf Astoria looking slim and elegant in a double-breasted suit, high collar, and bowler hat, carrying an immaculately furled umbrella, and wearing a gleaming pair of shoes. Eleven days later he appeared before the inquiry again after it moved to Washington. He was then allowed to return to England. On 4 June he appeared before the Board of Trade inquiry, and if he expected to be treated more gently by his fellow countrymen than by Americans his hopes were not fulfilled, for in London he was subjected to cross-examination that was as ruthlessly to the point as that of the senators, and more carefully planned.

He resented the way he was treated, especially in the United States. He wrote a captious private letter to Senator Smith during the Washington hearings, pointing out that he had been under 'severe mental and physical strain', and asking if he might now be released, 'in order that I may go home to my family'. Smith at once sent back an irritated reply: Ismay could certainly not leave before there had been the fullest inquiry into the circumstances of the accident, and he should 'continue to help me instead of annoying me and delaying my work by your personal importunities'. Ismay's feelings of persecution boiled over in public. The inquiry, he told reporters, was 'brutally unfair. They are going about it in a manner that seems unjust, and the injustice lies heaviest upon me. Why, I cannot even protect myself by having my counsel ask questions.'

Not everyone was against him, however. The correspondent of a Canadian paper, the *Morning Chronicle* of Halifax, wrote: 'And J. Bruce Ismay, the man whom a certain class of New York papers prefer to call "J. Brute Ismay", "coward", "white-livered", "the man who came home with the women and children". What of him? It is he who is the centre of attraction. It is to him that every eye constantly returns. He doesn't look [a coward] and his conduct does not show it. Ismay looks like a strong man. There is real power in the sun-tanned face and the square head with the crisp black curls.' The reporter noted Ismay's 'red eyes, with deep lines below them'. When a witness described the death cries of the *Titanic*, 'Ismay closed his eyes and gnawed his upturned black moustache'. Sometimes he put 'the middle joint of his finger between his teeth'. The reporter's last paragraph summed up his impressions: 'He seldom smiles, he shows no interest, no matter what the evidence may be. He shows every mark of great suffering.'

Ismay may have looked like a strong man, but he was a lacklustre witness. The most striking feature of all his appearances was the way he repeatedly countered questions by appeals to his own ignorance. His father had been one of the great shipowners of his time. He himself had been in the business for a quarter of a century. Although, as we have seen, his titular power was in practice severely circumscribed, he was nevertheless chairman of the company that owned the *Titanic*, and president of a huge American trust that controlled five British and two American shipping lines. Ships were the source of his fortune, his reputation, and his career.

Yet he seemed to wish to present himself as an amateur who had strayed aboard the *Titanic* almost by mistake. In London, he described himself as a 'passenger' until the Attorney-General asked him whether he had paid for his accommodation. In the United States he said he was 'not a navigator'. He was not a ship construction expert. He was 'not a sailor'. He repeated certain phrases: 'I saw none'; 'I could not tell you, sir'; 'That I could not answer, sir'; 'I really do not remember'. Senator Smith asked, 'What was the full equipment of lifeboats for a ship of this size?' 'I could not tell you that, sir,' Ismay replied. Smith also asked, 'What proportion of women and children were saved?' to which Ismay replied, 'I have no idea.' He did not know the full number of the crew. He presumed there were two wireless operators, but did not know. He did not know about the boiler construction on the *Titanic*. It was 'not possible' for him to judge the time it took to lower a lifeboat. He did not see the ship go down, and 'really could not say' when he last saw her. 'It might have been ten minutes after we left her. It is impossible for me to give any judgement of the time. I could not do it.' He did not observe any confusion. He did not see any passengers on deck when he entered the lifeboat. He did not hear an explosion. He did not look to see if there was a panic. He could not put a name to any of the passengers he saw aboard the *Titanic* during the hour and a half before she sank. He did not know whether the *Titanic* broke in two. At one extravagant moment in the British inquiry he went so far as to suggest that he did not understand longitude and latitude, which brought a sharp, incredulous rebuke from the Attorney-General. He told the American inquiry that the number of his stateroom had been B52. Then, when an English businessman said that he had occupied B52, Ismay thought he must have been in B56. Three weeks later in

London he was still confused about the number. He believed it must have been B52 after all, though he could not be sure; most remarkably, he was not certain whether his stateroom was on the port or the starboard side.

Did Ismay truly not know the many things he said he did not know? Had he decided that the less said the better? Or was he throughout the two inquiries in a state of nervous shock bordering on amnesia – before the disaster he was noted in shipping circles for his extraordinary memory. Possibly his performance was a mixture of all three. He does not seem to have set out to be obstructive. He combined professions of ignorance with assurances that he would do all he could to acquire from other sources the information sought from himself.

The Senate committee wanted answers to two questions above all, if only because they had been fastened on by the press and politicians. Why had he, the owner, been saved when the captain and many of the passengers for whose safety his company was responsible had been drowned? How far was he – as Senator Rayner of Maryland alleged – personally to blame for the high speed at which the *Titanic* had headed into a region of ice – perhaps looking for a record crossing?

Given the public uproar about Ismay's failure to do his duty by going down with his ship, the senators made surprisingly little attempt to investigate his conduct in detail. They did not, for instance, call another first-class male passenger who had got into the same boat as Ismay. This was the wealthy Mr William Carter from Philadelphia, whose beautiful and fashionable wife was a former Miss Polk, a member of the Scottish-Irish family that gave the United States its eleventh President. The Carters had two children at school in England – Lucille at Wycombe Abbey and William Jr at a prep school in Rugby – and the Carters had been spending a year in a

manor house they had leased in Leicestershire so that Mr
Carter could hunt. All the family had been saved, and
when Mr Carter reached New York he innocently
explained that he and Ismay had been advised to get into
the lifeboat by Chief Officer Wilde because they were
recognized as first-class passengers. Carter, who unlike
Ismay escaped all criticism, evidently thought this prefer-
ential treatment entirely reasonable. Whether Wilde gave
any such advice, however, is doubtful, though the senators might have been expected to show an interest in the
point. They must have been convinced that Ismay's simple
account of his action was truthful, as it probably was.

Both inquiries cross-questioned him much more closely
about whether or not he had as owner influenced the
Titanic's speed. He flatly denied any such influence. He
had never discussed the matter with Captain Smith. The
only conversation he had had with any officer about it
had been with the chief engineer before the ship left
Ireland. They had agreed that the *Titanic* should at some
stage be tried at full speed, but that was routine practice
for any ship on her first crossing. Of course the ultimate
decision would have remained with the captain. It was
true that he had spoken to passengers on the Sunday and
mentioned the plan to go at full speed on the Monday;
but there was no question of his having either ordered or
influenced the captain in this regard.

Captain Rostron gave Ismay useful support. It would
be unthinkable, said Rostron, for any self-respecting
captain – least of all Captain Smith – to take orders from
anybody while at sea. The captain was supreme. Nor did
Ismay have any difficulty in dismissing ill-informed talk
about the *Titanic* trying to set a transatlantic record.

The Marconigram that Ismay pocketed was more
troublesome. Captain Smith before lunch on the Sunday
had given him, without comment, the message from the

Baltic saying that a Greek steamer had reported icebergs and field ice. He, Ismay, had not really understood it, he said; he had 'attributed no special importance' to it. He was asked by the Attorney-General in London, 'Had you no curiosity to ascertain whether or not you would be travelling in the region in which ice was reported?' Ismay replied, 'I had not.' So he had put the Marconigram in his pocket as he went to lunch alone, and returned it to Captain Smith in the smoking room at ten past seven, before dinner, because the captain wanted to put it up in the chart room.

The Attorney-General slowly pushed Ismay into a corner. Ismay had seen a Marconigram warning of ice. He expected the *Titanic* to enter a region of ice that night – because of the Marconigram, he eventually conceded. How then could Ismay justify her speed?

Q: If you were approaching ice in the night it would be desirable, would it not, to slow down?
A: I am not a navigator.
LORD MERSEY: Answer the question.
ISMAY: I say no. I am not a navigator.

But the only reason for going fast in a region of ice, the Attorney-General suggested, would be to get out of danger as fast as possible. Ismay agreed; to get out of the region before, for instance, fog came down. Then it was Ismay's admitted view, said the Attorney-General, closing in, that it would be best for a ship's captain to go as fast as he could through an ice region at night? Ismay was in a hopeless tangle. He feebly replied, 'I say he was justified in going fast to get out of it if the conditions were suitable and right and the weather clear.' 'I think we understand,' said the Attorney-General.

Ismay was made to appear ridiculous over the ice warning; but nobody suggested that he personally was responsible for the *Titanic*'s failure to slow down as a result. The inadequate number of lifeboats showed Ismay in a more questionable light. The subject came up after the *Daily Mail* published an interview with the Rt Hon Alexander Carlisle, one of the *Titanic*'s principal designers from Harland & Wolff. Carlisle told the paper he had recommended the provision of forty lifeboats, but his proposal had been turned down. Called before the London inquiry, he said he had put his ideas, accompanied by designs, to two White Star directors. They had discussed the idea briefly before rejecting it. Who were these two directors? One of them was Ismay.

Ismay said he had never heard any mention of forty lifeboats. Yet even Ismay, with his professed ignorance of almost everything about ships, must have known that the modern and much discussed Wellin davit, as installed in the *Titanic*, was able to carry four lifeboats; he must also have been aware that the original plan was for each *Titanic* davit to carry two lifeboats. Besides, Carlisle's account of the way his suggestion was dismissed fits in with Ismay's apologia to the inquiry. The reason why the *Titanic* had not carried more lifeboats, Ismay said, was partly that she was not required to do so by Board of Trade regulations, but also because she was thought to be practically unsinkable, and was thus a gigantic lifeboat herself. She was given lifeboats not so much because anyone believed that her own passengers and crew might need them, but because they might be needed to rescue passengers and crew from other ships. This was the one shipping subject on which Ismay freely gave his views. His sudden articulateness suggests that it was indeed he who decided that more deck space for passengers was preferable to unnecessary lifeboats.

Ismay was cleared by both investigations; Lord Mersey noted briskly that if he had gone down with the ship he would merely have lengthened the casualty list. Two footnotes to the inquiry may be added. Three years after Ismay's death, John Thayer privately published his short account of his experiences. He wrote of Ismay:

There was some disturbance in loading the last two forward starboard boats. A large crowd of men was pressing to get into them. No women were around as far as I could see. I saw Ismay, who had been assisting in the loading of the last boat, push his way into it. It was really every man for himself. Many of the crew and men from the stokehole were lined up, with apparently not a thought of attempting to get away without orders. Purser H. W. McElroy, as brave and as fine a man as ever lived, was standing up in the next to last boat loading it . . . McElroy did not take a boat and was not saved.

This is a very different version of events from Ismay's, who gave the impression that the decks were deserted when he got into the boat. Ismay said repeatedly that there were no passengers on deck; but if there was 'a large crowd of men', would Ismay have known which were crew and which were passengers? Thayer's word 'push' is damaging. He knew Ismay well enough to recognize him. However, he was writing twenty-eight years after the event.

The other footnote comes from the third wife of Colonel J. J. Astor's son Vincent. In her autobiography, Brooke Astor describes a trip across the Atlantic in 1958 aboard the *United States*, in which her husband Vincent owned a large stake.

It was during the trip that I really saw Vincent in action. It was soon after the *Queen Elizabeth II* had been put in service, and it was said in the papers that she would break the Atlantic speed record for Atlantic crossing, thereby relegating the *United States* to a back seat. We were having a leisurely lunch in the upper deck dining room of the *United States* when a smiling waiter came up and said, 'If you look out of the window, sir, you will see the *Queen Elizabeth* just behind us.' Vincent took one look over his shoulder at the *Queen Elizabeth* looming over the horizon, and saying to me, 'I am going to the bridge,' threw down his napkin, and dashed out of the dining room.

Within five minutes as I was sipping my coffee, the whole ship began to shake, and the passengers, bewildered, jumped up to see what was happening. I went out on deck, and hanging onto the rail, watched as the *Queen Elizabeth* disappeared below the horizon behind us. Eventually, I went down to our suite, where Vincent appeared, beaming from ear to ear. 'Miss *United States* kicked up her heels, Pookie,' he said. 'She wants to keep her record, and we will dock hours before the *Elizabeth*.'

Considering Vincent Astor's ancestry, this incident throws an interesting light on Captain Rostron's blanket denial at the *Titanic* inquiry that owners ever intervened with their captains.

Ismay soon resigned the presidency of the International Mercantile Marine Company and the chairmanship of White Star. But his public ordeal was not over yet. Two years later, a long-deferred court case opened in New York to settle compensation claims against his old company. The hearings ranged over the whole question of White Star's incompetence and failures; but since it was part of the claimants' argument that the company's direct responsibility was proved by the part its chief executive had played in the disaster, Ismay's personal conduct repeatedly came up for blame and criticism.

The case centred on a $30,000 claim from Mrs William Renouf of Elizabeth, New Jersey, for the loss of her husband and two brothers. Total claims amounted to $16,804,112. Some of them were large. The Straus and Astor families did not sue, but Mrs H. B. Harris, the wife of a prominent theatrical producer, estimated her damages at a million dollars. The company submitted that its liability was limited to $97,972 and 12 cents, a ridiculously precise figure worked out by its lawyers and accountants when Ismay was still chairman.

So on 23 June 1915, at the US District Court in the Woolworth building, Charles Burlingham, proctor in Admiralty for White Star, who had attended all the Senate hearings, opened proceedings by arguing that White Star had taken every possible precaution for the *Titanic*'s safety, and that the line was therefore responsible only for the loss of freight and the passengers' financial losses. He gave as one example of White Star's prudence the doubling of lookouts when ice was reported, a precaution he had thought up himself.

A lawyer for the claimants, George Betts, at once introduced the name of Ismay. The company's chief executive, said Betts, had been 'practically allowed to captain the ship'. The *Titanic* had been going too fast; no practice lifeboat muster had ever been held; the lifeboats had not been properly manned. To underline the irresponsibility of sending the boats away half full, Betts produced Captain A. T. Lundin of the Wellin Marine Equipment Company, suppliers of the davits, who said – as was already well known – that each davit was capable of picking up and lowering four lifeboats one after the other, and strong enough to swing four times the weight of a single full lifeboat. This evidence was introduced to counter the excuse for the half full boats that had been put forward by *Titanic* officers during the Senate inquiry; they had assumed that the number of people that could be safely put into a boat being lowered was a matter of personal judgement.

Then came the young John Thayer. He said that he and his father had been constantly in the company of Ismay during the first few days of the run. He recalled a conversation on the Sunday of the sinking. The three of them had been chatting about the ship's speed and the time they would reach New York, and Mr Ismay had said, 'Two more boilers are to be opened up today' –

evidence of Ismay's interest in speed. Thayer added that he and his father (who, it will be remembered, was drowned) went to 'about eight boats' and asked which would take first-class passengers and each officer sent them to another boat, 'so we gave it up'.

Next came three women who had lost relatives. Mrs Renouf said her brothers could not get into one boat because it was being so badly lowered; it was 'almost vertical'. Mrs Kenyon from Connecticut, a first-class passenger whose husband drowned, said, 'No one warned us of the danger. It wasn't until my husband went up and spoke to Captain Smith that we knew the truth.' Her boat had contained only twenty-eight people, and the one person in it who knew how to row was not any member of the crew but the Countess of Rothes (this stalwart woman was on her way to join her fruit-farming husband in Canada). Mrs Horace de Camp said that there were only thirteen in her boat yet her husband was not allowed in; and he had been drowned.

A well-known tennis player, Karl H. Behr, said it was not until forty or fifty minutes after the collision that the passengers were given any warning of danger. He said Ismay had been giving orders in his shirt sleeves; Ismay had told the boat Behr was in to lower away although it contained only forty or fifty and could have taken fifteen or twenty more. Mrs Futrelle, the wife of an American writer, confirmed Behr's account of the delay before the officers warned the passengers; her husband had been assured by one officer that there was absolutely no danger at all. The Futrelles' first intimation that anything untoward had occurred came not from any information they were given by the ship's authorities, but from going on deck and finding that men were being separated from women by stewards.

Eugene Daly of Newark developed the theme of casualness and muddle. He had been told to go on deck by a steward, and when he got there had found a group of stewards smoking and laughing. He tried to get into a lifeboat and was threatened by an officer with a gun. He saw two men lying on deck and was told they had been shot (nobody else claimed to have seen these bodies). He had finally jumped into the sea and had been picked up by the very boat he had been refused permission to get into.

William Mellors from England told further stories of half-filled lifeboats, over-excited crew stopping people from getting into boats, and officers threatening male passengers with revolvers.

Then came the professionals. Captain Robert Niss of the *Bohemia* testified about ice conditions. He took the position that the International Ice Patrol takes today. Even on a clear starlit night, you could not guarantee to see ice far enough ahead to avoid striking it, he said. Even in moonlight you could miss it, unless the moon was behind the ice. Had he, like the captain of the *Titanic*, entered an ice zone, he would have slowed down to a speed that he was sure would give him room to stop in an emergency.

Captain Henry Meyerdierks, the captain of the Hamburg-Amerika Line steamship *President Grant*, said that if he had had the same warnings as the *Titanic*, he would have gone at least fifty miles south. Later Captain Niss took the stand again, this time carrying the 1912 log book of the *Pisa*, which had preceded the *Titanic* by thirty hours. The log showed that on 13 April the *Pisa* had encountered a large icefield, had sighted seven large icebergs, and had promptly sent ice warnings to all quarters. Niss, like Meyerdierks, spoke of the difficulty of seeing icebergs at night.

The indictment continued with the former chief of naval construction to the United States Navy saying that the *Titanic* had been built on traditional principles, but represented such an unusual increase in size that her builders should have produced a new theory of construction. There should have been an increase in transverse bulkheads to ensure reasonable safety. Rear-Admiral Richard M. Watt, another US navy construction expert, said that 'side rips' like the one that sank the *Titanic* were unknown in the US navy, but they had had 'bottom rips' from submerged reefs. If the *Titanic* had had a watertight deck extending to the top of her bulkheads, she would still be afloat. Longitudinal bulkheads would have increased buoyancy.

Twelve days after the case opened, the lawyer Roger Foster summed up for the claimants. 'Blames Ismay for Wreck' was the headline next day in the *New York Times*. Foster said the question of White Star's liability was to be determined by 'whether the company had knowledge that the *Titanic* was going at high speed knowingly, having been warned that there was obstruction ahead'. In answering that question, he continued, it must be remembered that Mr Ismay, the chief executive of the line, had spoken to the engineer about the speed, had told passengers about the two additional boilers to be opened up, and had carried in his pocket all day a Marconigram warning the *Titanic* of ice. The Marconigram should have been sent to the chart room and the position of the ice marked on the chart. 'It has been said that the captain is the supreme being on his ship, but this is not the case. The owner could dismiss him in mid-ocean.'

The case was settled out of court. In January 1916, three years and nine months after the *Titanic* went down, the claimants' lawyers and the company finally hammered out a compromise. White Star agreed to pay out

$2,500,000, and the claimants scaled down their more dramatic demands. The largest sum allowed for a death claim was $50,000, as against, for instance, the million dollars claimed by Mrs Harris. Smaller claims were not reduced by anything like the same proportion. Death claims for the immigrants had been filed at $1500; they were scaled down to $1000 each. These sums were not inconsiderable: on the day the settlement was announced, the 'oldest tea rooms in New York' on Fifth Avenue advertised breakfast for thirty-five cents; and Thomas Cook offered a five-day steamship tour to Bermuda for twenty-eight dollars.

The settlement was a compromise, but it was also a defeat and humiliation for White Star and Ismay. The company had been forced to admit that it was responsible for the disaster; and the world was reminded of the existence of the unfortunate J. Bruce Ismay.

Ismay had been trying to keep out of sight. While the British inquiry was still in progress he bought a retreat in Ireland, in County Galway, without seeing it. It was a sporting estate on the Atlantic, with a lodge, private boats, and three lakes, and when there was no salmon fishing there was fishing in the sea. He spent more and more time there; when it burned down in 1927 he had it entirely rebuilt. It was remarkable in that part of Ireland for the number of its bathrooms.

The Ismays had four children, two of them boys. One of them, George, used to recall in later life how he and his brother had been made to have cold baths every morning, even in winter. He also remembered how the children's part of the house was separated from their parents not by one but by two green baize doors. George worked for Cunard; one of the daughters married a Scotsman and retired to Mull. Ismay's wife lived until she was over 90, active to the end, giving bridge parties and concealing her age. She was a woman of strong character. By descendants, it is said that she would never allow her husband to talk about the *Titanic*.

He had sought in vain, after the disaster, to hold on to the chairmanship of White Star, but the Morgans – J. P. Morgan, now at the end of his life, and his son – were adamant that he could not do so. In any case, Ismay had been going to retire from the presidency of International Mercantile Marine in the summer of 1913; the *Titanic* was to have been a final triumph. But he retained a few directorships, one of them with the London, Midland and Scottish Railway. Though he spent more and more time in Ireland, he kept a house in Mayfair. His natural shyness became more marked. He enjoyed music; when he went alone to a concert, he bought two seats, one for himself and one for his hat and coat. When he travelled to Liverpool from London for a board meeting, he would reserve a whole compartment and be provided with a cold hamper, so that he did not have to enter the restaurant car. In Liverpool, he never revisited the White Star offices. Shortly before he died, he had a leg amputated, and rigged up a series of pulleys over his bath so that he could get in and out without help. He died in 1937 and was buried in Putney. His entry in the *Dictionary of National Biography*, written by the former editor of a shipping journal, does not mention the *Titanic*. Ismay would have welcomed that omission.

7

The Curious Behaviour of Marconi

One of the fascinations of the *Titanic* disaster is that more clearly than any other event, it reveals the modern world just starting to burst out of its Victorian chrysalis; so that the old world and the new can be seen almost simultaneously.

Ismay was the victim of a vicious assault by the new mass circulation press, led by William Randolph Hearst. Hearst's papers and their competitors were merely looking for stories and a target. At the same time, Ismay was judged and condemned by the moral standards of the old school; Admiral Mahan thought he should have behaved with 'a particularity of conduct' because of his station in life – a very Victorian notion that Hearst, for one, would not have dreamed of applying either to Ismay or himself.

Technology was also in transition; the motor car co-existed in New York with three million horses. The same was true of communications. Carrying out his constitutional duty to keep the sovereign informed, the Prime Minister, H. H. Asquith, wrote officially to King George V after every Cabinet meeting by hand – as he did after the Cabinet discussed the *Titanic*. To keep the Foreign Office and the Board of Trade (the Archbishop of Canterbury was still one of its ex officio members) in touch with the Senate hearings, the British Embassy in Washington could find no quicker way of doing so than by clipping newspaper reports and sending them to London by mail steamer. Two years earlier, however, Crippen the murderer had been unmasked as a result of wireless messages exchanged between the liner on which he and his mistress were travelling and Scotland Yard. Guglielmo Marconi, the pioneer of wireless communication, was one of the new men emerging from the chrysalis.

During the three and a half days that elapsed between the sinking of the *Titanic* and the arrival of the *Carpathia* in New York, nobody's fortunes dipped as low as Ismay's, and nobody's rose higher than Marconi's, as if they were two men on opposite ends of a seesaw. The more it became plain that the shipbuilding technology of the *Titanic* had failed – the double bottom, the watertight compartments – the more successful seemed the miraculous new technology of wireless telegraphy. But for Marconi and his invention, another seven hundred lives would have been lost.

Marconi companies boomed. Looking back now, though, it is hard to avoid the conclusion that Marconi came out of the *Titanic* disaster better than he deserved. The Senate inquired into the part he played in it – he happened to be in New York on business – but he escaped virtually unscathed. So did Marconi employees, one or two of whom behaved as ambiguously as their chairman.

Marconi was an undoubted genius who at a very early age captured the imagination of the western world. He was one of the scientists named by Henry Adams as having called into existence an invisible new universe whose infinite complexities someone with Adams's education could not begin to grasp; even though Adams 'wrapped himself in vibrations and rays', he achieved only 'a paradise of ignorance'. Before Marconi, the advances in communications since the middle of the nineteenth century had been more or less comprehensible to the educated mind. The first electric telegraph had been paid along the Great Western Railway between Paddington and West Drayton in 1843, making it possible for the first time in history to send a detailed message faster than the man who carried it. Eight years later England and France were joined by submarine cable; another cable was laid under the Atlantic in 1865; a link with India followed in 1870. The telegraph transmitted messages by code, usually Morse. Then came Alexander Graham Bell who discovered a way of sending the human voice down wires; Britain's first telephone exchange opened in 1879. The next giant step was Marconi's invention of wireless telegraphy.

The history of the new communications vocabulary is instructive. 'Telegraph' was first applied in 1792 to a simple device constructed by a Frenchman, a M. Chappe: an upright post with mobile arms that sent messages in accordance with a pre-arranged code. By 1805, the word was being used by cricketers to denote a scoreboard. 'Telegram' was an American coinage of 1857, a replacement for the clumsy 'telegraphic dispatch.'

A wholly new word was needed to describe Marconi's achievement. In 1887 the German physicist Hertz had found a way of generating radio waves by electrical spark discharges. Marconi (1874–1937) discovered how to send messages down these waves: hence, used for the first time in 1894, wireless ('wire sb, + less', as the *Oxford English Dictionary* explains). Marconi was shrewd as well as brilliant. He was barely out of his teens when he invented his apparatus. His father was a comfortably-off Italian and his mother a member of the Jameson Irish whiskey family. A Jameson cousin persuaded Marconi to move from Bologna to London in order to exploit his revolutionary device, and he had a well-publicized success in 1896 when, to the wonder of all, he sent a message, without benefit of wires, from the roof of the post office in St Martin's Lane to another roof in Queen Victoria Street, near St Paul's. Two years later he helped reporters covering Gladstone's last illness to send news from Bournemouth to Fleet Street; he always kept in with the press. The United States Navy invited him in 1899 to send messages between battleships, which he did, over a distance of twenty-five miles. Marconi apparatus was used in the Boer War. Sceptics maintained that radio waves travelled in a straight line and that the range of the apparatus would be limited by the curvature of the earth. Marconi routed them by bridging the Atlantic: he set up a transmitting station in Cornwall, arranged for the letter 'S' to be sent in Morse code, and picked up the signal on an aerial supported by kites and balloons in Newfoundland. No wonder Henry Adams's head spun. The dapper young Marconi became a popular hero: he was photographed with a strange twenty-foot-high cylinder erected on top of a steam bus; here was the first mobile wireless. The cylinder was an 'aerial' (a word first used to describe a wire for receiving or radiating the waves of wireless telegraphy in 1904).

The first British vessel to use Marconi's apparatus was the royal yacht, in 1898. By 1912, besides the *Titanic*, hundreds of British ships were carrying Marconi's machines, and only a very few, less than a dozen, the machines of his competitors. By then, he had an exclusive contract with the Italian government, had equipped German lightships, and had built a ring of stations on the North American coast, with a particularly important one at Cape Race, on the eastern tip of Newfoundland, to serve the ships using the St Lawrence Seaway and to provide information about snow and ice to shipping in the north Atlantic. Besides, he had landed a contract to construct a chain of wireless stations across the world to link up the British Empire, won a Nobel Prize for physics, and married the daughter of an Irish peer. As well as 'wireless' and 'aerial', another new word had had to be coined to describe his work: Marconigram, first used in 1902.

The invention had spread rapidly to ships, but was not properly adjusted to ships' needs. Marconi companies fitted the apparatus and supplied, with the shipping company's agreement, an operator, or, as was usual in the case of big ships, two operators. These men were trained and paid by Marconi, and it was their responsibility to maintain a commercial telegraphic service on board their ship. But they served two masters, since their hours of work were determined by the captain. In practice, since most captains were unable to judge, for instance, whether it would be better for the apparatus to be worked in the day, when its range might be 500 miles, or at night, when the range might double, the operators tended to decide their own duties. Thus it was sheer bad luck that the *Californian* operator had finished work for the night before the *Titanic* began to send distress signals; had he been at his machine, all those aboard the *Titanic* might have been saved; and it was sheer good luck that the operator on the *Carpathia*, who had already taken his coat off before turning in, decided as an afterthought to check an earlier message and, returning to his apparatus, picked up the *Titanic*'s call for help.

The chief operator of the *Titanic* who sent out that call at once became one of the heroes of the disaster. Memorials commemorating his heroism survive on both sides of the Atlantic, one in Battery Park, New York, and another in Godalming, Surrey. It was his 22-year-old junior colleague who created his posthumous fame. Of all the survivors' stories told immediately, Harold Bride's was by far the most arresting.

The arrival of the *Carpathia* in New York was chaotic. Since White Star officially admitted the sinking, the world had been three days without news. Nobody was quite sure who was alive and who was drowned. Thursday night began with rain and thunder. Morning paper reporters (sixteen from the *New York Times* alone) were hard pressed. It was already ten to eight when the *Carpathia*, trailed and occasionally illuminated by photographers taking flashlight pictures from a tug, passed the Statue of Liberty; twenty-five to ten before she tied up at the Cunard pier. Reporters and curious crowds were kept well away by police. When the survivors eventually came ashore, most of those who spoke English were swallowed up by weeping friends and relations.

Accurate reporting, under these circumstances, was not easy. News editors were clamouring for copy; some survivors were hysterical, or wishing to make a splash. Besides, as with most disaster stories, the less scrupulous reporters knew that what they wrote could never be checked. Friday morning's papers thus released a flood of unreliable information on the world.

'We had been crunching through ice all day,' Mr C. H. Romsacue of Georgetown, Kentucky, was reported as saying. A woman survivor claimed that 'Everyone rushed on deck and made for the same lifeboat. Many men made for the boats and were shot down by Captain Smith. Several fell to the decks mortally wounded before there was a semblance of order or discipline.' This fantasy was credited to Lady Duff Gordon. John Thayer was quoted as saying that he and his father had jumped overboard together. An Italian told an exciting tale of saving himself by clinging to 'a cake of ice'.

Some of the alleged quotes printed next day read as if they were spoken by re-write men. The *Grand Rapids Herald* quoted Quartermaster Moody, 'helmsman on the night of the disaster', on the dramatic moment when an officer had suddenly shouted at him, 'Port your helm!' – too late for the *Titanic* to avoid the 'submerged portion' of an iceberg. That a British sailor would have talked about the 'submerged portion' of anything is unlikely, and further doubt is thrown on the authenticity of the quote because the helmsman was called Hitchins, not Moody, and the order given was not 'port your helm' but 'hard-a-starboard'.

Among the dozens of survivors' stories, though, Harold Bride's stood out, both for its intrinsic interest and for its ring of truth. It was published on the front page of the *New York Times* under the headline 'Thrilling Story by Titanic's Surviving Wireless Man'. A standfirst explained that the account had been dictated the night before to a *Times* reporter. It reads like it. The reporter, concealing his trade, had managed to cross the police lines and board the *Carpathia* under the wing of Guglielmo Marconi himself, while all other reporters were being held back. Marconi and the reporter, Jim Speers, made their way to the tiny wireless cabin where Bride, his feet swathed in bandages, was still at work. Marconi was a famous man; he was also Bride's employer. The story Bride told was as follows:

In the first place, the public should not blame anybody because more wireless messages about the disaster to the *Titanic* did not reach shore from the *Carpathia*. I positively refused to send [answer] press dispatches because the bulk of personal messages with touching words of grief was so large. The wireless operators aboard the *Chester* got all they asked for. And they were wretched operators.[1]

They knew American Morse but not Continental Morse

---

[1] The *Chester* was one of two United States navy vessels sent by President Taft to give any help they could; he was privately anxious, besides, to learn the fate of his trusted aide, Archie Butt, who had been aboard the *Titanic*. But the *Chester* operators had been unable to extract any information at all from the *Carpathia*, although their calls were acknowledged.

sufficiently to be worth while. They taxed our endurance to the limit.

I had to cut them out at last, they were so insufferably slow, and go ahead with our messages of grief to relatives. We sent 119 personal messages today, and 50 yesterday.

When I was dragged aboard the *Carpathia* I went to the hospital at first. I stayed there for ten hours. Then somebody brought word that the *Carpathia*'s wireless operator was 'getting queer' from the work.

They asked me if I could go up and help. I could not walk. Both my feet were broken or something. I don't know what. I went up on crutches with somebody helping me.

I took the key and I never left the wireless cabin after that. Our meals were brought to us. We kept the wireless working all the time. The navy operators were a great nuisance. I advise them all to learn the Continental Morse and learn to speed up with it if they ever expect to be worth their salt. The *Chester*'s man thought he knew it but he was as slow as Christmas coming.

We worked all the time. Nothing went wrong. Sometimes the *Carpathia* man and sometimes I sent. There was a bed in the wireless cabin. I could sit on it and rest my feet while sending sometimes.

At this point it sounds as if the *Times* reporter was worried that Bride would never get round to the *Titanic*, and asked him to start further back.

To begin at the beginning. I joined the *Titanic* at Belfast. I was born at Nunhead, England, 22 years ago, and joined the Marconi forces last July. I first worked on the *Hoverford* [*Haverford*] and then on the *Lusitania*. I joined the *Titanic* at Belfast.

I didn't have much to do aboard the *Titanic* except to relieve Phillips from midnight until some time in the morning, when he should be through sleeping [the reporter's shorthand must have failed him here]. On the night of the accident, I was not sending, but was asleep. I was due to be up and relieve Phillips earlier than usual. And that reminds me – if it hadn't been for a lucky thing, we never could have sent any call for help.

The lucky thing was that the wireless broke down early

enough for us to fix it before the accident. We noticed something wrong on Sunday and Phillips and I worked seven hours to find it. We found a 'secretary' burned out, at last, and repaired it just a few hours before the iceberg was struck.

Phillips said to me as he took the night-shift, 'You turn in, boy, and get some sleep, and go [get?] up as soon as you can and give me a chance. I'm all done for with this work of making repairs.'

There were three rooms in the wireless cabin. One was a sleeping room, one a dynamo room, and one an operating room. I took off my clothes and went to sleep in bed. Then I was conscious of waking up and hearing Phillips send off to Cape Race. I read what he was sending. It was traffic matter.

I remembered how tired he was and I got out of bed without my clothes on to relieve him. I didn't even feel the shock. I hardly knew it had happened [until] after the Captain had come to us. There was no jolt whatever.

I was standing by Phillips telling him to go to bed when the Captain put his head in the cabin. 'We've struck an iceberg,' the Captain said, 'and I'm having an inspection made to tell what it has done for us. You better get ready to send out a call for assistance. But don't send it until I tell you.'

The Captain went away and in 10 minutes, I should estimate the time, he came back. We could hear a terrible confusion outside, but there was not the least thing to indicate there was any trouble. The wireless was working perfectly.

'Send the call for assistance,' ordered the Captain, barely putting his head in the door.

'What call should I send?' Phillips asked.

'The regulation international call for help. Just that.'

Then the Captain was gone. Phillips began to send 'CQD'. He flashed away at it and we joked while he did so. All of us made light of the disaster.

We joked that way while he made signals for about five minutes. Then the Captain came back.

'What are you sending?' he asked.

'CQD,' Phillips replied.

The humor of the situation appealed to me. I cut in with a little remark that made us all laugh, including the Captain.

'Send SOS,' I said. 'It's the new call, and it may be your last chance to send it.'

Phillips with a laugh changed the signal to SOS. The Captain told us we had been struck amidships, or just back of amidships. It was ten minutes, Phillips told me, after he had noticed the iceberg, that the slight jolt that was the collision's only signal to us occurred. We thought we were a good distance away.

We said lots of funny things to each other in the next few minutes. We picked up first the steamship *Frankfurt*. We gave her our position and said we had struck an iceberg and needed assistance. The *Frankfurt* operator went away to tell his captain.

He came back and we told him we were sinking by the head. By that time we could observe a distinct list forward.

The *Carpathia* answered our signal. We told her our position and said we were sinking by the head. The operator went to tell the Captain, and in five minutes returned and told us that the Captain of the *Carpathia* was putting about and heading for us.

Our Captain had left us at this time and Phillips told me to run and tell him what the *Carpathia* had answered. I did so and I went through an awful mass of people to his cabin. The decks were full of scrambling men and women. I saw no fighting, but I heard tell of it.

I came back and heard Phillips giving the *Carpathia* fuller directions. Phillips told me to put on my clothes. Until that moment I forgot that I was not dressed.

I went to my cabin and dressed. I brought an overcoat to Phillips. It was very cold. I slipped the overcoat upon him while he worked.

Every few minutes Phillips would send me to the Captain with little messages. They were merely telling how the *Carpathia* was coming our way and gave her speed.

I noticed as I was coming back from one trip that they were putting off women and children in lifeboats. I noticed that the list forward was increasing.

Phillips told me the wireless was growing weaker. The Captain came and told us our engine rooms were taking in water and that the dynamos might not last much longer. We sent that word to the *Carpathia*.

I went out on deck and looked around. The water was pretty close up to the boat deck. There was a great scramble aft, and how poor Phillips worked through it I don't know.

He was a brave man. I learned to love him that night and I suddenly felt for him a great reverence to see him standing there sticking to his work while everyone else was raging about.

I will never live to forget the work of Phillips for the last awful fifteen minutes.

I thought it was about time to look about and see if there was anything detached that would float. I remembered that every member of the crew had a special lifebelt and ought to know where it was. I remembered mine was under my bunk. I went and got it. Then I thought how cold the water was.

I remembered I had some boots and I put these on, and an extra jacket and I put that on. I saw Phillips standing out there still sending away, giving the *Carpathia* details of just how we were doing.

We picked up the *Olympic* and told her we were sinking by the head and were about all down [presumably, 'done']. As Phillips was sending the message I strapped his lifebelt to his back. I had already put on his overcoat.

I wondered if I could get him into his boots. He suggested with a sort of laugh that I look out and see if all the people were off in the boats, or if any boats were left, or how things were.

I saw a collapsible boat near a funnel and went over to it. Twelve men were trying to boost it down to the boat deck. They were having an awful time. It was the last boat left. I looked at it longingly a few minutes. Then I gave them a hand, and over she went. They all started to scramble in on the boat deck, and I walked back to Phillips. I said the last raft had gone.

Then came the Captain's voice: 'Men, you have done your full duty. You can do no more. Abandon your cabin. Now it's every man for himself. You look out for yourselves. I release you. That's the way of it at this kind of a time. Every man for himself.'

I looked out. The boat deck was awash. Phillips clung on sending and sending. He clung on for about ten minutes or maybe fifteen minutes after the Captain had released him. The water was then coming into our cabin.

While he worked something happened I hate to tell about. I was back in my room getting Phillips's money for him, and as I looked out the door I saw a stoker, or somebody from below decks, leaning over Phillips from behind. He was too busy to notice what the man was doing. The man was slipping the lifebelt off Phillips's back.

He was a big man, too. As you can see, I am very small. I

don't know what it was I got hold of. I remembered in a flash the way Phillips had clung on – how I had to fix that lifebelt in place because he was too busy to do it.

I knew that man from below decks had his own lifebelt and should have known where to get it.

I suddenly felt a passion not to let that man die a decent sailor's death. I wished he might have stretched rope or walked a plank. I did my duty. I hope I finished him. I don't know. We left him on the cabin floor of the wireless room and he was not moving.

From aft came the tunes of the band. It was a rag-time tune. I don't know what. Then there was 'Autumn'. Phillips ran aft and that was the last I ever saw of him alive.

I went to the place I had seen the collapsible boat on the boat deck, and to my surprise I saw the boat and the men still trying to push it off. I guess there wasn't a sailor in the crowd. They couldn't do it. I went up to them and was just lending a hand when a large wave came awash of the deck.

The big wave carried the boat off. I had hold of an oarlock and I went off with it. The next I knew I was in the boat.

But that was not all. I was in the boat and the boat was upside down and I was under it. And I remember realizing I was wet through, and that whatever happened I must not breathe, for I was under water.

I knew I had to fight for it and I did. How I got out from under the boat I do not know, but I felt a breath of air at last.

There were men all around me – hundreds of them. The sea was dotted with them, all depending on their lifebelts. I felt I simply had to get away from the ship. She was a beautiful sight then.

Smoke and sparks were rushing out of her funnel. There must have been an explosion but we had heard none. We only saw the stream of sparks. The ship was gradually turning on her nose – just like a duck does that goes down for a dive. I had only one thing on my mind – to get away from the suction. The band was still playing. I guess all the band went down.

They were playing 'Autumn' then. I swam with all my might. I suppose I was 150 feet away when the *Titanic*, on her nose, with her afterquarter sticking straight up in the air, began to settle – slowly.

When at last the waves washed over her rudder there wasn't

the least bit of suction I could feel. She must have kept going just as slowly as she had been.

I forgot to mention that, besides the *Olympic* and *Carpathia*, we spoke [to] some German boat, I don't know which, and told them how we were. We also spoke [to] the *Baltic*. I remembered those things as I began to figure what ships would be coming towards us.

I felt, after a little while, like sinking. It was very cold. I saw a boat of some kind near me and put all my strength into an effort to swim to it. It was hard work. I was all done when a hand reached out and pulled me aboard. It was our same collapsible. The same crowd was on it.

There was just room for me to roll on the edge. I lay there not caring what was happening. Somebody sat on my legs. They were wedged in between slats and were being wrenched. I had not the heart left to ask the man to move. It was a terrible sight all around – men swimming and sinking.

I lay where I was, letting the man wrench my feet out of shape. Others came near. Nobody gave them a hand. The bottom-up boat already had more men than it would hold and it was sinking.

At first the larger waves splashed over my clothing. Then they began to splash over my head and I had to breathe when I could.

As we floated around on our capsized boat and I kept straining my eyes for a ship's lights, somebody said, 'Don't you think we ought to pray?' The man who made the suggestion asked what the religion of the others was. Each man called out his religion. One was a Catholic, one a Methodist, one a Presbyterian.

It was decided the most appropriate prayer for all was the Lord's Prayer. We spoke it over in chorus with the man who first suggested that we pray as the leader.

Some splendid people saved us. They had a right-side-up boat, and it was full to its capacity. Yet they came to us and loaded us all into it. I saw some lights off in the distance and knew a steamship was coming to our aid.

I didn't care what happened. I just lay and gasped when I could and felt the pain in my feet. At last the *Carpathia* was alongside and the people were being taken up a rope ladder. Our boat drew near and one by one the men were taken off.

One man was dead. I passed him and went to the ladder,

although my feet pained terribly. The dead man was Phillips. He had died on the raft from exposure and cold, I guess. He had been all in from work before the wreck came. He stood his ground until the crisis had passed, and then he had collapsed, I guess.

But I hardly thought that then. I didn't think much of anything. I tried the rope ladder. My feet pained terribly, but I got to the top and felt hands reaching out to me.

The next I knew a woman was leaning over me in a cabin and I felt her hand waving back my hair and rubbing my face.

I felt somebody at my feet and felt the warmth of a jolt of liquor. Somebody got me under the arms. Then I was bustled down below to the hospital. That was early in the day, I guess. I lay in the hospital until near night and they told me the *Carpathia*'s wireless man was getting 'queer' and would I help.

After that I was never out of the wireless room, so I don't know what happened among the passengers. I saw nothing of Mrs Astor or any of them. I just worked wireless. The splutter never died down. I knew it soothed the hurt and felt like a tie to the world of friends and home.

How then could I take news queries? Sometimes I let a newspaper ask a question and get a long string of stuff asking for full particulars about everything. Whenever I started to take such a message I thought of the poor people waiting for their messages to go – hoping for answers to them.

I shut off the inquirers, and sent my personal messages. And I feel I did the white [*sic*] thing.

If the *Chester* had a decent operator I could have worked with him longer but he got terribly on my nerves with his insufferable incompetence. I was still sending my personal messages when Mr Marconi and the *Times* reporter arrived to ask that I prepare this statement.

There were, maybe, 100 left. I would like to send them all, because I could rest easier if I knew all those messages had gone to the friends waiting for them. But an ambulance man is waiting with a stretcher, and I guess I have got to go with him. I hope my legs get better soon.

The way the band kept playing was a noble thing. I heard it first while still we were working wireless, when there was a ragtime tune for us, and the last I saw of the band, when I was floating out in the sea with my lifebelt on, it was still on deck, playing 'Autumn'. How they ever did it I cannot imagine.

That and the way Phillips kept sending after the Captain told him his life was his own, and to look out for himself, are two things that stand out in my mind over all the rest.

It was a magnificent story, but was it accurate? It is disconcerting to find that Bride, when he appeared before the inquiries, somewhat changed his tune. One should perhaps bear in mind that he was only 22 (Phillips was 24), and that his experience of the world was confined to three trips to Brazil and three to New York. He had been a Marconi operator for only nine months.

In the interview, he said he saw the dead body of Phillips in the lifeboat as he was boarding the *Carpathia*. Under oath, he said he had 'heard' that Phillips had been seen in one of the boats. Again, in the interview he clearly implies that he alone, with murderous intent, knocked out the stoker who was stealing Phillips's lifebelt. Under oath, he said first that Phillips had held the man while he, Bride, struck him; but he later changed that account, too, saying that 'I held him and Phillips hit him.'

There are other, minor, inconsistencies. In the interview, describing his last sight of Phillips alive, he is quoted as saying that Phillips 'ran' aft; later, he said Phillips 'walked'. More puzzling, he said in the interview that he became impatient with the US navy wireless operators because they did not know Continental Morse; but Continental Morse was the system that the US navy employed.

When Bride appeared before the Senate committee his feet were still in bandages, and he was in and out of hospital. Many papers had published a photograph of him being carried down the *Carpathia*'s gangway, his arms round the shoulders of two helpers and his feet in the air. In court, he looked pale and ill, with black rings under his eyes. The senators did not press him.

Why did he change his story? It sounds as if the passage in the interview when he recognizes the dead body of Phillips was Jim Speers stretching a point for dramatic effect. If Bride really saw the body, or at the time thought he saw the body, he would have had no reason to change his story later. Perhaps he told Speers that Phillips might have been in the boat, and Speers could not resist firming the story up a bit. Who would ever know? On the other hand it seems likely that the original account of the attack on the stoker and the revision both came from Bride. He might have thought on reflection that it was imprudent to admit to an attempted – possibly a successful – murder. 'Ran' might again be the reporter.

Despite these changes, Bride's interview established two enduring *Titanic* legends: the heroism of Phillips, and the band that played on as the ship went down. Others testified about the band, and some said it was playing the hymn 'Nearer, My God, to Thee'. Colonel Gracie was sure it was not. 'If "Nearer My God, to Thee" had been one of the selections,' he wrote, 'I assuredly should have noticed it as a tactless warning of imminent death.' The 'Nearer, My God, to Thee' report seems to have come first from a story written by Charles F. Hurd, a staff correspondent of the New York *Evening World* who happened to be travelling in the *Carpathia*, and was thus in a position to question survivors at leisure before they got back to New York. He sounds like an honest reporter. At first, he was evidently sceptical about the hymn, but was convinced by the evidence. He wrote, 'To relate that the ship's string band gathered into the saloon[1] near the end and played "Nearer, My God, To Thee" sounds like an attempt to give an added solemn

---

[1] There was no 'saloon'. He was probably referring to the smoke room on the promenade (or A) deck.

colour to a scene which was in itself the climax of solemnity. But various passengers and survivors of the crew agree in the declaration that they heard this music.' Much argument has centred round this episode. The 'Nearer, My God, to Thee' school of thought was persuasively opposed by those who considered Bride to be the best witness and believed that the 'Autumn' he mentioned in his interview must refer to the musical setting of an entirely different hymn. However, the latest discovery, endorsed by Walter Lord in a recent essay, is that 'Autumn' was also the name often given to a popular waltz of the day called 'Songe d'Automne'. Bride did not say that 'Autumn' was a hymn.

But the interesting fact about Bride at the time had nothing to do with Phillips or hymns. It was that he had spent a large part of the voyage in the wireless room of the *Carpathia*, together with the *Carpathia*'s own operator, Harold Cottam. Between them, this pair had controlled the access of the outside world to news of the disaster; and they had kept it to themselves.

'Watchers Angered by *Carpathia*'s Silence', said the New York *Evening News*. 'Four Days of Terrible Suspense Breed Wild Rumours', said the seven-column headline over a feature in the *Springfield Sunday Union* a week after the disaster. 'Entire World's Thirst for News Only Assuaged When Rescue Ship Crept Into Port Through Fog and Darkness' read a second headline. The headlines were true. The Associated Press had tried every possible means to find out what had happened to the *Titanic*, beyond the bare fact of the sinking. So had the United States Navy, acting on behalf of the President of the United States. So had Marconi himself, who sent two messages to ask why the *Carpathia*'s captain did not supply some news. But the *Carpathia* refused to reply.

She transmitted partial lists of survivors and the private messages of survivors; nothing else.

Why? Perhaps the first point to note is that Bride and Cottam were not only young (Cottam was 21), but ill-paid. The British Marconi company claimed to start its operators at thirty shillings a week, rising to two pounds – half the American rate for the job. But in practice it sometimes paid less: after three years with the company Cottam was drawing £4.10s. a month; Bride was on £4. A second pertinent point is that both men would have been aware of the history of Jack Binns.

Three years earlier, Binns had been the Marconi operator aboard another White Star liner, the *Republic*, when she was in a serious collision off Nantucket. The wireless apparatus had been badly damaged, but Binns had contrived to repair it and send out distress signals. As a result, virtually all hands aboard the *Republic* had been rescued before the ship sank, and Binns had become a celebrity. Shortly afterwards, he resigned his job with the Marconi company and turned himself into a popular and well-paid writer on maritime topics.

The behaviour of Cottam and Bride required an explanation, to say the least. Ismay's Marconigram saying the *Titanic* had struck an iceberg and sunk did not reach the White Star office in New York for two days. The Senate committee was so astounded by this dilatoriness that they cabled Captain Rostron, of whom with good reason they had formed a high opinion, and asked if he could account for it. Rostron by this time was in Gibraltar. He cabled back to say that the message was given to the purser on the afternoon of the fifteenth, and that the purser had taken it to operator Cottam personally. He, Rostron, had particularly mentioned that everything possible must be done to get official messages away by the most convenient means; yet he now discovered that the Ismay message, which could and should have been passed to another ship for onward relay, had not been transmitted until the seventeenth, when the *Carpathia* was within range of the Marconi shore station on Sable Island, south of Nova Scotia. So Cottam and Bride had not only ignored requests for information from the head of their company, the United States Navy, the White Star Line, the Associated Press, and the President of the United States, but had declined to follow the instructions of the captain of the ship.

They gave three reasons for their conduct. First, the American operators were incompetent and ignorant of Continental Morse; to have dealt with their inquiries would have slowed up other traffic. Second, it was Marconi company practice not to send messages to shore stations via other ships; that was why, Cottam said, he had held back Ismay's message. Third, Captain Rostron had told them, given the pressure they were under, to deal only with official traffic and messages of survivors. That was why they had not answered queries from the press or Mr Marconi.

These reasons are unconvincing. The American operators knew Continental Morse. Marconi policy did not forbid operators to send messages via other ships, and in any case Rostron had told Cottam to use any means possible. The pressure was not so unrelenting that neither of them had time, in three or four days, to alert Rostron to what the *Springfield Sunday Union* described, accurately, as 'the entire world's thirst for news', of which both men were certainly aware. Neither of them lacked initiative. They slipped between the authority of the captain and the authority of their employers. Like Binns, they were at the centre of a marine drama that had attracted the world's attention, but they were much better placed to turn it to immediate advantage.

At the Senate inquiry, Senator Smith in particular tried hard, and with some success, to disentangle the nature of Marconi's relations with the *New York Times* after the disaster. How was it that the news for which the world had been waiting had not come from the *Carpathia*, and had only emerged after the *Carpathia* reached New York in the form of two exclusive interviews, with Bride and Cottam, in the *New York Times*?

The fact was that the *New York Times* for seven years had had a commercial arrangement with Marconi about transatlantic news. The paper had given a banquet in his honour a month before. Marconi and the *Times* managing editor, Carr Van Anda, knew one another. The *Times* historian, Meyer Berger, has described how, as the *Carpathia* approached New York, the *Times* day editor told his assembled news staff that the Associated Press had just sent the paper a note saying that the *Carpathia* 'studiously refuses to answer all queries'. It was therefore up to the reporters.

Around the same time, according to Marconi's chief engineer in New York, Frederick M. Sammis, the *New York Times* rang the Marconi office saying they wanted to interview any Marconi operators aboard the *Carpathia*, and would pay. Sammis thought this a good idea, and undertook to get word to Cottam. So he telephoned, he told the Senate inquiry, a fellow at the Seagate shore station near New York, a temporary operator hired for the crisis, and told him to try to get a message through. The temporary was a wit, and can scarcely have expected that his four cheerful Marconigrams would be intercepted by the United States warship *Florida*, passed on by her commanding officer to the Secretary for the Navy, and finally be read out before delighted reporters and a less delighted Senate committee.

'Say old man Marconi Company taking good care of

you. Keep your mouth shut and hold your story. It is fixed for you so you will get big money,' said the first Marconigram, in part. The second said, 'Arranged for your exclusive story for dollars in four figures. Mr Marconi agreeing. Say nothing until you see me' – 'me' was Sammis. Cottam was told to go to the Strand Hotel as soon as the ship docked.

Sammis insisted that he had had nothing to do with the phrasing of these messages. He realized they were not 'gems of English literature'. But he defended their general sentiments. Their phraseology, he considered, was designed 'to spruce the boys up a little', and he saw no reason to be ashamed of the part he had played in their inspiration. His superior, Mr Bottomley, knew of the exchanges, and he believed Mr Marconi did also. 'I am proud of the fact,' he said, 'that being an employer of labour and being the superior of poorly paid men, or mediumly paid men – men who do not see much of this world's goods – I will do them a good turn honestly if I can.'

Cottam, to the senators, at first tried to pretend that he had been off duty when the messages came in and had not read them properly. Then he admitted he had seen two.

As soon as the *Carpathia* was tied up, Cottam made off to the Strand Hotel. He was interviewed by the *New York Times*. Mention was made of a four-figure fee; nearly four years' wages. Cottam was not paid on the spot, but he got his money, $750, before the month was out. So did Bride, though the size of Bride's fee is not clear. He told the Senate inquiry it was $1000 but wrote to his boss in London saying it was $500.

But what was the role of Marconi? Senator Smith was out to discredit him. His organization had possessed

almost exclusive control over information about the catastrophe. That information should have been made immediately available as of right to everyone, especially the
distraught relations of the victims. Instead, Smith felt, it
had been held back for the benefit of a single business
partner, namely the *New York Times*. Here was an issue
that went far beyond a journalistic scoop or rivalry
between newspapers; the conduct of Marconi and his
employees raised the whole question of the malign grip
exerted by the spreading tentacles of business
monopolies.

Marconi said that he too wished that Cottam and Bride
had said something 'more explanatory' before reaching
New York. He had been 'exceedingly surprised' by the
Carpathia's silence, 'as everyone else was'. That was why
he had sent two messages – never answered – to ask why
the captain did not put out some news.

As for the *New York Times*, said Marconi, there had
been no deal. He had had no knowledge whatever of the
Marconigrams sent to Cottam about keeping his mouth
shut. He disapproved of them. Cottam had telephoned
him after the *Carpathia* arrived, saying that 'a journalist
wanted a story' and wanting to know if it was all right to
accept money for it. Marconi had said that it was all right
so far as the British Marconi company was concerned.
But he had certainly not known that the interviews with
Cottam and Bride were to be exclusive. He regretted
they had been exclusive: 'There was no idea of an
exclusive story in my mind.' That had been his position
all along.

Marconi's testimony cannot all have been truthful. On
the evening the *Carpathia* docked, Marconi dined with
the managing director of the American Marconi Company, John Bottomley, on the upper west side. During
dinner, a reporter, Jim Speers, arrived from the *New*

York Times, sent by Carr Van Anda. Marconi intended to drive down to the *Carpathia* later on to see the operators, after the survivors were ashore. Van Anda on the telephone from the *Times* office persuaded him to go at once and take Speers with him. Van Anda knew that no reporters were being allowed on board, but thought Speers might have a chance if he accompanied Marconi.

It was first expected that the *Carpathia* would arrive at one or two in the morning. The ship's position was unknown even to shore-based Marconi operators; the wit who telegraphed Cottam about the money ended one message, 'Where are you now?' When news spread that the ship would dock much earlier, a rush to the pier began. Seventh Avenue, asphalted for its whole length, was the main route downtown. By 8.15 P.M., as one paper reported, the street was jammed with 'racing autoists' in 'limousines, touring cars, smaller autos, and taxicabs.' Van Anda advised Marconi to avoid the roads and take the Ninth Avenue Elevated Railway to Fourteenth Street. Marconi abandoned his dinner and followed Van Anda's advice. At Fourteenth Street, he, Bottomley, and Speers were met by a taxicab ordered by the *Times* that took them as close as possible to Pier 54.

Estimates of the size of the crowd vary, but the figure of thirty thousand recurs. Two thousand people secured pier passes; the rest of the mob were kept back by several hundred police. Apart from friends and relations, those present on the pier included city officials, representatives of the Coroner's Office, doctors in white jackets, nurses in uniform, stretcher-bearers, the Immigration Commissioner and members of his staff, ambulance men with twenty or more ambulances, the drivers of fifteen trucks containing three nurses each and two hundred blankets supplied by a department store, Miss Eva Booth of the Salvation Army supported by a team ready to put up

male passengers at the Army's headquarters in Chatham
Square and female passengers at the Women's Hotel on
West Fifteenth Street, Monsignor Lavelle with ten Sisters
of Mercy, and a committee from the New York Stock
Exchange with $20,000 in cash to be distributed among
the needy; the money had been raised on the Exchange
by popular subscription and was carried by the President
of the Stock Exchange in a big oblong box.

At the gates of the pier, Bottomley was kept back by
the police, but Marconi and Speers were allowed through.

Now the obvious question arises: why did Marconi
think the managing editor of the *New York Times* was so
keen for him to fight his way downtown and covertly
escort a *New York Times* reporter into the presence of
the Marconi operators? Can he really have supposed that
Van Anda wanted interviews with his employees so that
the *New York Times* could distribute them to its rivals?
Marconi had dined in Bottomley's company, and travelled
downtown with him. Bottomley, according to the unchal-
lenged evidence later given to the Senate committee by
Sammis, knew the *New York Times* was ready to pay for
interviews with Cottam and Bride; he had sanctioned the
approach to Cottam. Even if Marconi, with uncharacter-
istic obtuseness, had failed to understand why Van Anda
so urgently sought his help, Bottomley would have
enlightened him. Marconi was sophisticated and worldly-
wise. He had been dealing with newspapers since the
death of Gladstone fourteen years earlier. He and his
apparatus had been commissioned by the *New York
Herald* to cover (exclusively) America's Cup races, and
the triumphant return to New York of Admiral Dewey,
the hero of Manila. He knew how newspapers worked.
He was present at the interview with Bride.

Later that night, Marconi went to the *New York Times*

office. Van Anda was there, directing the paper's fifteen-page coverage of the *Carpathia*'s arrival. The first edition went out at 12.30 A.M. with the Bride interview on the front page. The standfirst under the headline and above the opening paragraph read: 'This statement was dictated by Mr Bride to a reporter for the *New York Times*, who visited him with Mr Marconi in the wireless cabin of the *Carpathia* a few minutes after the steamship touched her pier.' Then came the italic line: 'Copyright, 1912, by The New York Times Company.'

It was after Marconi had returned to his hotel, the Holland House, that he was telephoned by Cottam. Marconi told the Senate committee Cottam had asked if it would be all right to give an account of his experiences. Marconi urged him 'to disclose anything he knew'. He also told Cottam he could accept payment for the interview. Cottam had telephoned very late, Marconi said, 'about two o'clock in the morning'.

Something is wrong about the timing here. When Marconi and Speers reached the *Carpathia*'s wireless cabin, Cottam had already left for the Strand Hotel nearby. Even allowing for the scrum, he cannot have arrived much later than ten o'clock. He told the inquiry he waited at the hotel for 'an hour or an hour and a half' to be interviewed, which is hard to credit, since the *New York Times* had hired a suite as a *Carpathia* news base and Cottam was one of the paper's main targets. But say the interview did not begin until 11.00 or 11.30 P.M. The reporter would have been in a hurry. Cottam must have finished his interview before he phoned Marconi. He said he thought it was over by midnight. Why then did he telephone at such an ungodly hour? He cannot have been seeking permission to give an interview he had already given. Perhaps the four figures 'talked of' again in the

Strand Hotel made him think he had better get Marconi's personal approval for the deal.

But whatever the substance and purpose of that call, it is clear that Marconi knew that Cottam, like Bride, was being paid by the *New York Times* in return for an interview. In both cases, Marconi personally acted as a go-between. What did Marconi think the *New York Times* was paying money for, if not for exclusivity?

The conclusion is inescapable. Marconi lied to the Senate committee when he said he did not intend the interviews to be exclusive.

The researches of the Michigan psychologist, Wyn Craig Wade, among Senator Smith's papers have shown that the senator considered Marconi's dealings with the *New York Times* to be anything but a trivial matter. A presidential election campaign was starting. The power of the big American trusts and monopolies was a prime issue; the trust-busters, of whom Smith was one, were keenly interested in the way the monopolies used their monopoly power. Marconi had a news monopoly over the *Titanic*, and had abused it, Smith strongly suspected.

The senator was usually an obstinate and persistent interrogator, but he let Marconi off the hook. He failed to expose, or try to expose, Marconi's pretences. The reason may have been, as Wade suggests, that Smith's fellow senators on the committee were reluctant to support him, fearful of the political unpopularity they might incur by attacking Marconi too roughly. His invention, after all, had just saved seven hundred lives.

Honours continued to be showered on Marconi. He concluded a deal with the Western Union cable company that marked another step towards his ambition of covering the world with a communications system. Later he became an Italian senator and an enthusiastic supporter of Mussolini. In Marconi House in the Strand, his behaviour became increasingly odd. He refused to share the lift with any employee he did not know personally. He died in 1937 – wireless stations everywhere closed for two minutes – at a moment when his political sympathies were beginning to put his English connections under strain.

Cottam remained in the Marconi service. Bride, on the other hand, left the company and disappeared. Even the dedicated researchers of the Titanic Historical Society have been unable to trace his later history. Perhaps he tried to follow in Jack Binns's footsteps on the road to prosperity, but failed.

8
Senator Smith and his 'Farce'

Like a murder that lifts the lid off a secret corner of society, the *Titanic* deaths suddenly exposed the hidden attitudes and tension of the Anglo-American world of 1912. Power was crossing the Atlantic from east to west, and causing strains. The American Civil War had left the United States momentarily the greatest military power on earth; Henry Adams, then at the legation in Grosvenor Square, observed that the unexpected display of American might left Londoners 'stupid with unbelief'. By the turn of the century, America had achieved great power status as it dismembered the old Spanish empire, establishing a protectorate over Cuba and annexing Puerto Rico and the Philippines. The half century before the *Titanic* disaster had seen also a vast explosion of industrial energy, and the creation of immense financial trusts and monopolies to exploit the continent's resources,

> The great metallic beast
> Expanding West and East.

The *Titanic* millionaires – Morgan, Guggenheim, Astor, Widener, Straus, Thayer – were beneficiaries of this unparalleled expansion.

As the balance tilted, the tensions began to show. The venom of the American attacks on Ismay cannot be explained by the objective facts about his conduct. He was vilified because he was a convenient symbol of the moral corruption of the old world, an effete aristocrat who seemed, with his disdainful and withdrawn British manner, to be looking down on the inhabitants of the new. Similarly, the British seized on Senator Smith, the inspirer and leader of the American inquiry into the disaster, as an example of an American who was too big for his boots, a man whose ignorance made him entirely unfit to exercise power – particularly over the British. In self-defence, the British turned him into a joke, a figure so comical that the London Hippodrome, with malice aforethought, invited him at the height of the inquiry to appear on stage and lecture on any maritime subject of his choice. When Smith declined, the manager said regretfully that he could have named his own price.

Outwardly, Anglo-American relations had never been closer, especially among the upper crust. They were helped by the new ease and speed of transatlantic travel. The liners carried Americans to Europe in search of pleasure, culture, health cures, and titled husbands, and Britons to the United States in search of business, relatives who had emigrated and prospered, and fees from lecture tours. At the top, neither society was difficult to penetrate. Visiting the United States on a lecture tour, John Morley found himself staying with President Theodore Roosevelt, who explained that the United States had moved into the Panama Canal because it was 'mush', and then with Andrew Carnegie, who arranged for Morley to visit his steel works but did not accompany him because, the manager explained, he hated the place.

The new American wealth enabled Americans to establish prominent social bridgeheads in England. One leading London hostess in 1912 was the former Maud Burke from California, Lady Cunard, who was renting the house of the Prime Minister, H. H. Asquith, in Cavendish Square. A second social magnet was Nancy Astor from Virginia, a close friend of the Prime Minister's wife. A third was the divorced first wife of Colonel J. J. Astor (and soon to become Lady Ribblesdale); she was credited with introducing a new fashion for breakfast parties. The elderly J. P. Morgan and his son were both well known at London dinner tables. The Strauses of Macy's knew the Burbages of Harrods. Henry James was not the only American who sought an ideal world in the 'well-appointed, well-administered' English country house; Lady Cunard's husband, Sir Bache, a direct descendant of the Samuel Cunard who founded the shipping line, converted himself entirely into an English country gentleman, with a great house in Leicestershire and his own pack of hounds. Sport was an important link. The Carters came for the hunting. John Thayer came from Philadelphia to England to play cricket, which was also the favourite game of Colonel Archibald Gracie. The amateur lawn tennis and rackets players knew one another.

The English kept an eye open for the new American money, selling off their daughters, or paintings, or shipping lines. But there was often an undercurrent of disdain. The patrician Asquith as Prime Minister could scarcely conceal his boredom with the American politicians he was compelled to meet. What could have been less interesting, he complained in a letter to Venetia Stanley, than a memorial service for poor Lady Hardinge followed by lunch with 'an American Senator Lodge'? If Asquith could find nothing in common with Lodge, as much a scholar, a lawyer and a patrician as Asquith, there was not much hope that he would be interested by any other American politician. Lloyd George described the frostiness when Teddy Roosevelt visited London and was a guest at the same table as Asquith: 'When R. declaimed trite statements, such as "I believe in liberty, but liberty with order," the PM glowered at him with a look of curiosity. I think Roosevelt saw it.' Asquith wrote to Venetia Stanley: 'Roosevelt held the floor practically the whole time, and talked to & at us as tho' we had been a public meeting or (occasionally) a Sunday school. What is it that makes all Americans so intolerably long-winded, and so prone to platitude?' English and Americans found it hard to appreciate one another's virtues. Asquith judged Roosevelt 'second-rate', though probably *au fond* a good fellow, with a passable sense of humour. Roosevelt judged Asquith second-rate too, describing him dismissively as 'able', in the limited sense that Woodrow Wilson and Taft were 'able'.

Over the *Titanic*, many British resented being called to account by Americans. The *Titanic* was a British-built ship, with a British crew; and the Atlantic was much more British than anyone else's. Their resentment was not allayed as they learned more about the man chosen to sit in judgement.

Senator William Alden Smith came from a poor family in Dowagiac, Michigan. He sold newspapers and popcorn as a boy to help the family finances, managed to become a lawyer in Grand Rapids, and despite the opposition of the moneyed power brokers got himself elected as a Congressman in 1895 and to the Senate in 1906, when he was 47. He was a Republican, but of a rather unorthodox kind. Like Roosevelt and Taft, he was anti-trust and had worked in the Senate against the J. P. Morgan interests well before the *Titanic* went down; his general political stance was in favour of 'the little man'. But when the Republican Party split between the old guard under President Taft and the progressives under Teddy Roosevelt – Roosevelt made his famous announcement, 'My hat is in the ring,' three weeks before the *Titanic* went down – Smith declined to join either group. In character, he could readily be made to fit the British stereotype of the sort of Americans who were wielding the new American power: bumptious, self-important, uninformed, provincial and full of zeal.

The trusts had reason to be wary of Smith. So had the British. The British ambassador in Washington when the *Titanic* went down was the formidable and learned James Bryce, for twenty years the Regius Professor of Civil Law at Oxford, and a former President of the Board of Trade and Chief Secretary for Ireland. After five years as ambassador, Bryce knew more than any Briton and as much as most Americans about America, especially American politics. He was 72; however, as Asquith said, he might look like Father Time but could still climb mountains (he had a peak named after him in the Canadian Rockies) and 'discourse at a moment's notice and at any required length on any topic, human or divine'. Bryce had had trouble with Smith. Twice Smith had frustrated him: once when he was trying to negotiate a trade treaty between Canada and the United States that Smith, with others, claimed would hurt Mid-west farmers and lumbermen; and again over a bilateral treaty between Britain and the United States on which Bryce had set his heart. The treaty was designed to show that Anglo-Saxons were uniquely able to settle their differences in a civilized manner by decreeing that all maritime disputes between the two countries should be settled by the arbitration court at The Hague. Smith was suspicious. Were the British trying to entangle the United States in their disreputable European struggles with Germany for naval supremacy? If the treaty was merely concerned, as the British claimed, with the peaceful resolution of international maritime disputes, then Germany should be included. The treaty foundered. Smith later opposed United States entry into World War One, declaring that Woodrow Wilson was in Britain's pocket.

Smith was put in charge of the Senate inquiry largely because it was he who inspired it. On Wednesday 17 April, as soon as the scale of the disaster was known,

Smith as a member of the Senate Commerce Committee introduced a resolution into a worried Senate directing that a sub-committee of Commerce should at once begin to investigate the causes of the wreck. His resolution was adopted unanimously. Before the day was out Smith was appointed chairman of the inquiry and had assembled a carefully balanced committee of Republicans and Democrats. Smith was up for re-election that autumn; but his motives in pressing for the inquiry do not seem to have been primarily inspired by a desire to win popularity in his home state, since he was confident of victory. He appears to have been genuinely stirred, even outraged, by the disaster; besides, it created a rare opportunity of marshalling public opinion behind an investigation into the way the shipping trusts operated. Legislation would follow.

Once his committee was appointed, and its considerable powers agreed, Smith set to work with tremendous energy. The US navy had intercepted Ismay's Marconigrams urging the White Star office in New York to hold the *Cedric*, so that Ismay and the *Titanic* crew could at once return to England. Smith went to see President Taft. Could a Treasury revenue cutter be sent to intercept the *Carpathia* before she docked, to ensure that witnesses the Senate wanted to question could not escape? Taft arranged it. Barely ten minutes after the *Carpathia* tied up, Smith, Senator Francis Newlands (a Democrat from Nevada), the Senate master-of-arms (who had powers to issue subpoenas), a sheriff, and Smith's private secretary hurried up the gangway and asked the whereabouts of J. Bruce Ismay.

In Ismay's cabin, Smith found P. A. S. Franklin, the White Star manager in New York. Franklin was ten minutes ahead of Smith, and it is easy to reconstruct the exchanges that took place between Ismay and Franklin in that time.

Ismay still did not know why Franklin had failed to hold the *Cedric*. Franklin would have told him, as he later told Senator Smith's committee, that it would have been disastrous to hurry the crew out of New York or agree to Ismay's sailing in the *Cedric*: 'We were here, and we were hearing the criticism.' Ismay had no choice but to make the best of it. When Smith came off the ship, he told reporters that he found no disposition in the White Star management to hinder the sub-committee's inquiry; on the contrary, he was sure they would do everything they could to co-operate. Smith had secured his star witness.

Then and later, Smith showed how nimble-footed and decisive he could be, and he was unafraid of using his powers to the full. The inquiry had scarcely started, in the gilded surroundings of the Waldorf Astoria Hotel – senators, witnesses, reporters, and spectators crammed into the East Room, later into the ballroom – before the White Star lawyer, Mr Burlingham, followed by Franklin, complained about the number of the company's employees being detained in New York. On a ship, a crew could be controlled, but once they were living ashore the line was virtually helpless. 'They get into endless troubles,' said Franklin. That was why all shipping lines made it a policy to get crews home again as fast as possible. Was it really necessary to hold two hundred of the *Titanic*'s crew? Smith was unmoved. 'We are not at all concerned,' he said. What mattered was not the convenience of the White Star Line, but the thoroughness of the inquiry.

In London, when news of these events arrived, the British Government reacted with alarm, for the alacrity with which the Americans had acted had taken it entirely by surprise. Agitated messages were sent from the Foreign Office to the Washington embassy saying that the Board of Trade urgently wanted to know whether the United States Senate had the power to investigate an accident to what was, after all, a British-registered ship. Cold comfort was sent back by Bryce. There was nothing to stop the Senate conducting an inquiry, and nothing to be done to keep it in check. Bryce on 22 April explained in a letter to the Foreign Secretary, Sir Edward Grey, that the inquiry was quite different 'of course' from the projected inquiry by the British Board of Trade. Formally, the aim of the Senate was to inquire into the causes of the wreck; but in truth it was merely responding to the press and public opinion, and those senators conducting the inquiry were doing so because they sought the limelight. Bryce explained the influence of the American press, especially the Hearst press, the *New York American*, the *New York Journal*, the *Boston American*, etc: 'However much may have been written about this school of journalism it is difficult for any person not residing in this country to realize to what extent their influence over the less well-educated classes is pernicious in its heartless exploitation of every calamity that has ever saddened, and of every scandal that has ever attracted attention in, this country.'

On 24th April Bryce advised London that he had discussed the Senate inquiry with the President. Taft had said it was nothing to do with him or his administration; it was entirely the initiative of the Senate. Bryce asked Taft how long he thought the inquiry would last – the ambassador, like the Board of Trade, was worried lest the British inquiry would be hampered because its witnesses were still being held in the United States. 'The President was of opinion that as long as the Chairman of the Committee thought it would keep him in the headlines the enquiry would go on.' Bryce two days later called on the Secretary of State. He agreed with the President and Bryce: the proceedings were 'mere self-advertisement'./

Bryce was wholly dismissive of Senator Smith. The ambassador was annoyed from the beginning by Smith's failure to inform the British of his motives and intentions, even though he was investigating an accident to a British ship. 'It might have been more courteous,' Bryce wrote to Grey, 'if some communication had been addressed to this embassy, though from persons so ignorant of the usages of international relations as most members of the Senate are no such action need have been expected.' Bryce referred to Smith's 'singular incompetence', then to his 'conspicuous incompetence', and, in case Sir Edward had failed to grasp his meaning, ended by saying it was 'generally admitted that Senator Smith is one of the most unsuitable persons who could have been charged with an investigation of this nature'. He was 'a person always anxious to put himself forward where any passing notoriety can be achieved'. By the time the inquiry had been in progress for ten days, Bryce was so indignant about what he thought was the irresponsible and time-consuming way that Smith was conducting himself that he advised London to make a formal protest. 'The chairman,' he wrote 'is now generally ridiculed,' and his committee 'now altogether abusing its powers.'

Bryce's general attitude was mirrored in London. 'I am told,' a Foreign Office official minuted, that 'the whole business has been engineered by Senator Smith of Michigan who is very hostile to the UK and Canada. The only upshot, I imagine, will be to discredit the US Senate.' However, the Foreign Office did not agree with Bryce that His Majesty's Government should make a formal protest. Nothing would be gained and much might be lost by complaining. Left alone, the committee would surely discredit itself more and more in American eyes; whereas if the British objected, American opinion might well rally to the senators on the ground that the British were trying to interfere. 'It can be left as it is,' Sir Edward Grey decided, in red ink. The Prime Minister agreed. He wrote to George V after a Cabinet meeting on 25 April to say that 'however ill-judged in some of its methods' the Senate committee might be, it was acting within its legal powers, and that was that.

The government resigned itself to watching the Senate's follies in a mood of intense irritation, almost contempt. But it presented an undisturbed face to the outside world, as represented by the House of Commons. MPs asked if British citizens were not being held against their will? No, the ministers replied, no suggestion of that kind had reached London; Foreign Office information was that all British witnesses had freely consented to help the US inquiry. But was the government aware that the senator conducting the inquiry had asked whether the purpose of watertight compartments was to provide a safe refuge for passengers at times of danger? The Hon. Member asking the question was advised not to depend too heavily on incomplete reports of the inquiry in the newspapers.

Smith was fully conscious of British suspicions and disapproval. He put his star witnesses on the stand immediately – Ismay, Rostron, Harold Bride – thus attracting maximum publicity before moving to Washington at the weekend. To ensure that his key witnesses moved with him, his committee issued subpoenas to Ismay, Franklin, all surviving *Titanic* officers, and twenty-nine members of the crew, instructing them to be on hand in the Senate when hearings resumed on the Monday. Five more crew members who should have been subpoenaed sailed from New York in the *Lapland*. Smith sent a vessel to bring them back.

As an interrogator, Smith could be faulted. He had a long-winded habit of repeating witnesses' replies that Asquith would have found painful to listen to. Sometimes he got himself into a muddle, unable to remember who was who, confusing the officers of the watch on the *Titanic* with those on the *Carpathia*. He argued about marine terminology, as in this characteristic exchange with Major Arthur Peuchen, a Canadian in the chemical business who was an experienced amateur yachtsman:

> SMITH: Did she [the *Titanic*] go down by the bow or by the head?
> PEUCHEN: Eventually, you mean?
> SMITH: Yes.
> PEUCHEN: She was down by the bow. You mean 'the head' by the bow do you not?
> SMITH: Exactly.
> PEUCHEN: It is the same thing.
> SMITH: No; not exactly the same thing.

But Smith had many virtues. He was convinced that he was a standard-bearer for the common man against the trusts, which made him impervious to outside pressure. He cut himself off from press criticism by ceasing to read the newspapers. He was indifferent to the insults from both sides of the Atlantic about his lack of expertise and his unfitness to be in charge of an investigation that required it. 'Energy is often more desirable than learning,' he said in his speech to the Senate after the inquiry was over (again, not a maxim likely to appeal to Asquith). He was above all dogged, with a sound instinct for where the bones were buried. He unearthed in the engine room of the *Olympic* a stoker formerly of the *Titanic* who supplied him with valuable evidence about the speed of

the *Titanic* before she struck. He required Marconi and
Franklin to produce all wireless messages.

Nor was the inquiry as amateurish as the British
especially liked to pretend; it was regularly attended and
assisted by experts from the US navy and the US steamship inspectorate. In any case, the much-despised ama-
teurism in some respects produced more interesting
results than the professionalism of the British inquiry.
The senators felt at liberty to investigate any aspect of
the disaster that they chose – the behaviour in the boats,
the last moments of Captain Smith, allegations of drinking
among the crew – and their informal procedures allowed
them to invite witnesses to describe their experiences at
length in their own words. In London, the format of
the inquiry, the judge, the distinguished lawyers, the
conventions and rules of the courts of law, meant that
every scrap of testimony had to be extracted piecemeal.
Lord Mersey was conducting a much more technical
inquiry than the Americans, with a long list of precise
questions to be answered; and he was impatient with
diversions.

The advantages of the American method over the
British, not in determining the cause of the wreck but in
illuminating the nature of the disaster, are well illustrated
by the record of testimony taken separately on the twelfth
day of the hearings, when the indefatigable Smith interviewed a Mrs J. Stuart White. One of the themes that
comes out of the American inquiry, here stated with
particular candour by Mrs White, was the resentment felt
by some first-class passengers over the way that lower-
class riff-raff had managed to survive, while more
upstanding males had drowned. Mrs White also exploded
the notion, which still persists, that everyone aboard the
Titanic underwent great suffering. As she said, people
ashore who could not find out what had happened to

their friends and relations experienced more and longer anguish than some of the *Titanic*'s passengers; and Mrs White's point is not weakened because those kept in suspense, in her case, were resident at the Waldorf Astoria.

SMITH: Do you make the Waldorf Astoria your permanent home, Mrs White?

MRS WHITE: My home really is Briarcliffe Lodge, Briarcliffe Manor, NY. That is my summer home. When I am in New York, I am always here at the Waldorf Astoria.

Q: I want to ask one or two questions, Mrs White, and let you answer them in your own way. You were a passenger in the *Titanic*?

A: Yes.

Q: Where did you get aboard the ship?

A: At Cherbourg.

Q: Where were your apartments on the *Titanic*? What deck were you on?

A: We were on C Deck.

Q: Do you remember the number of the room?

A: I do not believe I could tell you with any degree of certainty, at all. Miss Young and my maid could tell you.

Q: Miss Young or your maid would know the number of your room?

A: Yes. I never went out of my room from the time I went into it. I was never outside of the door until I came off the night of the collision.

Q: That was due, I believe, to a little accident that you had on entering the ship?

A: Yes, sir.

Q: You went directly to your apartment and remained there?

A: Yes; I remained in my room until I came out that night. I never took a step from my bed until that night.

Q: Were you aroused especially by the impact?

A: No; not at all. I was just sitting on the bed, just ready to turn the lights out. It did not seem to me that there was any very great impact at all. It was just as though we went over about a thousand marbles. There was nothing terrifying about it at all.

Q: Were you aroused by any one of the ship's officers or crew?

A: No.

Q: Do you know whether there was any alarm turned in [on] for the passengers?

A: We heard no alarm whatever. We went immediately on deck ourselves.

Q: On the upper deck?

A: Yes, sir.

Q: And Miss Young and your maid were with you?

A: Yes; and my manservant.

Q: What were they doing then?

A: Simply all standing around.

Q: Was anything being done about the lifeboats?

A: No; we were all standing around inside, waiting to know what the result was.

Q: The lifeboats had not then been cleared?

A: Nothing had been said about the lifeboats in any way, when suddenly Captain Smith came down the stairway and ordered us all to put on our life preservers, which we did. We stood around for another 20 minutes, then, I should think.

Q: Still on that deck?

A: No; on deck B.

Q: You went down to deck B?

A: Yes; he said we must go back again, to deck A, which we did, to get into the boats.

Q: Where did you enter the lifeboat?

A: I entered the lifeboat from the top deck, where the boats were. We had to enter the boat there. There was no other deck to the steamer except the top deck. It was a perfect rat trap. There was no other deck that was open, at all.

Q: Do you recollect what boat you entered?

A: Boat 8, the second boat off.

Q: On which side of the ship?

A: I could not tell you. It was the side going this way – the left side, as we were going.

Q: That would be the port side?

A: Yes. I got in the second boat that was lowered.

Q: What officer stood there?

A: I could not tell you that; I have no idea.

Q: What officer supervised this work?

A: I have no idea. I could not even tell whether it was an officer or the captain. I know we were told to get into the boat.

Q: Did you have any difficulty in getting into the boat?

A: None whatever. They handled me very carefully because I could hardly step. They lifted me in very carefully and very nicely.

Q: How far out from the side of the ship did the lifeboat hang? Were you able to step into it?

A: Oh, yes.

Q: Or were you passed into it?

A: No; we stepped into it. It did not hang far out.

Q: Did you see how far out it was?

A: No, sir; I have no idea. We got into it very easily. We got into the lifeboat without any inconvenience whatever. As I said, my condition was such that I had to be handled rather carefully, and there was no inconvenience at all.

Q: Did you see anything after the accident bearing upon the discipline of the officers, or crew, or their conduct, which you desire to speak of?

A: Yes; lots about them.

Q: Tell me about them.

A: For instance, before we cut loose from the ship two of the seamen with us – the men, I should say; I do not call them seamen; I think they were dining-room stewards – before we cut loose from the ship they took out cigarettes and lighted them; on an occasion like that! That is one thing we saw. All of those men escaped under the pretence of being oarsmen. The man who rowed me took his oar and rowed all over the boat, in every direction. I said to him, 'Why don't you put the oar in the oarlock?' He said, 'Do you put it in that hole?' I said, 'Certainly.' He said, 'I never had an oar in my hand before, but I think I can row.' Those were the men that we were put to sea with at night – with all those magnificent fellows left on board, who would have been such a protection to us. Those were the kind of men with whom we were put out to sea that night.

Q: How many were there in your boat?

A: There were 22 women and 4 men.

Q: None of the men seemed to understand the management of a boat?

A: Yes; there was one there, who was supposed to be a seaman, up at our end of the boat who gave the orders.

Q: Do you know who he was?

A: No; I do not know. I do not know the names of any of those men. But he seemed to know something about it.

Q: I wish you would describe, as nearly as you can, just what took place after your lifeboat got away from the *Titanic*.

A: What took place between the passengers and the seamen?

Q: Yes.

A: We simply rowed away. We had the order, on leaving the ship, to do that. The officer who put us in the boat – I do not know who he was – gave strict orders to the seamen, or the men, to make for the light opposite and land the passengers and get back just as soon as possible. That was the light that everybody saw in the distance.

Q: Did you see it?

A: Yes; I saw it distinctly.

Q: What was it?

A: It was a boat of some kind.

Q: How far away was it?

A: Oh, it was 10 miles away but we could see it distinctly. There was no doubt but that it was a boat. But we rowed and rowed and rowed, and then we all suggested that it was simply impossible for us to get to it; that we never could get to it, and the thing to do was to go back and see what we could do for the others. We only had 22 in our boat.

Then we turned and went back, and lingered around there for a long time, trying to locate the other boats, but we could not locate them except by seeing them. The only way they could locate us was by my electric light. The lamp on the boat was absolutely worth nothing. They tinkered with it all along, but they could not get it into shape. I had an electric cane – a cane with an electric light in it – and that was the only electric light we had. We sat there for a long time, and we saw the ship go down, distinctly.

Q: What was your impression of it as it went down?

A: It was something dreadful.

Nobody ever thought the ship was going down. I do not think there was a man on the boat who thought the ship was going down. They speak of the bravery of the men. I do not think there was any particular bravery, because none of the men thought it was going down. If they had thought the ship was going down, they would not have frivoled as they did about it. Some of them said, 'When you come back you will need a pass,' and 'You cannot get on tomorrow morning without a pass.' They never would have said those things if anybody had had any idea that the ship was going to sink.

In my opinion the ship when it went down was broken in two. I think it very probably broke in two.

I heard four distinct explosions, which we supposed were the boilers. Of course, we did not know anything about it.

Q: How loud were those explosions?

A: They were tremendous.

We did what we were ordered to do. We went toward the light. That seemed to be the verdict of everybody in the boat. We had strict orders to do that from the officer or whoever started us off – to row as fast as possible for that boat, land the passengers and come right back for the others. We all supposed that boat was coming towards us, on account of the rockets that we had sent up.

Q: Did you urge the man in charge of your lifeboat to go back?

A: One of us did.

Q: Did you urge him to go back to seek to pick up more people?

A: Not until we had gone out for half an hour and found it perfectly useless to attempt to reach that boat or that light. Then everybody suggested going back and we did, too, but we could not get there.

Q: You went back?

A: Yes. The sailor changed our course and tried to go back. That was after trying to reach that light for three-quarters of an hour. It was evidently impossible to reach it. It seemed to be going in the same direction which we were going, and we made no headway towards it at all. Then we turned and tried to go back.

Q: Did anybody try to get in or get out of your boat?

A: No.

Q: Did you land alongside the *Carpathia* with the same party with which you started from the boat deck of the *Titanic*?

A: Exactly.

Q: You all landed safely?

A: We all landed safely. We had a great deal of trouble, but we all landed safely.

Q: How many were there in your party?

A: Three; Miss Young, myself, and my maid. My valet was lost.

Q: Did you make any attempt to communicate with your friends, after you got aboard the *Carpathia*, by wireless or otherwise?

A: That was the first thing we did.

Q: Did you succeed?

A: No; we did not succeed. They never received the telegram until last Monday night in this hotel. They took our telegram the first thing when we got on board the *Carpathia*, Monday morning. They took our Marconigram. I think the people on land had a much more serious time than we had, so far as real suffering was concerned.

Q: Will you describe what you saw after daybreak, with regard to ice or icebergs?

A: We saw one iceberg in front of us. Of course, I could not see it, because I was standing this way (*indicating*). I did not even see the *Carpathia* until my attention was called to her. I stood up all night long because I could not get up onto the seats, which were very high, on account of my foot being bound up. I had no strength in my foot, and I stood all night long.

After we got on board the *Carpathia*, we could see 13 icebergs and 45 [four to five?] miles of floating ice, distinctly, right round us in every direction.

Everybody knew we were in the vicinity of icebergs. Even in our staterooms it was so cold we could not leave the port hole open. It was terribly cold. I made the remark to Miss Young, on Sunday morning: 'We must be very near icebergs to have such cold weather as this.' It was unusually cold.

It was a careless, reckless thing. It seems almost useless to speak of it.

No one was frightened on the ship. There was no panic. I insisted on Miss Young getting into something warm, and I got into something warm, and we locked our trunks and bags and went on deck.

There was no excitement whatever. Nobody seemed frightened. Nobody was panic-stricken. There was a lot of pathos when husbands and wives kissed each other good-bye of course.

We were the second boat pushed away from the ship, and we saw nothing that happened after that. We were not near enough. We heard the yells of the steerage passengers as they went down, but we saw none of the harrowing part of it at all.

As I have said before, the men in our boat were anything but seamen, with the exception of one man. The women all rowed, every one of them. Miss Young rowed every minute. The men could not row, they did not know the first thing about it. Mrs Swift, from Brooklyn, rowed every minute from the steamer to the *Carpathia*. Miss Young rowed every minute, also, except when she was throwing up, which she did six or seven times. Countess Rothe [Rothes] stood at the tiller. Where would we have been if it had not been for our women, with such men as that put in charge of the boat? Our head seaman would give an order and those men who knew nothing about the handling of a boat would say, 'If you don't stop talking through that hole in your face there will be one less in the boat.' We were in the hands of men of that kind. I settled two or three fights between them, and quietened them down. Imagine getting right out there and taking out a pipe and filling it and standing there smoking, with the women rowing, which was most dangerous; we had woollen rugs all around us.

Another thing which I think is a disgraceful point. The men were asked, when they got into our boat, if they could row. Imagine asking men that are supposed to be at the head of lifeboats – imagine asking them if they can row.

There is another point that has never been brought out in regard to this accident and that is that that steamer had no open decks except the top deck. How could they fill the lifeboats properly? They could not lower a lifeboat 70 feet with any degree of safety with more than 20 people in it. Where were they going to get any more people in them on the way down? There were no other open decks.

Just to think that on a beautiful starlit night – you could see the stars reflected in the water – with all those Marconi warnings, that they would allow such an accident to happen, with such a terrible loss of life and property.

It is simply unbearable, I think.

Q: There were no male passengers in your boat?

A: Not one.

Q: Do you know who any of the other women were in your boat?

A: Mrs Kenyon, Mrs Dr Leder, of Brooklyn, Mrs Swift, and the Countess Rothe [Rothes] who was at the tiller and her maid, and Miss Young, my maid and myself. I did not know any of the other ladies. Those were the ladies right round me.

I never saw a finer body of men in my life than the men passengers on this trip – athletes and men of sense – and if they had been permitted to enter these lifeboats with their families the boats would have been appropriately manned and many more lives saved, instead of allowing the stewards to get into the boats and save their lives, under the pretence that they could row, when they knew nothing whatever about it.

Q: I am very much obliged to you for your statement, Mrs White.

By calling so many passengers, Smith constructed a much more detailed and broader picture of the disaster than he could have obtained from the crew alone. Like Ismay, some of the crew felt that they were on trial; others, like Lightoller, thought it their duty to protect their colleagues and White Star. But the passengers were not on the defensive. Even as the *Carpathia* was making its way through the icebergs towards New York, a group of them led by Lawrence Beesley, the Dulwich schoolmaster, began to draw up a joint statement critical of White Star; on arrival, they issued it to the Associated Press. Lightoller and others might complain about the senators' maritime inexperience; but technical questions about watertight compartments or pumps were not the only points at issue. On these other matters, the senators were well qualified to ask awkward questions and the passengers – or some of them – were more likely to give candid and independent answers than the crew. The British inquiry called no passengers at all apart from the Duff Gordons, who appeared at their own request.

Consider the major in the Canadian militia, Major Peuchen. He had left the *Titanic* with honour. The quartermaster in charge of a half-lowered lifeboat sang out to say he needed another hand. Peuchen said to Lightoller, 'Can I be of any assistance?', adding that he was a yachtsman and could handle a boat. Lightoller ordered him to get aboard. Captain Smith himself, standing nearby, had told Peuchen, 'You had better go down below and break a window and get in through a window, into the boat.' Peuchen said he did not think that was feasible, and instead swung himself off the ship on a loose rope hanging from the davits and so down into the lifeboat.

He comes out of his testimony as pleased with himself, but he evidently remained calm throughout, and he was curious and observant. He had several fresh points to make. Cabin stewards had given evidence that they had woken up all passengers after the collision; but Peuchen was not so sure. On the *Carpathia* he had talked to two young ladies who claimed to have had a very narrow escape. They had slept through the crash and had not been awakened by their steward; luckily they had been woken up by chance by Mrs Astor, 'who was in rather an excited state.' He was 'rather surprised' that the sailors were not at their stations by the lifeboats; 'they seemed to be short of sailors'. He thought Lightoller could and should have allowed more men into the lifeboats instead of sticking rigidly to the 'women and children first' principle when there were no more women to be found and there was still room in the boats.

He had been impressed by the behaviour of crew and passengers. 'I never saw such order. It was perfect order. The discipline was splendid. The officers were carrying out their duty and I think, the passengers behaved splendidly. I did not see a cowardly act by any man.' He described how about a hundred stokers carrying their bags suddenly appeared on deck, crowding round in front of the boats, and how one of the officers – 'a very powerful one' – probably Wilde – came along and 'drove them, every man, like a lot of sheep, right off the deck'.

Peuchen was less complimentary about the quartermaster in charge of his lifeboat. This was Hitchins (he appears in the official transcript as 'Hichens'), who had been at the wheel when the ship hit the iceberg. Peuchen thought him unfit to be a quartermaster. Hitchins was evidently in a panic; before they shoved off he told Peuchen to 'get down and get that plug in' and then, when Peuchen fumbled in the dark, came rushing down the boat urging him to hurry up because the ship was going to founder – at least an hour before she did so.

After they pulled away (and after a stowaway, 'an Italian by birth, I should think', had mysteriously appeared from under the bow) they heard 'a sort of whistle' from the *Titanic*; an officer calling them back. Peuchen and the others thought they should go back, but Hitchins refused, saying 'It's our lives now, not theirs,' and insisted on Peuchen and the one other oarsman (Fleet the lookout) rowing further away.

Peuchen was plainly frustrated because Hitchins was at the tiller, which put him in control. 'He was a very talkative man. He had been swearing a good deal and was very disagreeable. I had one row with him. I asked him to come and row, to assist us in the rowing, and let some woman steer the boat, as it was a perfectly calm night. It did not require any skill for steering. The stars were out. He refused to do it, and he told me he was in charge of that boat, and I was to row.'

After the ship went down and they heard the cries for help, 'moaning and crying', Hitchins was urged a second time to go back but again refused, saying offensively there were 'only a lot of stiffs there', an expression the women very much resented. He asked one of the women for brandy 'and he also asked for one of her wraps, which he got'. He thought he saw a light (Peuchen was sure it was a reflection) and called out to another boat to ask whether they knew of any buoy around there, which 'struck me as being perfectly absurd, and showed me the

man did not know anything about navigating, expecting
to see a buoy in the middle of the Atlantic'.

Peuchen remained alert after the rescue. He was aston-
ished that when the *Carpathia* steamed very slowly
through the *Titanic*'s wreckage – 'something like two
islands' – he could not see one body. He had thought a
life-preserver was supposed to keep a person up, whether
alive or dead. He was sure nobody could have lived very
long in such cold water. He noted one telling detail: a
barber's pole floating among the debris. Since the barber's
shop was on C deck, he concluded that the force of the
explosions they all heard must have been tremendous, to
detach the pole – a deduction that was very probably
correct. He also noticed quantities of floating cork, whose
significance was, and is, obscure. On the *Carpathia* he
had heard talk that there had been no food or water in
some of the *Titanic*'s lifeboats, so he had made it his
business to inspect one or two of them and had found
hard tack in sealed containers and kegs of water.

Hitchins the quartermaster asked leave to make a
statement about taking the brandy and the woman's wrap,
a charge first levelled against him by Mrs Edgar J. Mayer
of New York.

I was very cold, sir, and I was standing up in the boat. I had
no hat on. A lady had a flask of whisky or brandy, or something
of that description, given her by some gentleman on the ship
before she left, and she pulled it out and gave me about a
tablespoonful and I drank it. Another lady, who was lying in
the bottom of the boat, in a rather weak condition, gave me a
half wet and half dry blanket to try to keep myself a little
warm, as I was half frozen. I think, it was very unkind of her,
sir, to make any statement criticizing me. When we got to the
ship I handled everyone as carefully as I could, and I was the
last one to leave the boat, and I do not think I deserve anything
like that to be put in the papers. That is what upset me and got
on my nerves.

Senator Smith did not ask Hitchins why, if he was 'half frozen', he rejected Peuchen's suggestion that he should share the rowing, which would have warmed him up.

A former naval rating, Edward Buley, in charge of the last lifeboat to leave, gave more evidence about bodies. His boat picked up four people alive, but

all the others were dead . . . There were a good few dead. Of course you could not discern them exactly on account of the wreckage; but we turned over several of them to see if they were alive. It looked as though none of them were drowned. They looked as though they were frozen. The life belts they had on were that much (*indicating*) out of the water, and their heads laid back, with their faces on the water, several of them. Their hands were coming up like that (*indicating*) . . . It looked as though they were frozen altogether.

Smith's address to the Senate on 28 May, after the inquiry was concluded, is a fine example of senatorial rhetoric, the prose equivalent of one of the *Titanic*'s baroque staterooms.

From the builders' hands, she was plunged straightway to her fate – and christening salvos acclaimed at once her birth and death. Builders of renown had launched her on the billows with every assurance of her strength, while every port rang with praise for their achievement . . . the ship went down carrying as needless a sacrifice of noble men and brave women as ever clustered about the Judgement Seat in any single moment of passing time.

The senator spoke of Captain Smith's 'clear eye and steady hand'; for forty years, 'storms sought in vain to vex him or to menace his craft'; he had been 'strong of limb, intent of purpose, pure in character, dauntless'. At the *Titanic*'s moment of crisis, 'the ice, resistless as steel, stole upon her and struck her in a vital spot.' Smith continued:

In our imagination, we can see again the proud ship instinct with life and energy, with active fingers again swarming upon her decks – musicians, teachers, artists, and authors; soldiers and sailors and men of large affairs; brave men and noble women of every land. We can see the unpretentious and the lowly progenitors of the great and strong turning their back on the Old World, where endurance is to them no longer a virtue, and looking hopefully to the New. At the very moment of their greatest joy, the ship suddenly reels, mutilated and groaning. With splendid courage the musicians fill the last moments with sympathetic melody. The ship wearily gives up the unequal battle . . .

It was an emotional occasion, and senators and spectators were duly moved. But besides the rhetoric, Smith's speech contained a series of precise and devastating criticisms:

1. Captain Smith's indifference to danger was a direct cause of the disaster: he was over-confident.
2. The organization of the escape was haphazard.
3. A higher proportion of steerage passengers was lost because they were given no warning before the ship was doomed.
4. Some lifeboats were only partially loaded; none had compasses and only three had lamps. They were so badly manned that if their rescue had been delayed they would have been crushed by the advancing ice floe, 'nearly thirty miles in width and rising sixteen feet above the surface of the water . . . Nearly five hundred people were needlessly sacrificed for want of orderly discipline in loading the few (boats) that were provided.'
5. Some crew never reported to their stations and deserted their ship too quickly. Some were shockingly indifferent to the plight of others, remaining at a safe distance in partially-filled boats while others drowned.
6. The use of wireless at sea must be reformed. Wages should go up, to discourage operators from exploiting tragedies. Wireless apparatus should be manned night and day.
7. Captain Lord of the *Californian* deluded himself about the presence of another ship between himself and the *Titanic*. There was no such ship. He bore a heavy responsibility. By contrast,

Captain Rostron of the *Carpathia* should be honoured throughout the ages.

8. Ismay was not to blame for the *Titanic*'s high speed in a
region of danger; but his presence on board, and that of Thomas
Andrews from Harland & Wolff, unconsciously stimulated
greater speed.

The senator's speech and his committee's simultaneous
report were a serious blow to British shipbuilding and
mercantile marine. Smith recommended, and the Congress approved, the award of the Congressional Medal of
Honour to Captain Rostron (it was later presented to
him by President Taft). Tribute was paid to the unselfish
men and women and the faithful officers who went down
with the ship. But for those who survived, speech and
report contained little comfort. Even Lightoller, who
might be thought to have conducted himself with exceptional courage and professionalism, was by implication
found guilty. He had defended the ship's speed to the
inquiry; he had been one of the principal organizers of
the manning and loading of the lifeboats – the very points
on which the committee was most critical.

What did Smith and his committee achieve in the long
run? Some changes had already been made by the time
the committee reported. Shipping lanes were moved
further south, away from the ice. The US navy assigned
two scout cruisers to patrol the Grand Banks (one of
them was the *Chester*, the ship whose wireless operators
had been so scorned by Harold Bride); this was the
beginning of the International Ice Patrol. Ismay himself
at once decreed that no White Star liner must in future
sail without lifeboat accommodation for everyone aboard.

But Smith also did much to prod a reluctant US
government into legislative action. The Smith bill laid
down new rules about bulkheads, lifesaving equipment,
pumps, the number of skilled crewmen for each boat,

and the designation of a particular place in each lifeboat for each passenger and member of the crew. The near-anarchy of wireless operation was stopped: all vessels with over fifty passengers must be equipped with a wireless set with a range of at least 100 miles; all sets must have auxiliary power; direct communication must be provided between wireless operators and the bridge; wireless apparatus must be manned day and night. On rockets, the bill made it a misdemeanour to send up rockets except as distress signals.

Smith also called for new international agreements to regulate sea traffic. The first Safety of Life and Sea conference met in London between 12 November 1913 and 20 January 1914, producing an unprecedented degree of international co-operation. Many of the measures had been prefigured by the Smith bill. Lifeboats must be provided for everybody. Ships approaching ice at night must slow down or alter course. Rockets were officially recognized as international distress signals, and banned for any other purpose. All ships were to carry wireless with an auxiliary power source; the power of existing sets was to be increased. The United States agreed to continue and expand its ice patrol, which was to be financed by thirteen nations.

In the United States, Smith's efforts eventually led to new laws about lifeboat drills and the training of seamen assigned to lifeboats. Besides, Smith's bill took a crack at the trusts; it sought to ensure that all companies carrying passengers in or out of US ports disclosed more infor-mation than hitherto about their ownership and finances, and brought them under the Sherman Anti-Trust Act which, in theory at least, outlawed conspiracies in restraint of trade and all monopolies. More generally, the public attention first focused on conditions at sea by the *Titanic* disaster – and deliberately kept on the boil by

Smith – helped to produce the LaFollette Seaman's Act of 1915, which gave the oppressed men of the American mercantile marine, largely foreigners, the rights they had long been denied.

The *Titanic* disaster also led to the regulation of wireless. Communication between shore and ships had been seriously compromised by the interference of amateur operators; henceforward, all radio operators in the United States were required to be licensed – the beginnings of the FCC.

This burst of regulation and law-making cannot all be ascribed to Senator Smith, but it could not have happened without the climate of opinion he helped to create.

In Britain, the reception of his committee's report was mixed. Some of those who had been scornful of the committee's competence changed their tune when they read the sober report. Bryce was one of them. Lightoller was not. Twenty-three years later, he wrote that the only achievement of the inquiry was to 'make our seamen, quartermasters, and petty officers look ridiculous'. It was a farce, he said, 'wherein all the traditions and customs of the sea were continuously and persistently flouted'. Lightoller, though a fine seaman and an admirable man, was scarcely impartial. At the very least Smith and his colleagues – who particularly referred to the Board of Trade's 'laxity' – produced a weight of embarrassing and even shameful testimony that the Board's own simultaneous inquiry and subsequent report would not be able to ignore.

When the US committee started work, the correspondent of the London *Times* – reflecting the attitudes of the British Embassy – loftily stated his view that Senator Smith and his colleagues were 'not likely to elicit much important or even sensational information'. Not for the first time, or the last, British disdain had underestimated American doggedness.

9

Lord Mersey and the Whitewash Brush

From the beginning, suspicious people thought that the British inquiry into the sinking was bound to be unsatisfactory. The news itself had appalled the nation. For twenty-four hours, in Britain as in the United States, there was a strong disposition to believe that the ship, since she had been called unsinkable, must somehow be safe. In response to an anxious message from the Board of Trade, the White Star office in Liverpool sent back a telegram saying that although the *Titanic* had indeed struck an iceberg, the *Virginian* was standing by and 'there was no danger of loss of life'. When the truth was known, the shock was all the more devastating. Crowds besieged the White Star offices in Liverpool, Southampton, and London. The Lord Mayor of London, the *Daily Mail*, and others opened appeals for bereaved families. The Bishop of Winchester pronounced what became the commonplace verdict on the disaster, describing the *Titanic* as 'a monument to human presumption'. The two-hundred-and-fifty-strong choir of the Leeds Orchestra, performing in Paris, opened its concert by singing 'Nearer, My God, to Thee'. The nation mourned.

The Cabinet met on the morning of 16 April. Afterwards, Asquith wrote to George V: 'Mr Buxton reported the latest news as to the sinking of the *Titanic* – one of the saddest maritime disasters of our time.' Sydney Buxton was President of the Board of Trade, and thus head of the department responsible. An inquiry under Board of Trade auspices would have to be held: two separate shipping Acts required it. But there was a difficulty. The Board of Trade had certified as safe a ship that, on its maiden voyage, had proved to be spectacularly unsafe. How then could a Board of Trade inquiry into the causes of the disaster be impartial? Mr Martin, MP, put down a question for the Prime Minister. Since the Board of Trade 'must necessarily be itself on trial', he asked, would it not be more appropriate if the inquiry was conducted by a select committee of the House? Asquith's private secretary was Eric Drummond, later the sixteenth Earl of Perth and, in the 1930s, ambassador to Rome. He noted in the weary tones of an intelligent man who knows he is stating the obvious: 'I suppose the line to take is that the Court of Inquiry though appointed by the Board of Trade will be independent of them, and can report favourably or adversely as they may think fit with regard to Board of Trade regulations and actions.' Drummond's grasp of the procedures was imperfect. The inquiry was required to report to the Board of Trade; but the person who presided over the inquiry – a Wreck Commissioner of the United Kingdom, an ancient office seldom revived – was appointed by the Lord Chancellor; and the five expert assessors appointed to help the Commissioner were nominated by the Home Office. This convenient confusion allowed the Home Office to pass on complaints about partiality to the Board of Trade, and the Board of Trade to do the same to the Home Office.

The Bradford & District Trades and Labour Council soon sent the Home Office a resolution expressing 'no confidence in the Court of Inquiry' and describing it as 'an attempt to lull public confidence and to whitewash those who are most responsible for the terrible loss of human life'. This may have been the first time the word 'whitewash' was applied to the inquiry, but it was not the last. Second Officer Lightoller used it in 1935. In 1969, Geoffrey Marcus published *The Maiden Voyage* expressly to expose 'the whitewash so liberally applied by Lord Mersey and his assessors'. Patrick Stenson, in his biography of Second Officer Lightoller, published in 1984, endorses Lightoller's comments about 'the whitewash brush'.

The announcement of the name of the Wreck Commissioner – Lord Mersey – was made on 27 April. Almost immediately, the Prime Minister was having to defend it in the House. Sir Edward Carson asked, 'Does the right honourable gentleman imagine that Lord Mersey will be influenced by the Board of Trade.' Asquith replied, 'No, sir. It is an insult to Lord Mersey to suggest such a thing.'

But who was Lord Mersey, in whose independence Asquith put such trust, and what sort of man was he? The accusation that the report on the *Titanic* was a whitewash can only be sensibly examined in the light of Mersey's background and connections. To begin with, he was not an aristocrat, as some Americans at the time – because of his title – assumed. He was born John Charles Bigham, the second son of a Liverpool merchant. The only distinctive fact in his ancestry was that his great-grandfather, a farmer in Kirkcudbrightshire, was a friend of Robert Burns, who, when he was an excise man at Dumfries, used to ride over and sit by the fire, smoking his pipe and telling stories.

Mersey's own roots were entirely in Liverpool. His father, brought up in what Mersey used to describe as 'grinding poverty', started his career very modestly as a clerk in a riverside shipping office. Soon, however, he saved enough money to buy a small schooner, which was stolen by one of his sea-captain brothers-in-law; he chased him to San Francisco, a journey of four months, and arrived in time to see the ship's masts disappearing over the horizon. Back in Liverpool he was declared bankrupt. But he was a strong and industrious character, and did not despair. During the American Civil War, he cornered the rosin and turpentine market; after the war, he dealt successfully in insurance shares. By the time of his death, in 1880, he had become a rich man and a substantial figure – though of lesser standing than the Ismays and Holts – in Liverpool's civic and maritime life.

Mersey had a strict upbringing. He called his parents 'sir' and 'ma'am', and was forbidden to sit down when he took meals in their company. He was sent to school in Germany where he acquired a passion for the opera and theatre that he never lost; his first ambition was to go on the stage. He had a good baritone voice, and in later life would entertain his guests after dinner with old English songs and arias from Verdi and Gounod operas. He was slow in coming to the law. For seven formative years he worked in his father's office, making some money, learning about maritime affairs, and acquiring a strong distaste for business. While reading for the Bar he also picked up a degree at the Sorbonne, adding French to his German. He was called to the Bar in 1871, married the daughter of a prosperous Liverpool outfitter, and before long, helped by his local connections, was established as one of the leading counsel on the northern circuit, with a large share of the commercial business in Liverpool. Though without physical advantages, being small with a weak voice, he was learned, industrious, and quick-witted. A difficult judge said to him one day, 'Well, Mr Bigham, I may be able to teach you law, but I cannot teach you manners.' He replied, 'My lord, I agree.'

He took silk in 1883, the beginning of his real success. He became the friend of the Lord Chief Justice, the Master of the Rolls, and the Attorney-General. He sent his sons to Eton. Though not particularly interested in politics, he stood as a Liberal – unsuccessfully – for the Toxteth division of Liverpool in 1885, and successfully for the Exchange Division in 1895. By now he was in the front rank of the Bar, with an enormous practice. During the short time he was an MP, he played a leading part in the House of Commons committee set up to inquire into the Jameson Raid. The question was whether the British had connived at this abortive attempt, inspired by Cecil Rhodes, to instigate a rising against President Paul Kruger of the Transvaal. The committee cleared the government, but Boers and many British were sceptical. Mersey's role in this inquiry, when he conducted much of the cross-examination, was the reason why some people, when he was put in charge of the *Titanic* inquiry, mistrusted him; they thought that, having helped with what they regarded as one whitewash, he was fully capable of presiding over another.

He went from strength to strength. Aged 57, after twenty-six years at the Bar, he became a high court judge and travelled to Windsor to be knighted by Queen Victoria. In 1901, he was one of the judges summoned to advise at Lord Russell's trial for bigamy in the House of Lords. He went to South Africa on a royal commission on martial law. In 1909 he was made president of the Probate, Divorce, and Admiralty Division, but suffered a series of alarming heart attacks and quickly had to retire. Henceforward, though soon recovered and as industrious as ever, he undertook only *ad hoc* assignments.

Mersey was the obvious choice as *Titanic* Wreck Commissioner. He was wholly familiar with the shipping business and maritime law; his coat of arms, acquired when he was raised to the peerage in 1910, featured barebreasted supporters carrying an oar and an anchor. His legal experience included every kind of litigation except murder cases, which he loathed.

In the light of the accusations, it should be noted that although his connections were wide, and although his career had brought him membership of the small circle of the English governing class, he was little interested in politics and did not move in political society. He had an essentially crossbench mind. One of his protégés was Lord Sankey, who went out of his way to thank Mersey for his early encouragement after he was appointed Lord Chancellor in Ramsay MacDonald's second Labour government. His domestic life was peaceful, with a handsome and cultivated wife and two successful and devoted sons. He had no financial worries; he saved more than he spent. For leisure, he travelled to France, or read – his favourite authors were Dickens, Balzac, and Daudet. His friends came from the world of the theatre and music – Lillian Bayliss and both Gilbert and Sullivan among them – and above all from the Bar. The law and lawyers were his passion. To the end of his life, as an extremely old man, he would still totter off to dine with the Benchers of the Middle Temple.

Some of Mersey's critics assume or imply that he intended the *Titanic* inquiry to be a whitewash from the start. This is highly improbable. When he was appointed, Mersey was in Newcastle, acting as chairman of a Minimum Wage Committee. His first act was to get hold of his son, invite him to be secretary to the inquiry, and ask him to get on with the preliminaries: to hire a hall, prepare a list of the first witnesses, find a small office, and make arrangements for counsel, shorthand writers, and the press. (The son in turn enlisted the help of his father's clerk, Arthur Donis, always called A. Donis because of his agreeable nature and striking good looks – qualities he transmitted to his two actress daughters, Zena and Phyllis Dare.)

Captain the Hon. Clive Bigham, then aged 39, was in some ways a more remarkable man than his father. Like his friend Aubrey Herbert, the model for John Buchan's

Greenmantle, he was stimulated by foreign exploits that served a patriotic need. He was given a conventional education – the Eton connections were useful to him later on – and decided, somewhat against his father's wishes, who hoped he would choose the law, to become a soldier. For a time he enjoyed the light duties required in those days of an officer in the Grenadier Guards (a captain could expect six months' leave a year), and the opportunity to explore London night life. Then he grew bored. He therefore approached his Etonian friends in the diplomatic service and secured a temporary post as a Queen's Messenger, which enabled him to travel at public expense on the Orient Express to Constantinople.

During the next five years he enjoyed a life of high adventure. He learned the Turkish language and investigated the causes of the Armenian massacres taking place in little-known parts of Asia Minor, reporting his conclusions to the Foreign Office. He covered the Turco-Greek war of 1897 for *The Times*. He travelled unceasingly in the remoter parts of Asia, Russia and China. A journey of ten thousand miles in the eighteen provinces of China, by river and horse-back, was particularly intrepid, since he was often among people who had never before seen a European, and whose reactions were unpredictable. His purpose was to make a report on a projected Russian railway through Manchuria. When, after one or two narrow escapes, he came at the end of this year-long journey to within striking distance of Peking, where he hoped to arrive in time for a reunion dinner of Old Etonians, he found himself in the midst of the Boxer rising. He acquitted himself bravely; at 28, he became the youngest person ever to be awarded a CMG.

All members of the governing classes in those days knew all other members. Back in London, through friends, Bigham found a job in military intelligence. Almost his first task was to go to Paris and try to stop the attacks of two low-class newspapers on Queen Victoria; he silenced them without difficulty, settling up with the editors for a few five-pound notes. He had already written books about his travels. He now wrote military handbooks on Abyssinia, Arabia, and Morocco, three of the few countries he had never visited. At the general election of 1906, he stood as a Liberal in Windsor. He was defeated, but with the Liberal victory, though he was still attached in some obscure fashion to the Grenadier Guards, he began a new career as an itinerant investigator for the government. He was well read and a concise writer. He knew everyone. Like his father, he believed in disposing of the matter in hand as expeditiously as possible. In a very short time, as if extracting chocolate bars from a slot machine, he himself or the committees to which he was secretary had produced reports and sometimes recommendations about freight rates, the regulation of motor cars, railways, the administration of lighthouses, vivisection, and the prevalence of alcohol consumption in Great Britain (less prevalent than it used to be, was his conclusion).

To round off this sketch of father and son: Lord Mersey was promoted viscount in recognition of his services in World War One, when he had been constantly at work on shipping claims, or conducting an inquiry into hospital out-patients, or sitting as a Lord of Appeal; he died in 1937. Bigham during the war served at Gallipoli, made friends with T. E. Lawrence, had four narrow escapes from death – from a bullet through his car, a shell through his tent, a bomb in his room, and a torpedo – but survived to become a member of the British delegation to the peace conference at Versailles. He later wrote several more books, one of them a history of the Roxburghe Club, a select group of scholarly bibliophiles to which he belonged. He died in 1956, leaving a library of 10,000 volumes.

An old photograph shows Lord Mersey and his secretary arriving at the London Scottish Drill Hall, near St James's Park station, for the first day of the inquiry. Lord Mersey looks confident and well equipped, with top hat, tail coat, umbrella, wing-collar, tie pin, eye-glasses, and watch chain. His son, deceptively elegant in top hat and frock coat, looks as though he had never ventured east of the Savoy Hotel, nor encountered any foreigner more outlandish than the Savoy's head waiter, Monsieur Ritz.

They were principals in a considerable event. Under Captain Bigham's supervision, the drill hall had been turned into a makeshift courtroom; long curtains concealed the brickwork; a dais at one end supported Lord Mersey's desk and, at a slightly lower level, the desks of the assessors; a table, chair and decanter of water for witnesses stood to Lord Mersey's right; and one wall was occupied by a large model of the *Titanic* supplied by White Star and a chart of the North Atlantic.

Facing Lord Mersey were some of the most eminent lawyers in Britain: the Attorney-General, Sir Rufus Isaacs, KC; the Solicitor-General, Sir John Simon, KC; Mr Butler Aspinall, KC; Mr S. T. Rowlatt; Mr Raymond Asquith (the Prime Minister's son); Sir Robert Finlay for the White Star Line; Mr Thomas Scanlan for the National Sailors' and Firemen's Union; Mr Clement Edwards for the Dockers' Union; Mr W. D. Harbinson for the third-class passengers; Mr Henry Duke, KC, for Sir Cosmo and Lady Duff Gordon; Mr C. Robertson Dunlop for the owner, master and officers of the *Californian*. The hall was packed, and remained so throughout the hearings.

The Attorney-General opened with an eloquent statement of sorrow about the disaster, followed by Sir Robert Finlay for White Star. 'There is only one thing,' said Sir

Robert, 'that gives some consolation, and to that the Attorney-General has alluded, that this disaster has given an opportunity for a display of discipline and of heroism which is worthy of all the best traditions of the marine of this country.'

The preliminaries were followed by complaints. Lord Mersey had set himself twenty-six precise questions to answer, but they had been 'very hurriedly typewritten' and the 'very few copies' were not enough to go round. Next came complaints about the 'great difficulty of hearing. This hall was not built for the purpose of holding inquiries of this kind and its acoustic properties are very bad indeed.' The Attorney-General agreed; it was 'most difficult to hear and most inconvenient.' Lord Mersey was brisk, as he remained throughout the inquiry. 'We must go on here until we find another room,' he said, not mentioning that the hall had been chosen by his son. That ended the proceedings for the first day. The second day began with the calling of Archie Jewell, one of the lookout men. He proved to be the first of ninety-four witnesses.

Every word spoken at the inquiry is to be found in the *Evidence, Appendices, and Index of the Formal Investigation into the Loss of the SS* Titanic, published by His Majesty's Stationery Office as a single large volume in 1912. The pages of the copy in the Marine Library of the Department of Transport are crumbling, their corners, unless the reader is careful, liable to break off. A vandal has marked in ink the passages referring to Captain Lord of the *Californian*. But all the spoken evidence on which Mersey based his alleged whitewash is readily available.

Evidence about behind-the-scenes activity at the Board of Trade is less complete. Yet the files kept in cardboard boxes at the Public Records Office tell us something. The first point liable to strike the reader who comes to

these yellowing documents after reading contemporary
newspapers is that he is now seeing traces of a great
government department run by clear-headed bureaucrats
expertly preparing to defend its flanks. The writers of
these minutes are little concerned with the subjects exciting the newspapers and general public. There is no trace
of any departmental interest in the conduct of those in
the *Titanic*, or in the *Titanic*'s speed, or in questions of
negligence, or in who escaped and why. These are matters
for the court or the company. The Board's concern is first
to examine their own vulnerability. The question of the
impartiality of the inquiry can be left to ministers – if
necessary the Prime Minister. The Board's main anxiety
– and it was already under attack – was to find out
whether their Marine Department had been negligent.
Were the Board's regulations about lifeboats out of date,
as seemed to be the case? Had the *Titanic*'s sea trials
been properly carried out? Had the *Titanic*'s equipment
been properly tested? The court – if not Lord Mersey,
then one or other of the phalanx of lawyers – would
demand precise answers to these questions, and the
department must at once discover where it stood.

Reading between the lines, it looks as though the civil
servants very quickly, and correctly identified lifeboats as
their main weakness. The outside world already knew
that more lives would have been saved if the *Titanic* had
carried more lifeboats; and the world also knew that the
Titanic had carried more lifeboats than Board of Trade
regulations required. That horse had bolted; but at least
the stable door could be shut. Within the week, the
Board summoned all British shipping lines to a meeting.
What action were they taking about lifeboats in the light
of the disaster? The White Star representative said that
Mr Ismay, in his capacity as chairman of the International
Mercantile Marine, had already publicly announced that

all component companies – White Star, Leyland, Atlantic, Red Star, American – must in future ensure that their ships carried enough lifeboats to accommodate all passengers and crew. The representative plainly thought that Ismay had acted precipitately. The chairman had given his order without consulting his nautical advisers, who might raise objections. Nor had he considered the difficulty of obtaining enough boats. Cunard and the other lines said they were reviewing the matter urgently. For the moment, pending the outcome of the inquiry, there was little more the Board could do. They would have to be satisfied with a half-shut stable door.

With equal speed they established, at least to their own satisfaction, that they were not vulnerable over the tests and trials carried out by their inspectors. In Belfast, the Board's surveyor repeated a test on a lifeboat of the type supplied to the *Titanic*; it was designed and certified to carry sixty-five persons; he had put sixty-six aboard and there was no difficulty in using the oars. Precise details of the materials used in the lifeboats' construction were forwarded to London. Lifebelts had also been correctly tested, he assured the Board, with iron attached.

By the time Lord Mersey was appointed, the Board had already conducted, by chance, a small-scale inquiry of their own into the fundamental cause of the disaster. Professor J. H. Biles of Glasgow University, a recognized expert on the structure of big ships who had himself designed some of them, was acquainted with a senior civil servant at the Board, Sir R. Chalmers. A week after the *Titanic* sank he wrote to Chalmers: 'Does it interest you to know what I think of the *Titanic*? If it does not, don't waste any more time in reading this letter.' He went on:

We have never known of a ship being lost by a collision with an iceberg – some cases of mysterious disappearance have been suspected of having been caused by ice. Many cases of collision with other ships have been known and can be provided against because the amount of *damage* that can be done by collision is limited. The worst is that a ship may be struck on a watertight bulkhead and so flood two compartments. Provision is usually made for safety in such an event.

In the earlier smaller ships it was necessary to carry bulkheads to the upper deck to give the necessary safety. As the size of ship and number of decks increased, the added space above the upper deck was left undivided in order to give greater freedom in arranging passenger quarters. If these spaces had been subdivided by carrying the bulkheads up through them, more than two compartments could have been flooded and the *Titanic* would have remained afloat very much longer and probably might have been towed into port . . .

I think the public outcry about the boats is likely to obscure the real causes of the trouble: the neglect to carry the bulkheads as high as possible.

Why the ship ran into the ice we shall probably never know, but it is obviously the sailor man's business to keep clear. It is the owner's business to make the ship as safe as possible.

Chalmers circulated the letter. 'Much in what Professor Biles has written,' concluded Captain Young of the Board's technical staff. 'I agree with his main contention,' wrote the principal ship surveyor. Someone at the Board of Trade presumably spoke to someone at the Home Office. A few days later, Professor Biles became one of the Court of Inquiry's assessors. It appears to have been a significant appointment. At the end of July, when after much questioning of ship construction experts by the lawyers Lord Mersey presented his report, one of his main recommendations concerned the extension of bulkheads to a greater height – essentially the point made by Biles a week after the disaster. In due course, the Biles doctrine led to new regulations, and hence to the reconstruction of many of the passenger ships afloat.

At the time, the Board could take some comfort from

Biles's opinion that bulkheads not lifeboats were the culprits. The Board alone was responsible for laying down the number and type of boats carried by liners, but it did not carry sole responsibility for the rules governing bulkheads; these were drawn up by a Bulkhead Committee partly composed of outside experts.

Other problems dealt with by the Board during this period were, by comparison, routine. The Imperial and Royal Austro-Hungarian Consulate-General wanted to know how many of the crew were Austrian or Hungarian nationals; the answer was one, a steward. The Armenian Patriarch solicited assistance for the relations of four drowned Armenians; they were sent £25 each, pending further inquiries. From Sofia came news of a Royal Ukase that sanctioned a grant of £200 for proceedings against White Star with a view to claiming indemnities for Bulgarians who had perished. New rates of compensatory pay for witnesses attending the inquiry had to be worked out in consultation with the Treasury; alarm was expressed about the large leap, under the revised rates, in the pay of the chief baker. The files contain an acrimonious correspondence with Fourth Officer Boxhall, who complained that he had been underpaid by £3.10s. and that his letters were 'utterly ignored' (it was not until September that he was finally told he had been paid the same as the third and fifth officers and had no grounds for complaint). Lists were compiled of those drowned, showing their country of origin: seventy-three Irish had been lost in steerage.

One laborious administrative task, relating to Captain Lord and the *Californian*, concerned a ship with a black funnel and a white band reported to have been seen near the sinking. British representatives all over the world were asked to pursue inquiries with foreign governments, port authorities and shipping lines. The investigation was meticulous; a British consul suspected that the funnel of one ship might have been re-painted, and surreptitiously scratched it with his knife. But although answers to the Board's inquiries were still coming in as late as 1913, no ship fitting the description was found.

As the prolonged and scrupulous search for the ship with the black funnel indicates, the inquiry was thorough, within the limits it set itself. During thirty-six days of sittings, the ninety-four witnesses were asked 25,600 questions. The lawyers were efficient, pursuing – unlike Senator Smith – carefully thought-out lines of questioning; Sir Rufus Isaacs was particularly brilliant, demonstrating the advantages of getting up shortly after dawn, his invariable custom, to read briefs.

Lord Mersey liked cases before him to bowl along as fast as possible. He discouraged diversions. His mind was usually a step or two ahead of everyone else's in court, and he was inclined to become restless when he felt he had heard enough evidence to answer one of his twenty-six questions. Captain Lord later complained to the Board of Trade about this characteristic, since he was sure Mersey had decided on his, Lord's, guilt before he had heard all the evidence. When lawyers put blurred questions, Mersey re-phrased them, always more concisely. He was sharp from time to time with the third-class passengers' counsel, Harbinson, but never seriously hampered him. With the crew, he was polite: 'Thank you, Jewell,' he told the first witness, 'and if you'll allow me to say so, I think you have given your evidence very well indeed.'

The report is clear and well-written. Perhaps Clive Bigham had something to do with it; he had a taste for straightforward prose, and it was he, as secretary, who officially sent the finished document to the Board of Trade (who pointed out that he had got the date of a shipping Act wrong by forty years on page one). The Board made special arrangements to publish the report as quickly as possible, authorizing the printers to pay extra for overtime and work over the Bank Holiday; and asking for specially large type. These arrangements were made before the Board knew the report's contents. By the shipping journals and the serious newspapers, the reception was on the whole favourable. The report recommended many changes: to wireless, to lifeboat regulations, to methods of ship construction. The Board of Trade did not escape censure. The files show, however, that the bureaucrats were relieved to have got off relatively lightly, at least by comparison with the charges of sloth and dereliction of duty that had been levelled at them before the inquiry began.

But the most remarkable point about the report was that it did not find Captain Smith and the White Star Line guilty of negligence. This is where the charges of whitewash come in. The report said that Smith could not be convicted of negligence because in maintaining his ship's speed, despite the presence of ice, he was following the long-established practice of the North Atlantic. What was foolhardiness in Smith's case, however, would be negligence in similar cases in future. Mersey had said in court that he did not wish to be too hard on a man who could not be present to defend himself. Having let off Smith, the inquiry could scarcely convict the company that employed him; and here the report implicitly accepted the Lightoller theory that the accident had happened only because conditions that night had been exceptional. Mersey and Isaacs had discussed openly in court the question of Lightoller's reliability as a witness; both were sceptical. Mersey wondered whether Lightoller really could remember exactly what Captain Smith had said to him during his watch. Even so, the report took his word for it that the conditions – an exceptionally calm sea, a starry night, an iceberg that was invisible – formed 'a combination that would not happen again in a hundred years'.

Years later, Lightoller wrote of the inquiry: 'A washing of dirty linen would help no one. The BOT had passed that ship as in all respects fit for sea, in every sense of the word, with sufficient margin of safety for everyone on board. Now the BOT was holding an inquiry into the loss of that ship – hence the whitewash brush.'

The charges of whitewash may be summed up as follows: Smith may indeed have been conforming to the practice of mail steamer captains; several of them had testified to that effect in court. Nevertheless that practice was reckless – as the inquiry report itself stated. That Smith's recklessness imitated that of others was no reason to excuse him from negligence.

As for White Star, its regulations stated that the safety of the ship must always be the captain's prime consideration. Yet the chairman of the line, J. Bruce Ismay, had been handed a Marconigram by the captain which reported the proximity of ice; he knew the ship was travelling at nearly full speed. Ismay could not reasonably claim, though he attempted to do so, that he was a mere passenger. Like Smith, he should have taken steps to ensure the safety of the passengers. But he had done nothing. The company was therefore as negligent as Smith. Unlike the American inquiry, the British inquiry was silent about the subtle pressure that the presence of 'the owner' might have exerted on Captain Smith to chalk up an impressive maiden voyage.

A further point made in support of the whitewash charge is that Mersey brushed aside the criticism that there were not enough seamen on the *Titanic* to handle the lifeboats properly. But the evidence pointed to a shortage of seamen: certainly of seamen in the right place at the right time. Lightoller ordered a passenger, Major Peuchen, into a boat because he could not find any member of the crew capable of helping Quartermaster Hitchins.

The inquiry had other weaknesses. It blandly concluded that there had been no discrimination against steerage passengers yet did not examine a single steerage passenger – though here Lord Mersey could point to the fact that Harbinson, the counsel for the third class, agreed that there was no evidence that they had been unfairly treated. The inquiry also failed to investigate properly the practices among Marconi operators. Nor did it bring out the very important fact that the officers did not know that the life-saving equipment was strong enough to allow the lifeboats to be filled to capacity at the davits, if necessary.

But was it a whitewash? There is no evidence of collusion between Mersey and the Board of Trade. There is no evidence of the fabrication or suppression of facts. The inquiry was under the close scrutiny of the Bar: twenty-eight lawyers were usually in court. Mersey would have been much more alert to what barristers and judges would think of his performance than of what politicians or public or shipowners would think. Even if he had wished, he would not have dared to reach conclusions that would not command general professional support. He also had to get the agreement to his report of the five assessors. He was not the sort of man to risk his standing simply to protect officials in the Board of Trade, or a dead merchant navy captain, or the directors of a shipping line owned by American capital.

Yet he was much too easy on Smith, the builders, the owners and the Board of Trade. Professor Biles had made the relevant points in his private letter of 21 April to the Board of Trade. It was the sailor's business to

steer clear of danger; and it was the owner's business to
make the ship as safe as possible. Neither had done so.
Why then did Mersey give them the benefit of the doubt?
He may have thought that since Captain Smith was dead,
there was no point in censuring him too harshly. He may
have been influenced in letting off the company by the
industrial unrest in the shipping business: White Star
faced a virtual mutiny during the inquiry when the crew
walked off the *Olympic* as a protest against inadequate
life-saving equipment. He may have said to himself that
the object of the inquiry was to find the facts and make
recommendations for improved public safety, not to judge
people guilty or not guilty. Or he – and the assessors –
may consciously or unconsciously have been deterred by
the spirit of the times from making unnecessary trouble
for members of the governing classes; after all, the only
person who might have broken the law was Captain Lord,
by failing to assist a vessel in distress. But whatever went
on in Mersey's mind, and it is not impossible that he
thought of nothing except justice, his report reached the
very peculiar though unstated conclusion that, despite
failures here and there, nobody at all was responsible for
the worst maritime disaster in history. It was not a
deliberate, conscious, calculated whitewash, but it was a
whitewash nevertheless.

In Britain as in the United States the inquiry was
sooner or later followed by a string of reforms: to wireless
regulations, navigation practices, provision of lifeboats,
ship construction. If nobody had been negligent, the
reforms would not have been necessary.

But the real proof that Mersey had been too indulgent
came sixteen months later. An Irish farmer who had lost
a son in the *Titanic* sued White Star for compensation.
Some of the same cast of characters reappeared: Scanlan
and Duke among the lawyers; Lightoller, Lee and Fleet

of the crew. After much of the ground had been gone over again, the jury found no negligence about lookouts but did find negligence about speed. White Star appealed. In February 1914 the Court of Appeal upheld the jury's verdict. The question was, said Lord Justice Vaughan Williams, whether the danger had been unforeseen and unforeseeable. If so, there could not have been negligence. But the dangers had been foreseen. Lightoller had ordered the lookouts to keep a special eye out for ice; Captain Smith had ordered an alteration of course to the south of the regular shipping lane; both actions showed that danger was foreseen. If danger was foreseen, it was not unforeseeable. The verdict was upheld.

So, having been exonerated by Lord Mersey in 1912, White Star was found guilty by the Court of Appeal in 1913, and settled the American compensation out of court in 1916, which was a tacit admission of guilt. The later events did not confirm the Mersey verdict.

Looking back, it is clear that one of the most prominent people in the inquiry ought not to have been part of it at all. Rufus Isaacs (1860–1935) enjoyed one of the most spectacular careers of the century. The fourth of nine children of a Jewish fruit merchant in Spitalfields, in the East End of London, he finished his schooling before he was 14, yet rose to become Attorney-General, Lord Chief Justice, an ambassador to Washington, Viceroy of India, Foreign Secretary, and a marquess.

His early years were uncertain. He signed articles as a ship's boy when he was 16 for a wage of ten shillings a month. (Charles Booth, in *Life and Labour of the People in London*, published in 1888, drew the 'poverty line' at thirty shillings a week.) In Rio, he jumped ship, but was caught. Back home, he worked briefly in the drudgery of his father's fruit business before becoming a stock jobber;

he next had the disastrous experience of being 'hammered' on the Stock Exchange. Then his mother took a hand and made him read for the Bar. He had a fine, handsome presence, expressive hands, and 'an alert glance', as a contemporary put it. He rapidly made his mark. In 1904, it was Isaacs who prosecuted Whitaker Wright for fraud in a case in which Mersey was criticized for unjudicial bias against the accused. In 1910, he became Attorney-General and thus official head of the Bar. In 1911, he led for the prosecution in a criminal libel case brought as a result of an allegation that George V, then on the eve of his coronation, had been married before he married Queen Mary. In the same year, he was knighted and made a privy councillor.

Now it so happened that around the time Rufus Isaacs became Attorney-General in 1910, his brother Godfrey became joint managing director of the Marconi Wireless Telegraph Company. The company was famous and making progress, but its performance was not outstanding. But in March 1912, Godfrey Isaacs and Marconi secured an important contract from the British Government – the department principally concerned was the Post Office – to construct and operate the ambitious long-distance wireless telegraphy service that would link up the Empire. The law officers were not consulted. The right-wing journal *Eye Witness*, edited by G. K. Chesterton's brother, Cecil, alleged nevertheless that the monopoly obtained by the Marconi company was due to the influence exerted by the Attorney-General in favour of his brother. It was said that Rufus Isaacs, as well as Lloyd George, and the Liberal chief whip, the Master of Elibank, were seeking to make money out of the contract.

These allegations, inspired by anti-semitism, were untrue. What was true, though not publicly known, was that Godfrey Isaacs had acquired a large block of shares in the American Marconi Company; and on 9 April 1912, over lunch at the Savoy Hotel, he offered to dispose of some of them to his brothers Rufus and Harry. That was the day before the *Titanic* sailed. Rufus Isaacs declined the offer, on the grounds that he preferred not to have any dealings with a company in commercial relations with the government. Harry Isaacs accepted.

The *Titanic* sank on 15 April, and the world, as it waited anxiously for details, realized fully for the first time the revolutionary significance of Marconi's invention. On the morning of 17 April, for instance, the paper that W.T. Stead used to edit, the *Northern Echo*, carried a story from its New York correspondent as follows:

It is more than 36 hours since the greatest disaster in the history of the Atlantic Ocean occurred, and New York has not received a single dispatch from any eyewitness, or any journalist within a thousand miles of the spot off the Newfoundland Banks where the *Titanic* went down.

Every message so far has been by wireless, and has come from some steamship officer or land station officer who has picked up others emitted from the keyboard of the *Carpathia*, the *Olympic*, the *Parisian*, the *Virginian*, the *Baltic*, or the *Californian* and intercepted in their mysterious passage through the air.

The tremendous anxiety of the relatives of the *Titanic*'s 1400 passengers to ascertain the names of the survivors has found expression in the greatest avalanche of Marconigrams ever dispatched up the Atlantic coast.

That very day, Harry Isaacs offered to sell his brother Rufus some of his share in the American Marconi company. This time, the Attorney-General accepted. He bought 10,000 shares at £2; a substantial purchase, the equivalent of about £690,000 at today's prices, according to the Central Statistical Office. On the same day he transferred 1000 of them to each of his ministerial friends,

Lloyd George and the Master of Elibank, keeping 8000 for himself.

The *Titanic* inquiry opened on 2 May. The Attorney-General played a leading part, questioning, among others, Marconi; the Mersey report was duly published at the end of July. But rumours about share dealings persisted. On 11 October, the Postmaster-General, Herbert Samuel, moved in the House of Commons for the establishment of a select committee to investigate the Marconi affair. Then the Attorney-General spoke. He strongly denied (as did Lloyd George) that he had ever had any interest in the English Marconi company. But he did not think it necessary to refer to his holdings in the American company. 'It was a lamentable error of judgement,' Lord Simon wrote after Isaacs's death (Simon in 1912 was Solicitor-General and at Isaacs's side during the *Titanic* inquiry; later he became Lord Chancellor). Indeed, the information about Isaacs's holdings in the American Marconi company came out only in January 1913, during a libel action against a Paris newspaper, *Le Matin*. The final report of the Commons select committee said that ministers had acted in the sincere belief that their share dealings were not in conflict with their public duty; but it was a majority, not a unanimous report, and it was accepted by the House only after fierce party controversy. On 18 June 1913, Isaacs admitted, 'It was a mistake to purchase those shares.' The mistake, however, did not interrupt his career; four months later, Asquith after some hesitation appointed him Lord Chief Justice of England.

An outcry followed. Kipling was provoked to write one of the most vitriolic poems in the language, about Gehazi, Elisha's swindling servant in the Old Testament, which opens:

result of government regulation – the prospects for the shares appeared bright.

So it has proved. My brother Godfrey and Mr Marconi were in the United States to arrange for the American Marconi company to buy out a rival company, United Wireless, that had gone bankrupt. The news of this deal was publicly announced on the day that the *Carpathia* reached New York: the day after I bought my 10,000 shares. It was also announced that the American Marconi company had done a second deal, this time with the Western Union Cable Company, to build long-range stations in the United States and outside. I had known about this announcement before I bought my shares.

Now the news of this expansion certainly helped the shares. But it does not account for the exceptional sharpness of their rise that started before and continued after the announcement. Before the *Titanic* sank, nobody had contemplated for a moment that they would rise so fast. Formal dealings in the American shares opened on the London Stock Exchange on 19 April. The shares I had bought for £2 opened at £3.5s. During the day, I sold nearly half my holding at an average price of £3.6s.6d. and thus recouped much of my total cash liability, leaving me with a very good paper profit – made in the two days after the disaster – on my original investment.

I should add that I engaged in further dealings in these shares on 3 May, the day after this inquiry opened. The position today is that I still hold 4430 American Marconi company shares, for which in effect I paid £1.5s.3d. each, but which now stand substantially higher. Their prospects, I believe, remain bright – particularly since it is now extremely likely that as a result of this inquiry the governments of Britain and the United States will in future require all sizeable ships to carry wireless.

Now, with your permission, my lord, I shall resume my examination of Mr Marconi.

Would Lord Mersey have allowed Sir Rufus to continue?

There were striking contrasts between the way the Americans and the British handled Marconi. The senators took the position that wireless telegraphy was a boon, but the disaster had revealed grave defects in the system, as it certainly had. They questioned Marconi closely about his relations with the *New York Times*, the reasons why the Marconi operators aboard the *Carpathia* had not answered Marconigrams, the hours and low pay of Marconi employees, the interference of wireless amateurs with official communications, and the extent of Marconi's business interests and their possible tendency towards monopoly. At times, the Americans' treatment of the great inventor was overtly hostile. The British inquiry, on the other hand, treated Marconi as a purely technical witness. It confined itself to the priorities given to different types of message, working hours, the diagrams issued to operators to advise them when shore stations and other ships would or should be within call, and the replacement of the CQD by the SOS distress signal. Many questions aimed to establish the *Californian*'s degree of blame for her failure to pick up the *Titanic*'s desperate calls. The difference between the two inquiries was summed up at the end of Marconi's London appearance when Lord Mersey turned to the silent Sir Robert Finlay, counsel for the White Star Line, and said, 'Do you want to ask anything, Sir Robert?'; and Finlay replied, 'I only want to say we are very glad to have had the honour of seeing Mr Marconi.'

When over a year later in May 1913 the House of Commons select committee into the Marconi affair questioned Sir Rufus about his Marconi shares, nobody noticed that he had bought them immediately after the British inquiry had begun. The chairman of the committee, Sir Albert Spicer, asked Isaacs, 'What did you understand from your brother [Harry] was the reason of the great advance in the American prices?' Sir Rufus replied, 'The purchases in America.' He was referring to the purchase of United Wireless. He did not mention the huge boost given to the Marconi system by the *Titanic* disaster; nor that it was after the disaster that he took the opportunity, on his brother's advice, to get in on the ground floor.

Whether, but for the Attorney-General's shareholding, Marconi would have been more closely examined at the British inquiry, as he was in the United States, about the evident defects of his system, is a matter for conjecture.

10
The Titanic *Rediscovered*

During the years that followed the Mersey report, no doubt because a greater disaster supervened, in Britain and the rest of Europe interest in the *Titanic* as an historical event slowly faded away. The name of the ship settled deeply into the general consciousness as a metaphor of calamity; but the accident itself was half-forgotten, recalled briefly in a local newspaper when a survivor died or a features editor remembered an anniversary. Things might have been the same in the United States had not the Grand Theater on Main Street, Indian Orchard, Massachusetts, shown in the fall of 1953 the film *Titanic*, starring Clifton Webb and Barbara Stanwyck. From this seed we may date the birth, in an improbable spot, of modern *Titanic* scholarship.

The cinema was owned by a Polish-American, Henry Kamuda, who had inherited it from his father. One of Henry's children, then aged 14, was called Edward; and this is the man who now knows more about the *Titanic* and her fate than anyone else – certainly much more than was known to those who went down in her, or to any of the survivors. In 1953 he was working around his father's cinema, putting up posters in the town, doing odd jobs. He saw the film and was enthralled. It was the beginning of an obsession. He read about the *Titanic* in encyclopaedias. He asked an old bookstore to look out for *Titanic* books. He made contact with another enthusiast, who had spent a year and a half building a model of the ship and had corresponded with Harland & Wolff and with J. G. Boxhall, one of the surviving officers.

Then came what Kamuda calls 'my big break'. In 1958, the J. Arthur Rank Organization made a film of *A Night to Remember*, loosely based on Walter Lord's book of the same name. The script was by Eric Ambler; Kenneth More starred as Lightoller, and Alec McCowen played Cottam, the *Carpathia*'s radio operator. The lifeboat scenes were shot in the Ruislip reservoir, near Pinewood Studios, and the engine room scenes at Cricklewood Pumping Station.

The film, advertised as 'an incredible, spellbinding story of six hours unlike any other six hours the world has ever known!', was well received. In the United States, to drum up trade, the Exploitation Department of Rank Film Distributors in New York sent local cinema owners 'business builders', or ideas for local promotions – fashion tie-ups, questions for quiz shows, 'radio spot platters'. One of the 'spots' said:

At night the sounds on board a luxury liner at sea are varied . . . bits of honeymoon conversation filter through the Edwardian mahogany panel . . . somewhere two lovers whisper in muffled tones . . . a door closes softly . . . the 'Blue Danube' drifts from the first-class saloon down to second-class ears . . . then quite suddenly you notice it . . . the smooth hum of the great engines has died . . . and the *Titanic* is dying, too . . . 'She can't sink! . . . she's unsinkable . . . she can't float . . . how long will she last . . . another hour and a half' . . . For you, one of the few in the tiny lifeboats, it is indeed A NIGHT TO REMEMBER . . . the *New York Times* calls it 'tense, exciting, and supremely awesome drama on the screen' . . . never before seen on screen or television . . . Walter Lord's thrilling best-seller, A NIGHT TO REMEMBER.

All these items came to Indian Orchard and were exciting enough, but the one that particularly stirred Edward Kamuda, now 18, was a list of *Titanic* survivors. The idea was that if any of them happened to live in the district where the film was shown they could be exhibited along with the film. Kamuda wrote to every single survivor, and to his surprise many of them wrote back. Next, a hobbies magazine featured him in a series about people interested in obscure subjects. Thus he made contact with others similarly obsessed, until in 1963 he and his new friends, though scattered across the United States, decided to form a society, to which they gave the not wholly happy title of the Titanic Enthusiasts of America. Next, with Kamuda as editor-in-chief, the enthusiasts started a journal, *The Marconigram.* The headline on the first story read, 'Bristol' – meaning, Bristol, England – 'has *Titanic* lifeboat'. The story was wrong, which determined Kamuda to tighten up his standards of scholarship. There was another setback. The Marconi company in London objected to the title, since it associated them more closely than they would have wished with the *Titanic.* The enthusiasts accordingly changed the name to the *Titanic Commutator.* A commutator, in one of its meanings, is a device that records a ship's list, but since few people know the word the journal is often called the *Titanic Communicator.* When it started, Kamuda had only forty-five subscribers, and only fifteen of those paid the annual subscription of $5. He himself was far from rich; and his first issues were crudely produced on a mimeograph owned by the Army National Guard, of which he was a member, with Kamuda himself meeting the cost of paper and postage.

But gradually the membership grew and more subscribers paid their subscriptions, and the society began to acquire *Titanic* relics, usually from survivors. One of the events that shocked Kamuda into starting the society was his discovery, after a survivor died in New York, that his collection of memorabilia had been dumped in the city garbage. The society's greatest coup was to secure the lifebelt worn by the pregnant Mrs Astor when she was rescued. The story goes, according to Mr Kamuda, that when she was being hoisted out of the lifeboat by one of the *Carpathia*'s crew she promised him $5000 for helping her. Either the promise was never made or it slipped Mrs Astor's mind after she got aboard and was accommodated, with other rich first-class passengers, in the captain's cabin. In any event, all her rescuer got was the lifebelt, which he took home to Michigan and stowed in a closet. Sixty-seven years later, his son was in New York when he learned about the Enthusiasts on the radio and, after negotiations, handed over the lifebelt. These days it can be studied at close quarters in a glass case at the Philadelphia Maritime Museum, where it forms part of a permanent *Titanic* exhibit.

The fact that this exhibit is in Philadelphia, five hours from Indian Orchard, is proof of the magnanimity of Mr Kamuda and the other officers of what is now, following a prudent change of name, the Titanic Historical Society. A few years ago they began to think they ought to stop keeping their *Titanic* collection in their own widely scattered homes and turn it over to a properly equipped museum for safe keeping. Their choice alighted on the relatively new Philadelphia Maritime Museum, which had been set up through the gusto, and with the funds, of a well-connected Philadelphia lawyer, Welles Henderson. He had acquired an old building in the historic heart of Philadelphia, next to the site of Benjamin Franklin's house, and with civic help equipped it with the most up-to-date filing and storage systems, as well as high security and controlled temperatures. Here now is by far the best collection anywhere of *Titanic* books, tapes, films, videos, photographs, cassettes, letters and objects.

The objects are not numerous, but few visitors to the museum fail to be affected by them. Mrs Astor's lifebelt, the label reads, was 'presented by Dr Gottlieb Rencher, senior attendant-in-charge to the surgeon of the *Carpathia*. The imprint of the manufacturer, "Forberry, London", is faintly visible over the cloth covering over the cork blocks'. The cloth is a rusty brown. The lifebelt rests on a wooden deck chair with a broken straw back; this was not a first-class deck chair, since the first-class chairs had wooden slats at the back, but it might be second-class – though some evidence suggests that second-class deck chairs had slats also. Nearby is an English silver flask in an alligator leather case given to R. Norris Williams, the tennis player, by his father. The father, after the collision, felt sure he would not survive and passed on the flask to his son, advising him to have it filled up. The barman refused to serve the young Williams on the grounds that the time was well after midnight and the bar was closed; so Williams put the flask in his pocket, where he found it after his father perished and he was rescued.

Other objects turned over to the museum by the Society include a nine-inch piece of wood from a *Titanic* lifeboat seat; a straight razor once the property of Dining Saloon Steward Frederick Ray of Bristol; a bracelet worn by Lillian Black, damaged when she dropped and trod on it in a lifeboat; the discharge book of the lookout who saw the iceberg, Fred Fleet, which, in the column headed 'Description of Voyage', says 'Intended New York', and elsewhere describes Fleet as five foot eight inches, with grey eyes, brown hair, and 'dark Indian spots on both hands'; a White Star button from the coat of Steward C. W. Fitzpatrick of Southampton; an oblong bread board 'believed' to have come from the *Titanic*; a wooden sliver of ship's rail; a menu; writing paper; and a strip of green carpet that a steward squirrelled away to take home to show his wife. Most remarkable of all are the relics of

Selina Rogers Cook, an Englishwoman who was 22 at the time and who died in 1964. She was on her way to visit her sister in the United States and she not only saved but cherished for the rest of her life two champagne corks, one comb, one coin purse, one wedding-ring box from London, one third-class return railway ticket (revised fare 5½d.) from Southfields, Wimbledon, to Walham Green, Hammersmith, the pale blue veil she tied round her head to keep her hat on when she entered her lifeboat, and a tooth she had had extracted but kept.

Mr Kamuda does not regret the transfer of these treasures to Philadelphia, but wishes they were closer, so that he could visit them regularly. He has been seeking out and collecting every morsel of *Titanic* information for thirty years, but his appetite is undiminished, stemming, he thinks, principally from the stories of heroism, and from the beauty of the doomed ship.

Mr Kamuda's place of work is a museum in itself. He is a sentimentalist. His father, when he owned the theatre opposite, had two shops, one on either side of the entrance. One sold jewellery, the other candy. When television spoiled the theatre business in the 1960s, he sold the cinema and opened Henry's Jewelry Store directly across the street, in a single-storey building the shape of a shoe-box, with a dark green side wall and a retractable awning. This is where, since his father's demise, Edward Kamuda spends his time. Inside, among the merchandise – watches, jewels, greeting cards, photographs of the Pope, Catholic devotional objects, wineglasses engraved 'bride' and 'groom' – are signs of Mr Kamuda's passion: cinema posters of every *Titanic* film; postcards of a *Titanic* model at Fall River, Massachusetts, (with the incorrect '*Titanic*, Southampton' instead of '*Titanic*, Liverpool' painted on its stern), and a photograph of the *Olympic* on its way to the breaker's yard. Prominent also are portraits of Mr

Kamuda's father and mother. His office at the back of the shop is a happy clutter of watch and jewellery repair tools, a Virgin Mary thermometer, a souvenir of the Empire State Building, a coloured picture of the *Titanic*, a clock with a *Titanic* face, and a pen-holder attached to a miniature brass ship's wheel, *circa* 1930.

Mr Kamuda is not married: 'You could say I'm married to the *Titanic*.' He is quiet in manner, and when I visited him during business hours was wearing blue trousers, brown slippers, a white shirt, and – a present from his mother – a blue tie with a ship's wheel motif, attached to the shirt by a *Titanic* tie-clip. An assistant asked *sotto voce* if she should charge $20 for a mended watch. 'No,' said Kamuda. 'Eighteen dollars.'

Mr Kamuda's society had 2000 members before the wreck was found in September 1985, and 2700 very soon afterwards. Most members live in the United States, but there are at least a hundred in the United Kingdom, forty in Australia, and others in Germany, France, Holland, Belgium, Norway, Hawaii, and Malaysia. The society has held three conventions: thirty-five people attended the first and six hundred the third in 1982, in Philadelphia, where the participants met six of the dwindling band of survivors, listened to speeches, attended a memorial service, and sat down to a banquet featuring Caprice of Fruit Southampton; followed by Poached Breast of Capon White Star with Carpathian Baby Carrots, or Baked Filet of Sole Queenstown with Cape Race Parsley Potatoes; followed by Chocolate Mousse Titanic. The oldest person present was one of the survivors, Edwina Mackenzie from Hermosa Beach, California, aged 97. (She died in 1984, aged 100, having lived to receive birthday greetings from the President and Mrs Reagan and, via Western Union, Queen Elizabeth; at her funeral the priest referred to her part in the reform of maritime safety laws.)

When Kamuda started writing to *Titanic* survivors – 'our survivors', he sometimes calls them – he did so tentatively, fearing he might be disturbing memories they had tried to forget. Not all of them wished to be made honorary members of the Society, but many were pleased and grateful. He had a particularly ready response from the United Kingdom, he told me: 'They valued the human feelings a little bit more.'

One point that had struck me, talking to the descendants of survivors, was that the American children and grandchildren of the *Titanic* immigrants all seemed to have moved up in the world – one of them worked for a bank on the 111th floor of the New York Trade Center – whereas the British descendants of the crew seemed to have remained in the lowly social stratum occupied by their fathers or grandfathers in 1912. The point had struck Mr Kamuda also. In retrospect, Senator Smith's rhetoric about the *Titanic* steerage passengers who had abandoned the old world for the new because they no longer regarded endurance as a virtue seemed fully justified.

I asked Mr Kamuda, as we sat in his store, what he felt about the dramatic discovery of the *Titanic* wreck. He was less enthusiastic than I had expected. Ten years earlier, Kamuda thought they would never find it. Two years before they did find it, he changed his mind. Now that his obsession had been located, scrutinized, and photographed, his feelings were mixed; he was afraid that the mystique. the mystery and veneration that had always swirled round the ship would somehow be dissipated, though he was sure that the heroism shown and the beauty of the ship itself could never be tarnished. His passion, I felt, was shifting towards the *Titanic*'s sister ship, the *Olympic*: 'She was a ship that did her job, yet man broke her up instead of saving her.' There was at least no danger of the *Olympic*, her dignity in tatters, ending up at Disneyland.

But it would be unfair to give the impression that Kamuda and his fellow members are eccentrics sunk in nostalgia. Nobody could be more up to date than the scientist who discovered the *Titanic* wreck, Dr Robert Ballard; and he was stimulated and helped by Titanic Historical Society members. The American-French expedition he led was based at Woods Hole, on the southern tip of Cape Cod, which is not far from Indian Orchard.

I arrived there, as it happened, at a time full of depressing echoes for anyone interested in the *Titanic*. Three days earlier, the American space shot carrying *Challenger* aloft had exploded in flames off Florida, killing all the astronauts: it was by far the worst accident in the history of the space programme. It had struck Kamuda, as it must have struck everyone familiar with the *Titanic* story, that there were disturbing parallels between the two disasters. Suddenly in 1986, as in 1912, people felt that man had been taking far too much for granted, putting exaggerated faith in his own powers and infallible technology. Some of the leading articles, with the change of a word or two, could have been lamenting not *Challenger* but the *Titanic*. A senior official of the National Aeronautics and Space Administration, which was responsible for the launch, expressed incredulity at what had happened: he had thought such a thing 'impossible'. P. A. S. Franklin, head of the White Star Line in New York, said much the same when he learned that the *Titanic* had sunk. Even the proximate cause of both accidents – cold weather – was the same.

At Woods Hole, I found that Dr Ballard and the team which had discovered the *Titanic* were on stand-by in case they were needed to search for the remains of

Challenger in the Atlantic. So was the underwater vehicle used in the *Titanic* hunt, the *Argo*, named after the mythological vessel that carried Jason on his quest for the Golden Fleece.

Between the *Titanic*, *Challenger*, and *Argo* there was a direct link. All three vehicles had to do with 'frontier' technology: the conquest of the Atlantic, the conquest of space, the conquest of the ocean floor. Ballard has compared the conquest of the ocean floor to the conquest of space, calling it the 'last frontier'; and has described another of Woods Hole's underwater vehicles, the *Alvin* – a large shiny silver ball that carries three people – as an undersea space capsule. The word 'conquest', in retrospect, seemed misplaced.

Wandering round Woods Hole, I detected a further link: a public relations ingredient common to all three. The size of the *Titanic* was a public relations exercise in itself, to attract publicity and bookings. NASA had put a woman schoolteacher aboard *Challenger* solely in order to stimulate public interest in the manned space programme, and thus attract public support and funds. Public relations was an element too in the discovery of the *Titanic*. Nothing could have been better calculated to draw attention to the work of Woods Hole, and to encourage the funding, public and private, on which it depends. Most people had never heard of Woods Hole or Dr Ballard before the discovery of the *Titanic*.

There is yet another link. All three of these technical wonders had a military side. The British Government looked favourably on the building of the *Olympic* and *Titanic*, as it did on the crack Cunarders, because they would be invaluable assets in the event of war. The space programme had military implications. So did the search for the *Titanic*. Ballard is an ex-navy man. Woods Hole is partly funded by the navy. The Woods Hole research vessels and underwater vehicles belong to the navy. The navy gave permission for them to be used to look for the *Titanic* as a good test of underwater technology that the navy is interested in for reasons entirely unconnected with nostalgia.

Ballard's prime concern is not with the *Titanic* either. His real interest is in the Mid-Ocean Ridge, the almost entirely unexplored chain of mountains that runs round the globe underwater like the stitching on a baseball. Unknown before the 1960s, this immense range is said to be 45,000 miles long and to cover no less than 23 per cent of the world's surface. It is not wholly underwater. It comes out of the Pacific in California, for instance, where it turns into the San Andreas fault. Almost all the world's earthquakes are believed to occur on this ridge, and one of the things that concerned Ballard when he was planning the *Titanic* search was the thought that the ship might have been buried by the tumultuous underwater earthquake that severed submarine cables in the area in 1928.

It was not his interest in the Mid-Ocean Ridge, however, but his discovery of the *Titanic* that made Ballard a national, even an international figure – the third underwater explorer that the man in the street has heard of, in succession to Piccard and Cousteau. He looks the part: tall, good-looking and athletic. He is also intrepid, and easily holds the record for underwater dives. He has made three hundred descents in *Alvin*, sometimes to 13,000 feet, or two and a half miles, which is the depth of the *Titanic* wreck. He was born in Kansas in 1942; studied chemistry and geology at the University of California; went to two graduate schools of oceanography, at the University of Hawaii and the University of Southern California; spent five years in the armed services, first in army intelligence and then the navy; and later picked up a Ph.D. in marine geology and geophysics at the University of Rhode Island. It was as a naval liaison officer that he first came in contact with Woods Hole.

Apart from the Scripps Institution of Oceanography in California, Woods Hole is the largest oceanographic institution in the United States. The staff numbers some 900 scientists, including Nobel prizewinners. Yet it is easy to miss, since Woods Hole is no more than a village and the scientific buildings are tucked away. Few of the thousands of holidaymakers who take the Woods Hole ferries in the summer to visit the fashionable offshore island of Martha's Vineyard – some of them on their way to gaze at the bridge at Chappaquiddick where Senator Edward Kennedy had his accident – realize they are a quarter of a mile from a scientific powerhouse. In the winter, Woods Hole has a more serious feel; making visitors remember Herman Melville and the old whaling stations nearby at Bedford or Nantucket, and the square clapboard houses at Edgartown, on the Vineyard, where the whaling captains used to live.

The Oceanographic Institution is private, founded in 1930 with three million Rockefeller dollars. It acquired its military connections, and expanded greatly, during World War Two, when among other things it developed anti-fouling paint for ships' bottoms and worked on winds and tides before the Normandy landings. It now carries out every sort of research from the effect of carbon dioxide build-up in the oceans to 'aquaculture' possibilities, plankton distribution, 'sediments of the abyss', natural petroleum seeps, salmon ranching, and the use of underwater acoustics. It is organized like a university, with some scientists having tenure, and a board of trustees. Of its $50 million a year operating budget, $20–25 million comes from the National Science Foundation, $10 million from the Office of Naval Research, and the rest from business.

Dr Ballard is a senior scientist in the Ocean Engineering Department and head of the Deep Submergence Laboratory, whose mission is to explore the deep-sea floor – less than one tenth of 1 per cent of which has ever been seen by the human eye. Since 1948, Ballard has also been a consultant to the deputy chief of naval operations for submarine warfare. He first became interested in finding the *Titanic* in the early 1970s, purely as a technical challenge, but could find nobody to put up the money. The reason he thought of the *Titanic* was because of a technological advance; *Alvin*, the little round three-person submarine, had originally had a steel hull, and could dive to 6000 feet; but then she was given a titanium hull, which enabled her to go down to 13,000 feet – as deep as the presumed site of the *Titanic*. Pursuing his researches into where the ship might be, Ballard came across one of the Titanic Historical Society fanatics, the late William H. Tantum IV, who taught him that the *Titanic* was more than just another wreck. Still, Ballard could get no backing, though he twice tried, and nor could Tantum, who formed an organization in 1978 called Seaonics International expressly to find and film whatever might be down there.

Tantum died in 1980, and Ballard, while continuing his work on the Mid-Ocean Ridge, had to sit in frustration on the sidelines while a brash Texan oilman named Jack Grimm mounted three expeditions, in 1980, 1981 and 1983, that flopped – he was sure he had found the *Titanic*'s propeller, but it was only a rock – and made the whole idea of finding the wreck seem still more outlandish.

Grimm used an ultra-sophisticated research vessel, first-rate sonar housed in a 'fish' towed along the ocean floor, and scientists from the Scripps Institution of Oceanography. Ballard's reaction to his failures was to conclude that the key to success for any future expedition must be to spend much more time in the area, and to be ready to explore some 150 square miles in case the ship was not where she was supposed to be. For collaborators, since the appropriate Woods Hole research vessel could be made available for one month in a year but not two, he turned to the French, and in particular to an engineer, Jean-Louis Michel, whom he had come to respect during a joint Franco-American exploration of the Mid-Atlantic ridge by submersible in 1973–4. Apart from the Americans, the French and Japanese are most advanced in underwater technology and Michel worked for the Institut Français de Recherches pour l'Exploitation des Mers, a government organization based in Toulon.

This time, the third time of asking, the US navy raised no objections because the technology that Ballard proposed to use was new and needed a work-out. One reason why the navy is interested in the inventions of Ballard's team is obvious, considering the list of maritime nuclear accidents. The nuclear submarine USS *Thresher* was lost off Cape Cod in 1963; she was found and photographed at some 8000 feet, scattered in pieces. In 1968, a Russian submarine armed with nuclear weapons exploded and sank 750 miles north-west of Hawaii, at a depth of some three miles. A month later, another nuclear submarine, the USS *Scorpion*, sank near the Azores. The Russians failed to find their submarine, but the Americans found her, surreptitiously, and raised her a reported 5000 feet before she snapped and dropped back to the ocean bed. Bits of the *Scorpion* were photographed at 10,000 feet. A more alarming event occurred in January 1966 when as a result of a mid-air collision over Spain several H-bombs fell on land and one into the Mediterranean.

The bombs on land were soon found; to find the one in the sea the US navy called in Woods Hole and *Alvin*. After a month's search *Alvin* was successful; and a 'deep submersible', the Reynolds Aluminum Company's *Aluminaut*, designed to operate at 15,000 feet, retrieved it. 'That was when people started taking *Alvin* seriously,' the Woods Hole Information Manager, Shelly Lauzon, told me.

Like the building of the *Titanic*, the space programme, and the military underwater programme, the programme to explore the *Titanic* was not so much an example of man inventing machines in order to accomplish a necessary task, as an example of an undertaking entered into by man as a way of finding something useful-sounding for his new machines to do. The French were eager to join in the search for the *Titanic* because they too had new equipment to test: a revolutionary sonar system.

On 11 July 1985, with Ballard aboard, a French vessel started work, sweeping back and forth across the 150 square miles search area, plotted by Michel, as if 'mowing a lawn' (this became a favourite phrase to describe how the ship was found). The French carried out an 'acoustical search', trailing one underwater vehicle able to take soundings in several directions at once, followed by a magnetometer reporting whether objects found by the first vehicle were made of metal or not. Both vehicles were attached to the parent ship by cable; strong surface currents made their control difficult, and the ship ran into a gale. On 7 August, the French search ended; they had found nothing, but had nevertheless 'mown' 80 per cent of the big square and, as it turned out, had been at one point within a hundred yards of success.

In mid-August the Woods Hole (but US navy-owned) research vessel *Knorr* took over. She is 2000 tons and 245 feet long, with a satellite navigation system and 'cycloidal' propellers that allow her to be driven sideways as well as forwards and backwards – the captain talks about 'right', 'left', 'up', 'down', 'nose up', 'nose down', 'stall the ship'. On board were twenty-six crew and twenty-three scientists, including three Frenchmen led by Jean-Louis Michel. Also on hand was a naval officer from a military establishment in San Diego that operates miniature submarines.

The French search had been acoustical; the American search was visual. The *Knorr's* most important piece of equipment was *Argo*, newly developed by Woods Hole with millions of the US navy's dollars. The *Argo* is an unmanned search and survey vessel, the size of a small car, which is equipped with high-class sensors, three cameras in the front, and powerful strobe lights in the back to light up the ocean floor, which at 13,000 feet is in total darkness. The novelty of *Argo* is that unlike previous search vehicles, whether manned or unmanned, it can stay submerged for days; a dramatic improvement. It trails behind its parent surface vessel on a cable, and has no driving power of its own.

The terrain the *Argo* had to inspect was partly canyons, partly mud, and the *Knorr* crew watched with increasing boredom as it sent its pictures back up the cable. There was a monitor screen in the ship's library where the captain of the *Knorr* used to relax when he was not 'driving'. 'I'd watch this camera go along the bottom,' Captain Bowen said later, 'and look at mud and more mud and sand dunes and a few rocks. Every time we saw something dark come up we'd say, "Gee, is this it?" This went on for days.' The captain was 'amazed' that although they were near one of the junction points on the great circle routes which, until a few years ago, ships used to follow religiously (now they use 'weather routing'), 'there wasn't a lot of junk on the bottom. Seventy-five years of cargo ships dumping hundreds of beer bottles overboard, and passenger liners . . . it shows how big the ocean is, I suppose . . . never saw anything . . . not even a bottle.'

Finally, at 1.40 A.M. on the night of 1 September the dispirited screen-watchers in the control room suddenly saw a shape they thought must be one of the *Titanic*'s gigantic boilers. Someone was sent to wake Ballard. He came rushing into the control room, jumpsuit over his pyjamas, took one look at the screen, and cried, 'That's it!' He said later, 'It was incredible. All those years and all those efforts and days and days with the French and days and days before and *bang*. There it was.' Ballard has a sense of occasion. He led a group on to the stern where he held a short memorial service in memory of the *Titanic*'s 1500 dead. Then he raised a Harland & Wolff flag.

For the next four days Ballard and his associates scarcely slept. The weather window was closing. They 'flew' the *Argo* as close to the wreck as they dared, working from the bows towards the stern to avoid the rigging, and then sent down a smaller vehicle to take 35 mm coloured still photographs. In four days, the cameras shot more than 20,000 frames of film.

The great ship was more or less upright, but retained only two funnels. With increasing wonder, the crew of the *Knorr* saw strange white objects that they eventually realized must be porcelain dishes; a chamber pot; a tray possibly of silver; wine bottles identified later by experts consulted by the *National Geographic Magazine* as Madeira, port, and a probable Bordeaux and a Riesling; a set of bedsprings; a first-class smoking room tile; lumps of coal; a generator; and a second-class smoking room window. Ballard said he felt like an archaeologist opening a Pharaoh's tomb.

Of the ship's structure, they saw a giant hole left by the

forward funnel when it crashed into the sea and nearly killed Lightoller; the bridge; the side of the bridge where Captain Smith was photographed leaving Queenstown; anchor chains; the forward cranes still in position; bollards that still seemed to be shiny; empty davits. Captain Bowen found most moving of all the pictures of the crow's nest, with what appeared to be a telephone line dangling out of it, the line down which Fred Fleet shouted, 'Iceberg right ahead!' and got the reply, 'Thank you'.

Ballard was surprised, when he tried to approach the stern, not to be able to find it. On the way back to Woods Hole, examining the film images, he realized that he had seen it after all, but in pieces. It was strewn in a 'debris field' stretching more than a mile behind the wreck.

Going home, after Woods Hole had told the world of the find, the *Knorr*'s radio operator handled a hundred commercial radio calls, forty radio telegraph messages (the radio telegraph, a radio signal sent in Morse code, is still used extensively), eighty-one ham radio phone calls, and numerous calls from coast stations. Portishead Radio in England called to say they were holding hundreds of calls for the *Knorr*. Ballard was interviewed on radio by ABC, NBC, CBS, and the *New York Times*. At Woods Hole, helicopters whirring overhead, the ship was given a hero's welcome.

What did the discovery reveal? Ed Kamuda surveyed the arguments of seventy-three years. Some maintained that the liner would have levelled off at 1000 feet, turned on her side like a falling leaf, and hit the floor at a moderate speed, masts and funnels snapping off. Others thought she had broken in two and would have hit the bottom at 100 mph, smashing herself to pieces. Others again believed she would have nose-dived deep into mud, leaving two thirds of her sticking out almost upright. 'Only a few guessed that the ship landed on an even keel, gently, and would be found in pristine condition.' Those who said the boilers had smashed down through the ship and possibly crashed through the hull were proved right; they had been scoffed at over the years on the grounds that the *Titanic*'s hull was too strong for that.

Ballard said he found the wreck some ten miles further towards the east than it was supposed to be. He protected its precise location, but stated flatly that the position given by the *Titanic* in her distress signals was incorrect. Her navigator thought she was going faster than she was. The indications were, said Ballard, that 'a south-easterly current was slowing *Titanic* and putting her off her track'.

Why, then, had Rostron of the *Carpathia* congratulated the *Titanic* navigator on a 'splendid' position that enabled him, coming from the south-east, to set a course straight to the lifeboats? Rostron assumed the boats had moved more or less east, whereas in fact they had moved more or less south.

Ballard and his French colleagues concluded, after they found the wreck, that the *Californian* must have been much closer than Captain Lord had claimed. He had said eighteen or nineteen miles; Ballard thought the true answer was well under ten miles, and perhaps as little as five. To that, the Lordites instantly replied: if the *Californian* was so close, why – on such a clear night – did not people in the *Titanic* see an unmistakable blaze of lights? And *vice versa*.

The principal result of the discovery, though, was to raise questions about the *Titanic*'s future, not its past. Could it be salvaged? Mr Grimm, the oilman, at one stage seemed confident that the job could be done; but then he had also seemed confident at one stage that expeditions financed by him could find a hole in the

North Pole, Noah's Ark in Turkey, the Abominable Snowman in Tibet, and the Loch Ness Monster in Scotland. Had he found the *Titanic* on one of his three expeditions, he intended to employ robots equipped with blow torches to cut a hole in the hull, and extract any valuables they might come across inside; Mr Grimm would then consider presenting these items to the Smithsonian Museum in Washington, DC.

Another person who got into the papers by talking about salvaging was an Englishman, Douglas Woolley, who had experience as a farmhand, railway signalman, male nurse, and porter in a Ford motor factory. He claimed to be the *Titanic*'s owner, by securing title in the last unliquidated stock share in White Star, and a disclaimer from its successor, Cunard. At one time or another he had set up four companies – Seawise and Titanic Salvage Ltd., Titanic Salvage Co., Seawise Salvage Co., and Deftpoint Ltd. – and, with two Hungarian scientists, Ambros Balas and Laszlo Szaskoe, planned to use a bathysphere with mechanical arms to wrap hundreds of plastic containers round the *Titanic*'s hull; they would next pass an electric current through the water inside the containers to break up the water into gases that would lift the ship gently to the surface. Then she would be towed back to Liverpool, refitted, and housed in a dry dock as a maritime museum.

More recently, a salvage engineer in Stamford, Connecticut, has proposed to pack 180,000 tons of petroleum jelly into polyester bags stowed inside the hull; he has said that the jelly would harden and cause the *Titanic* to become buoyant. John Pierce, a British enthusiast who helped to recover artefacts from the *Lusitania*, has spoken of a 'giant iceberg' scheme, whereby the *Titanic* would be wrapped in a wire net, liquid nitrogen would be pumped through the net, the nitrogen would turn into an iceberg, float upwards, and hey presto. Mr Pierce has also spoken of a simpler-sounding plan of raising the ship by means of giant air bags filled with compressed air – as used to salvage the sabotaged Greenpeace boat, *Rainbow Warrior*, from Auckland harbour in 1985. In either case, it would be Mr Pierce's intention to take the ship back to Harland & Wolff, restore her full 1912 glory, and sail her on another maiden voyage, hoping for better luck next time.

Successful salvage techniques have involved compressed air, or pontoons, or the injection of polyurethane foam. None of these would work, experienced salvage people say, at a depth of two and a half miles.

Dr Ballard has said bluntly, 'To raise the *Titanic* is foolish.' Lord Grade, after he financed a disastrous film, *Raise The Titanic*, said, 'It would have been cheaper to have lowered the Atlantic'; and many people who have considered the costs say much the same about a real-life attempt. Mr William Summers, writing to *The Times* soon after the discovery of the wreck, put the cost at over £100 million. Mr Summers, a member of the steel-making family of the same name, and the person responsible for jacklifting the *Mary Rose* out of the Solent in 1982, pointed out that steel was in its 'early manhood' in 1910, and the evidence was that the *Titanic* suffered serious damage in her descent. 'This would make complete support of the structure necessary, very much as for the *Mary Rose* – but for an 852-foot, 46,328-ton item!' An armada of recovery vessels would be needed to put in place a system of controlling the ascent of such a huge, fragile shell; and the armada would surely run the risk of storm, or indeed icebergs, either during the lift or the laborious tow to shore. Even if the ship could be recovered and put on show, any conceivable revenue would be mopped up by the costs of preventing corrosion.

Scrap steel, he concluded, fetches only £35 to £40 a ton. Captain Bowen has said, 'Salvage would be impossible. It would be like trying to lift an old Cape Cod barn with a crane. It would just crumble into a thousand pieces.'

Dr Ballard and all those who helped to find the *Titanic* said as soon as they came ashore that she should be allowed to rest in peace, and so, shortly afterwards, did all the survivors and the descendants of survivors whose views were canvassed. But Ballard was not confident that the realism of Mr Summers would necessarily deter some of those whose eyes were fixed on the wreck. Even if it became plain to everyone that a salvage operation was a fantasy, greedy treasure-hunters might easily send down instruments to trawl through the wreck and inflict great damage. Nobody, it turned out, not even Mr Woolley, owned the *Titanic*, and there was no law that could stop anybody from meddling with her.

For these reasons, urged on by Dr Ballard and survivors, the House of Representatives Merchant Marine and Fishing Committee approved a bill in November 1985 to 'recognize the sanctity of the shipwreck *Titanic* as a maritime memorial', bar Americans from indiscriminate salvage operations, and seek an agreement with other nations, including Great Britain, France, and Canada, 'to protect the wreck's scientific, historical, and cultural significance'. The administration supported the bill.

But the discovery of the *Titanic* provoked much wider questions than the future of one old ship. For the first time, the world at large was suddenly made aware of the burgeoning of underwater technology. If it was possible not only to find the wreck at a depth of two and a half miles – a feat described by someone at Woods Hole as like dangling a needle into a soda bottle from the top of the Empire State Building – but to photograph a bottle of *Titanic* port, what else might be done down there?

Dr Ballard was on hand to explain. He and his fellow oceanographers live among jargon – they 'multiplex' things, or see 'imaged areas' – and Ballard has invented a new word to describe the next advance in his science, which is to establish man's 'telepresence' on the ocean bed. He told the House Merchant Marine Committee that the technology used in finding the *Titanic* was in the vanguard of the technology that man would soon be using to project his eyes, ears and eventually his hands to the ocean floor. Going to the movies, watching television, using a telephone were all crude forms of 'telepresence'. Exploration of the ocean floor was not driving the technology, but was benefiting from it; the driving forces were the space programme, with its robots on Mars and Venus, the commercial world, with its developing television and cinema techniques, and the military, with 'their desire to remove humans from the risks of combat'.

Deep-sea exploration indeed seems to be following the example of the exploration of space, replacing expensive and not particularly efficient manned vehicles by the equivalent of unmanned space probes. Ballard's Deep Submergence Laboratory has been developing an unmanned vehicle named *Jason* that can do everything, and more, that has been done over the past fifteen years by their manned workhorse *Alvin*.

When fully developed, the system will work as follows. The research vessel will position itself to within a few yards of where it wants to be by using satellites in 'geostationary orbit' 22,000 miles in space. The Global Positioning System will be plugged into *Argo*, so that it too will know exactly where it is. *Argo* will conduct a general survey of the terrain. Then it will be kept still at a height of some 100 metres above the floor. *Jason* then leaves *Argo*, though still tethered to it, and equipped with stereo colour television and robot arms, zooms in for a close look, picking up samples if required and taking them back for *Argo* to store. Both vehicles can keep up this work for days at a stretch.

Up top, the operator can see what *Jason* sees through its stereo eyes. Simultaneously, he can watch *Jason* through the eyes of *Argo* poised overhead. This is what Ballard means by man being able before long to establish a 'telepresence' on the ocean floor.

This is what he had in mind when he told the House committee: 'I strongly believe that if the *Titanic* is left alone, within the next few years, beginning as early as next year, robot vehicles will be able to enter its beautifully designed rooms and document in colour its preserved splendour – a feat that no salvage operation could duplicate.'

At great depths, wrecks are preserved as in a giant refrigerator; down there, freezing temperatures and darkness inhibit, where they do not prevent, the biological activity that consumes wood or metal in shallower water. Round the world, hundreds and hundreds of well-preserved wrecks are 'awaiting mankind', Ballard has said. After his *Titanic* triumph, he began to wonder about the chances of finding the most spectacular wrecks of all: the four hundred Roman vessels sunk by a storm after their victory over the Carthaginians in the Second Punic War of 225 BC.

Ballard is an adviser to the Walt Disney World Company as well as to the US navy. He is in the strange position of being able to interest them both in the same technology. One day, he imagines that tourists in Orlando, Florida, will be able to sit in a capsule and watch direct telecasts relayed via satellite from *Argo* and *Jason* on the ocean floor. At the same time, the technology has implications for submarine warfare.

Soon after his return from the *Titanic* Ballard took

Argo on its first purely scientific expedition. Off the coast of Mexico, he surveyed parts of the East Pacific Rise, looking at recent volcanic activity and hydrothermal vent fields, or underwater geysers. Thanks to *Argo*, he saw more of the world's underwater mountain range in a few days than all scientists put together had seen of it in the previous decade.

Ballard would be first to admit that the abiding power of the *Titanic* legend has helped him and his Deep Submergence Laboratory to advance his underwater ambitions. As Shelly Lauzon, the Information Manager at Woods Hole, put it, 'What better thing could you find to make people aware of these programmes than the *Titanic*?'

11
Graveyard of a Legend

For those seeking to recapture the feel of the far-off days when the *Titanic* went down, certain places are especially evocative: the central square in Southampton with its memorial to the engineers; the cracked and empty concrete of the Belfast slipway; the Straus park in New York on the site of their old family farm. But the most evocative place of all is Halifax, Nova Scotia. It is barely mentioned in the voluminous *Titanic* literature – perhaps what happened there in the aftermath of the sinking is too grisly to have found a ready slot in what has become, otherwise, a not unenjoyable legend.

Unlike other substantial towns or cities washed by the Atlantic on the north-east American coast, Halifax at once makes the visitor aware of its strong connection with the British Isles. It is named after an earl of Halifax, not the Yorkshire town; and over the years there has been much marrying of Halifax girls by British soldiers and sailors. One of the town clocks, still going, was erected by Queen Victoria's father, the Duke of Kent, who was a stickler for punctuality. The city's chief maritime distinction is that it gave birth to the transatlantic shipping business, since the most successful Haligonian of all was Samuel Cunard. The great shipping line shut its office here in the 1960s, defeated by jet aircraft, but the dark green tankers of the S. Cunard Company – an oil and gas firm started by one of Samuel's sons – are still to be seen filling up the central heating tanks of Halifax citizens; an imposing pair of gates survives from an old

Cunard residence; there is a Cunard Street; and, at the Holiday Inn, a Cunard Room for functions.

Although Halifax today, with a population of 250,000, is four times as big as it was in 1912 and has the usual quota of high-rise office blocks, it has not changed beyond recognition. It is an architectural historian's hunting-ground of styles and fusions of different cultures – British, French, American. Government House is a magnificent Georgian mansion; so is the parliament building. Some of the Georgian houses during the nineteenth century were crowned with French mansard roofs. There are many New England-style white clapboard houses, and a profusion of churches including one, an old Protestant church in mid-town, St Paul's, built in the best New England manner, which is the only church in the world, it is safe to say, to contain a stained-glass window that commemorates a clergyman who was blown through it. He was one of those killed in the great and terrible Halifax explosion of 1917, when two ships, one of them carrying TNT, collided, causing 2000 deaths and 8000 injured: the largest man-made explosion, according to local historians, before the atomic bomb.

Historically, the importance of Halifax as a frontier post and fortress, and later as a commercial and military city, arose from its harbour, which is long, narrow and safe: one of the best harbours in the world. As elsewhere these days, from Liverpool to Baltimore to Melbourne, the old port, its warehouses made unnecessary by containers, is being tastefully refurbished with harbourside hotels, fish restaurants, museums, restored shops and boutiques. But the waterfront is still busy, and still a naval base; and it is not difficult, with the help of the maps and small displays of *Titanic* relics in the museums and public archives, to think oneself back to 1912, when Halifax witnessed the last and saddest scenes in the

Titanic drama. More Haligonians knew the North Atlantic in those days than they do now: a thousand fishing vessels then operated out of Halifax. They were the inheritors of a tradition that stretched back to the seventeenth century, when the French fished the Newfoundland Banks for cod, using hand-held lines, each man protected against the wind by an individual canvas wind-shield.

Halifax was part of the *Titanic* story from the beginning, since it was the site of a shore wireless station that relayed messages from ships at or near the scene of the disaster. At one moment a wild rumour circulated that the *Titanic* had not sunk: she was being towed in the direction of Halifax and would be beached on Sable Island nearby, where she would disembark her passengers before being towed on to Halifax harbour.

It was to Halifax that the White Star company turned to collect the *Titanic* corpses. For hours after the sinking, it was hoped against hope that some ship or ships other than the *Carpathia* had picked up survivors; but gradually a dreadful fact had to be faced: some 1500 men, women and children were still out in the Atlantic. The fact was all the grimmer because survivors' accounts agreed that although there had been a shortage of lifeboats, there had been no shortage of lifebelts; the overwhelming majority of passengers and crew had been wearing them. The corpses would still be floating.

White Star chartered a cable ship, the *Mackay-Bennett*, to recover as many bodies as she could. She sailed on 17 April (the day Sir Rufus Isaacs bought his Marconi shares), loaded with some hundred coffins, embalming fluid, the leading local undertaker, John Snow of Snow & Co., and the Reverend Canon Kenneth Hind of All Saints Cathedral. Fog and squalls made her task difficult, but at dawn on the third day bodies were sighted and, though heavy seas were running, boats lowered. Fifty-one bodies were recovered that day, and twenty-four buried at sea, after a service taken by Canon Hind, because they were badly decomposed. During the day, it was later reported, the ship's company sighted a woman's red skirt tied to an oar. A photograph shows one of the *Mackay-Bennett*'s boats, with four men at the oars, in the act of hauling a body inboard.

As each corpse reached the parent ship, the purser filled in a careful list: male or female, appearance, estimated age, clothing, effects. Each body was tagged with a number; the effects, if any, were put into separate canvas bags. Bodies not buried at sea were embalmed and laid out in coffins or canvas shrouds on deck.

By Thursday 25 April, White Star had sent another ship, the *Minia*, to relieve the *Mackay-Bennett*, and next day, following a joint search, the *Mackay-Bennett* set course for home, 'having as many on board as we could look after', as the captain later explained. He and his crew had recovered three hundred and six bodies, and buried at sea a hundred and sixteen. The *Minia* stayed on until 3 May, in bad weather; she recovered seventeen bodies and buried two at sea. One of those brought back by the *Minia* was Charles M. Hays, President of the Canadian Grand Trunk Railroad, whose last known conversation was with his fellow-Canadian, Major Peuchen, when he told him, after the collision, that 'this boat is good for eight hours'. Two other ships sent to join the search found only five more bodies.

In Halifax, arrangements for the return of the *Mackay-Bennett* were drawn up with care and reverence. The authorities were aware of the turmoil that had accompanied the *Carpathia*'s arrival in New York. It was accordingly decided that the ship would dock at a jetty protected on the landward side by a ten-foot brick wall with only two gates; the usual guards were doubled. Press and photographers were to be strictly controlled. Up the hill, in the middle of the city, the Mayflower Curling Rink was converted into a temporary mortuary and heavily draped in black. The city's flags flew at half-mast.

The *Mackay-Bennett* sailed slowly into the Halifax approaches on the overcast morning of 30 April, after almost two weeks at sea. Thousands lined the shore in silence, the men with their heads bared; the crowds could see bodies laid out on the fore-deck and coffins piled high in the stern. Naturally, the big international wire services had sent squads of reporters and technicians to get the first news about which bodies had been recovered; they had erected their own wireless mast. However, a *Halifax Chronicle* reporter, Jim Hickey, had had the foresight before the *Mackay-Bennett* sailed to make a private arrangement with Canon Hind. As the ship approached, the co-operative clergyman tossed a list of names down to the reporter who had come alongside in a hired tug. Back ashore, the reporter ran two blocks up the street to the *Chronicle* office; and the local man's enterprise is still remembered in Halifax as the *Chronicle*'s one world scoop.

After the ship was secured, one of the first people up the gangway was Captain Roberts, the captain of Colonel J. J. Astor's yacht.

The bodies were carried down the gangway on canvas stretchers by the ship's crew and handed to the undertakers, whose horse-drawn hearses stood on the jetty. Snow & Co. had brought in forty extra undertakers and embalmers from all over the Maritime Provinces. Bodies not in coffins were put in coffins; then the hearses set off slowly to the curling rink. A reporter noted with surprise that only about a hundred people had assembled on the jetty, and that onlookers were few on the streets between jetty and curling rink.

At the rink, friends, relations, and agents identified and claimed the dead. A young Widener from Philadelphia thought at first he had found his father, but it was his father's valet, wearing his father's coat; the *Chronicle* added that the underclothing was 'not of the texture' worn by Widener Senior. Upstairs at the rink there was a temporary coroner's office. Certificates of death and burial permits were issued for each body, but formalities were reduced to a minimum. The railroads made special arrangements for the transport of coffins; they could be sent by express on the payment of two first-class fares.

The purser's lists needed remarkably little revision. They were quickly printed; and one of them, divided into two parts, on folio sheets with a crumbling brown paper cover, survives in the possession of Mr Russ Lownds, whose father was the chief accountant on the staff of the White Star agents in Halifax.

These lists make poignant reading. I found that I first searched instinctively for J. J. Astor, as no doubt many others, for similarly vulgar motives, had searched seventy-odd years before. I wanted to see if it was true, as the legend tells, that his body was identified by the amount of money he carried. There it was: No 124.

Male; estimated age, 50; light hair and moustache. Clothing – Blue-serge suit; blue handkerchief with 'A.V.'; belt with gold buckle; brown boots with red rubber soles; brown flannel shirt; 'J.J.A.' on back of collar. Effects – Gold watch; cuff links, gold with diamond; diamond ring with three stones; £225 in English notes; $2440 in notes; £5 in gold; 7s. in silver; 5 ten-franc pieces; gold pencil; pocketbook. First class.

Name – J.J. Astor

So he was identified not by his money but by the initials on the back of his collar, a humdrum clue to identity.

The diamond ring was a surprise; would a rich Englishman of the time have worn anything similar? Who was 'A.V.'?

Colonel Astor's body was one of the first to leave Halifax; his young son and heir, Vincent, his lawyer, Nicholas Biddle, as well as the captain of his yacht, had come up from New York in a private railway car named 'Oceanic'.[1]

Next on the list I read:

Female; estimated age, 22; dark black hair. Clothing – Blue dress and blouse; black shoes. Effects – Purse with miniature photo; key; few coins; photo locket. No marks on body or clothing. Probably third class.

And probably Irish, I thought. I remembered that Lawrence Beesley, compiling a list of third-class survivors aboard the *Carpathia*, noticed that whereas all the Swedish immigrants had brought money away from the *Titanic*, none of the Irish girls had a penny.

Another entry, obviously an aspiring immigrant: Leslie Gelinski. His estimated age was 30, and he had been carrying when he drowned a primer of the English language.

Almost every entry prompted speculation:

E. Gilbert Dambon: gold watch and chain; opal and ruby ring; bracelet; lady's watch and chain; solitaire diamond ring;

---

[1] In his will, Colonel Astor left the two children of his first marriage, Vincent and Alice, $87,000,000 and $5,000,000 respectively. He left his second wife, Madeleine, $1,695,000 and his unborn son, who became John Jacob Astor VI, a trust fund of $3,000,000 with $5,000,000 when he came of age. Madeleine Astor married, secondly, in 1919, a stockbroker named William Dick; and thirdly, in 1931, an Italian boxer named Enzo Fiermonte. Six years later she committed suicide. John Jacob Astor VI married three times; when his half-brother Vincent died in 1960, leaving $129,000,000 divided between the Vincent Astor Foundation and Brooke Astor, his third wife, 'Jack' Astor contested the will; but without success.

cheque $1315.79 Security Bank, Sioux City, Jewel case, $266 in notes, $30 in gold.

Was E. Gilbert Dambon a real name? It sounded invented. He was carrying a lot of money for someone in steerage. Since the third-class return to Europe in the *Titanic* was advertised by White Star as $36.25, E. Gilbert Dambon had enough cash on him for sixteen crossings. Had he been a migrant, despite his unlikely name, he would scarcely have been carrying a cheque for more than a thousand dollars drawn on a bank in Sioux City. He must have been an American. Perhaps he was a jewel thief who worked maiden voyages; or perhaps the lady's watch and chain, and the bracelet, and the opal and ruby ring, were presents for his sisters bought in Paris, following a big win at Longchamps.

Another entry was bleak: Estimated age 30, blue suit, no marks, brown hair and moustache; no effects.

Another immigrant: Female, about 25, hair fair. Sum of 150 Finnish marks sewed into clothing.

The saddest of all was No 328.

Four foot six inches. Age about 14, hair golden brown. Marks: very dark skin, refined features. Lace-trimmed red-black overdress, black underdress, green striped undershirt, black woollen shawl and felt slippers. Probably third-class passenger.

But there was one mystery that puzzled Halifax citizens then and continues to puzzle the public archivists now. There were two people with Halifax connections aboard the *Titanic*. One, a Miss Slayter, survived (she complained about the number of crew who had been saved by comparison with the number of passengers who had been drowned). The other was George Wright, a very prominent local figure, rich and exceptionally well travelled. He was a big man, who wore a moustache with waxed tips. He had made a fortune as a developer; a street is named after him. He was a leading local yachtsman, the owner of a fifty-seven-foot boat, a winner of yachting cups, at home on the sea. He was also mildly eccentric: he objected to what he regarded as the growing vulgarity and lewdness of language and campaigned against *The Girl of the Golden West*, thinking it improper. He was a local benefactor, a pioneer of trade directories and amateur photography: all in all, the sort of man that strangers noticed. He liked to travel in the latest and best, and he took the *Titanic*; at least, his name is on the first-class passenger list. Yet none of the survivors mentioned meeting or seeing him, and he was not among those brought back to Halifax. A friend of his said he could only think that, as a heavy sleeper, he had never woken up.

Besides this list of the drowned, Halifax possesses a good crop of other *Titanic* memorials and relics. Captain de Cartaret of the *Minia* salvaged from the floating wreckage the one surviving object, so far as I am aware, that must convince the most sceptical that the interminably repeated assertions about the *Titanic*'s luxuriousness are true. This is a piece of wood, two and three-quarter feet long and a foot wide, elaborately carved in baroque Grinling Gibbons style in the shape of seeds, berries, leaves, and birds. It is not veneer, but done in one piece. 'You would need to be an expert to be confident that this wasn't seventeenth century but early twentieth century,' said the archivist who showed it to me. Any amateur would certainly assume he was holding a decorative fragment of a Wren church altarpiece or organ casing. Where it fitted into the *Titanic* the archivists do not know, despite intensive study of contemporary photographs. They think it might have been part of the main stairway.

The Maritime Museum owns a *Titanic* steamer, or deck chair: slatted, heavy, well made. A vandal has stolen the brass frame on the back that once held a passenger's visiting card. Some people in Nova Scotia own another *Titanic* steamer chair that they use in summer on the lawn. The Maritime Museum chair is definitely authentic. The surprise is that so few *Titanic* items survive. Apart from the Halifax graves, the most moving relics are the letters in the Halifax archives from relations of the drowned. One of them is a letter of July 1912 from Mr C. Jupe of 74 Buller Road, Southampton, barely literate, stamped 'Received Jul 20 Provincial Secretary's Office'.

Dear Sir I have been inform by Mr F Blake Superintendent Engineer of the White Star Line Trafalgar Chambers on the 10th that the Body of my Beloved Son Herbert Jupe which was Electrical Engineer No 3 on the Ill-Fatted Titanic has been recovered and Burried at Sea by the Cable Steamer "Mackey-Bennett" and that his Silver Watch and Handkerchief marked H.J. is in your Possession. He bought him half a doz of the same when he was at Belfast with the R.M.S. Olympic to have a new blade put to one of her Perpellors we are extremely oblidged for all your Kindness to my Precious Boy. He was not married and was the Love of our Hearts and he loved his Home But God gave and God has taken Him Blessed be the Name of the Lord. He has Left an Aceing Void in our Home which cannot be filled.
  Please Send along the Watch and Handkerchief marked H.J.
  Yours Truly C. Jupe.
  His Mother is 72 Last april 4th.
  His Father is 68 Last Feb 9th.

Mr Russ Lownds possesses a framed receipt from the Provincial Secretary's office that he inherited from his father. Dated 30 April 1912, it confirms that the Provincial Secretary has received from Mr Lownds, agent of the White Star Line, two hundred and forty-five canvas bags 'alleged to contain valuables belonging to persons drowned off the *Titanic*'. Herbert Jupe's watch and handkerchief would have been returned. But what happened to the unclaimed canvas bags and their contents? The public archivists think they may still exist, mislaid in some government vault.

The unclaimed bodies, a hundred and fifty in all, were buried in Halifax: a hundred and twenty-one in the Protestant cemetery, Fairview Lawn, nineteen in the Catholic cemetery, Mount Olivet, and ten in the Jewish cemetery, the Baron von Hirsch. An unseemly dispute broke out between Christians and Jews about the proper destination of some of the bodies; four bodies removed to the Jewish cemetery were discovered to be Roman Catholics.

Fairview Lawn Cemetery lies in a suburb on a slight wooded slope some two and a half miles or so from the jetty where the *Mackay-Bennett* docked, and almost within sight of it, on the seaward side of one of the arms that open out into the harbour approaches. Big railway yards are visible nearby. The *Titanic* graves are arranged in straight rows, mostly small low gravestones with the surnames, where known, in bold plain letters across the bevelled tops.

In this sad, anonymous place, I drew up a mental balance sheet of the effect of history on the classic form of the legend.

★ The legend said that the *Titanic* had been billed by her builders and owners as unsinkable. This was not true. Edward Kamuda of the Titanic Historical Society had been searching for evidence of this myth for thirty years, but failed to find it. The one pertinent fact is that the journal *Engineering* used the words 'practically unsinkable'.

★ The *Titanic* was going for a record crossing. Not true.

It was impossible for her, with less power and more weight, to challenge the record-holding Cunarders. She may have been travelling too fast, but that is another matter.

* Captain Smith exhorted passengers and crew to 'Be British'. The evidence is flimsy.

* As the ship went down, the orchestra was playing 'Nearer, My God, to Thee'. Almost certainly untrue. But the evidence is strong that the orchestra played a hymn; and the weight of it favours 'Autumn'.

* The *Titanic*'s distress rockets were seen from the *Californian*; and Captain Lord therefore stands condemned for not rescuing all on board. The Scottish verdict of Not Proven is appropriate.

* Discipline was superb. On the whole, discipline was good. But many crew left the ship before ordered to do so. Many did not appear at their boat stations.

* Lord Mersey engineered a whitewash. He did not engineer a planned, conscious whitewash. There was no conspiracy. But his report was a whitewash, nonetheless.

* Senator Smith was a headline-seeking ignoramus who produced a comically inadequate report. Untrue.

* J. Bruce Ismay was a coward who used his position to get off the ship as soon as he could. Untrue.

* One man escaped dressed as a woman. Not true, in its classic form. A man put a shawl over his head and was briefly mistaken for a woman.

* A British aristocrat bribed the crew of his lifeboat not to go back to pick up drowning people. Not proven.

* In the *Titanic*'s safes were gold bars and jewels. Highly improbable.

* Steerage passengers were deliberately discriminated against by the ship's authorities, to keep room in the lifeboats for the better-off. Not true.

* The rich behaved badly. Untrue.

★ Four first-class passengers in evening dress played bridge as they went to their doom. It is true that men played cards after the collision, but for the legend in its pure form there is no evidence.

★ Sir Cosmo Duff Gordon commandeered an empty lifeboat and three fellow bridge players and played bridge in the boat. Alas, no corroboration for this anecdote exists.

Incontrovertible and undented, on the other hand, are the reputations of the engineers, the orchestra, Phillips the Marconi operator, Astor, the Strauses, Gracie, Andrews, Lightoller, Father Byles. Captain Rostron's conduct, which brought him a Congressional Medal of Honour, survives intact. Captain Smith, open to criticism on grounds of his seamanship before the collision, cannot be faulted for the way he behaved after it.

For whatever reason, many passengers and members of the crew, perhaps most, did behave with dignity – in some instances, no doubt, because they did not fully realize their danger. Some showed a heroic sense of duty, for instance the engineers; it is true, in the most direct way, that these men laid down their lives that others might live. The same could probably be said of others, if we only knew.

In a graveyard, no explanations are offered. Some of the inscriptions at Fairview Lawn are brief. One of them says, 'John Law Hume, Died, April 15 1912.' He was the violinist in the *Titanic*'s orchestra. J. Fred Clarke, the bass player, is buried in the Roman Catholic cemetery.

Two gravestones in the Fairview cemetery have longer inscriptions than the others. One says: 'In Memoriam Ernest Edward Samuel Freeman, last surviving son of Capt. S. W. Kearney Freeman, RN., Husband of Laura Mary Jane Freeman Lost in the *Titanic* disaster April 15,

1912. He remained at his post of duty, seeking to save others, regardless of his own life and went down with the ship. Erected by Mr J. Bruce Ismay to commemorate a long and faithful service.' One wonders whether Ismay wrote this inscription himself. The last few words have become obscured, but Mr Russ Lownds one day in his garage pulled out a box that contained old glass photographic plates belonging to his father. One of them was of the Freeman stone, and shows the complete wording.

Another inscription, commemorating a trimmer, reads: 'Sacred to the memory of Everett Edward Elliott of the heroic crew SS *Titanic* died on duty April 15, 1912. Aged 24 years.

> Each man stood at his post
> While all the weaker ones
> Went by, and showed once
> More to all the world
> How Englishmen should die.

There is also a special gravestone, taller than the rest, 'erected to the memory of an unknown child whose remains were recovered after the disaster to the *Titanic* April 15th 1912'. The child, who was 2 years old, with fair hair, has been tentatively identified as one of four children named Paulson who joined the *Titanic* at Southampton with their mother.

There is nothing else to see. At the entrance to the cemetery, on a white wooden board in need of paint, is the one word in capital letters TITANIC.

Appendix One

CARGO MANIFEST RMS *TITANIC*
OWNERS: White Star Line/I.M.M.

VOYAGE: #1 CAPTAIN: E. J. Smith
CHIEF PURSER: Hugh McElroy

PORT OF LOADING: Southampton
(Also loading at Cherbourg & Queenstown.)

PORT OF DISCHARGE: New York
SAILING DATE: 10 April 1912. ARRIVAL DATE: 17 April 1912

cse=case, cs=cases, bls=bales, bgs=bags
bndl=bundle, bbl=barrel, hhd=hogshead

CONSIGNEE	DESCRIPTION OF GOODS
Wakem & McLaughlin.	1cse Wine.
Thorer & Praetorius.	3 bls Skins.
Carter W.E.	1 cse Auto.
Fuchs & Lang Mfg. Co.	4 cs Printers Blankets.
Spaulding A.G. & Bros.	34 cs Athletic Goods (golf clubs).
Park & Tilford.	1 cse toothpaste, 5 cs Drug sundries, 1 cse Brushware.
Maltus & Ware.	8 cs Orchids.
Spencerian Pen Co.	4 cs Pens.
Sherman Sons & Co.	7 cs Cottons.
Claflin & Co.	12 cs Cotton Laces.
Muser Bros.	3 cs Tissues.

Isler & Guye.	4 bls Straw.
Hydeman & Lassner.	1 cse Tulle.
Petry, P.H. & Co.	1 cse Tulle.
Metzger, A.S.	2 cse Tulle.
Mills & Gibbs.	29 cs Cottons, 1 cse Gloves.
Field, Marshall & Co.	1 cse Gloves.
N.Y. Motion Pictures Co.	1 cse Films.
Thorburn, J.M. & Co.	8 cs Bulbs.
Rawstick & H. Trad. Co.	28 bgs Sticks.
Dujardin & Ladnuck.	10 bxs Melons.
Amer. Exp. Co.	25 cs Mdse.
Tiffany Co.	1 cask China,
	1 cse Silver Goods.
Lustig Bros.	4 cse Straw Hats.
Kuyper P.C. & Co.	1 cse Elastic Cords,
	1 cse Leather.
Cohen, M. Bros.	5 pkgs Skins.
Gross, Engel Co.	1 cse Skins.
Wilson, P.K. & Son.	61 cs Tulle.
Gallia Textile Co.	1 cse Lace Goods.
Calhoun Robbins & Co.	1 cse Cotton Laces,
	½ cse brushware.
Victor & Achilles.	1 cse Brushware.
Baungarten, Wm. & Co.	3 cs Furniture.
Speilman Co.	3 cs Silk Crape.
Nottingham Lace Works.	2 cs Cottons.
Naday & Fleischer.	1 cs Laces.
Rosenthal, Leo J., Co.	4 cs Cottons.
Wakem & McLaughlin.	25 cs Biscuits,
	42 cs Wines.
Leeming T. & Co.	7 cse Biscuits.
Crown Perfume Co.	3 cs Soap Perfumes.
Meadows, T. & Co.	5 cs Books, 3 bxs Samples.
	1 cse Parchments.
Thomas & Pierson.	2 cs Hardware, 2 cs Books.
	2 cs Furniture.
Amer. Exp. Co.	1 cse Elastics,
	1 cse Gramaphone,

4 cs Hosiery, 5 cs Books,
1 cse Canvas, 3 cs Prints,
1 cse Rubber Goods,
5 cs Films, 1 cse Tweed,
1 cse Sero Fittings
   (Syringes),
A quantity of Oak
   Beams,
1 cse Plants,
1 cse Speedometers,
1 pkg Effects,
2 cs Samples,
8 cs Paste, 4 cs Books,
2 cs Camera and Stand.

Sheldon, G.W. & Co.	1 cse Machinery.
Maltus & Ware.	15 cs Alarm Apparatus,
Hempstead & Sons.	4 cs Orchids,
	30 cs Plants.
Brasch & Rothenstein.	2 cs Lace Collars,
	2 cs Books.
Isler & Guye.	53 pkgs Straw.
Baring Brothers & Co.	68 cs Rubber,
	10 bags Galls (suspenders?).
Altman, B. & Co.	1 cse Cottons.
Stern S.	60 cs Salt Powder.
Arnold, F.R. & Co.	6 cs Soap.
Schieffelin & Co.	17 pkgs Wool Fat.
American Motor Co.	1 pkg Candles.
Strohmeyer & Arpe.	75 bls Fish.
National City Bank N.Y.	11 bls Rubber.
Kronfeld, Saunders & Co.	5 cs Shells.
Richard, C.B.	1 cse Films.
Corbel, M.J. & Co.	2 cs Hat Leather, &c.
Snow's Express Co.	2 cs Books.
Van Ingen, E.H. & Co.	1 cse Woollens.
Lippincot, J.B. & Co.	10 cs Books.
Lazard Freres.	1 bale Skins.
Aero Club of America.	1 crate Machinery,

	1 cse Printed Matter.
Whitcombe, McGeachim & Co.	386 rolls Linoleum.
Wright & Graham.	437 casks Tea.
Ullmann, J.	4 bales Skins.
Arnold & Zeiss.	134 cs Rubber.
Brown Brothers & Co.	76 cs Dragons Blood,
	2 cs Gum.
American Shipping Co.	3 cs Books.
Adams Express Co.	95 cs Books.
Laskee & Bernstein.	117 cs Sponges.
Oelrichs & Co.	2 cs Pictures &c.
Stachert, G.H. & Co.	12 pkgs Periodical.
Milbank, Leamann & Co.	3 cs Woollens.
Vandergrift, F.B. & Co.	53 cs Champagne.
Downing, R.F. & Co.	1 cse Felt, 1 do Meal,
	8 do Tennis Balls,
	1 do Engine Packing.
Dublin, Morris & Kornbluth.	2 pkgs Skins.
Hersog, Simon & Sons.	4 pkgs Skins.
International Trading Co.	1 cse Surgical Goods,
	1 cse Ironware.
Fitt & Scott.	4 cs Printed Matter,
	1 cse Cloth.
Davies Turner & Co.	4 cs Printed Matter,
	1 cse Machinery,
	1 do Picture,
	1 cse Books, 1 do Mdse,
	1 do Notions, 1 do Photo.
Sheldon, G.W. & Co.	1 cse Elastics, 2 cs Books,
	1 box Golf Balls,
	5 cs Instruments.
American Express Co.	2 parcels Merchandise.
Vandergrift, F.B. & Co.	1 cse Merchandise.
Budd S.	1 parcel Merchandise.
Lamke & Buechner.	1 parcel Merchandise.
Nicholas, G.S. & Co.	1 cse Merchandise.
Walker, G.A.	1 cse Merchandise.
Adams Express Co.	4 rolls Linoleum,

	1 cse Hats,
	3 bales Leather,
	5 cs Books,
	6 cs Confectionery,
	1 cse Tin Tubes, 2 cs Soap,
	2 cs Boots.
Wells Fargo & Co.	3 cs Books, 2 cs Furniture,
	1 cse Pamphlets,
	1 do Paints,
	1 cse Eggs, 1 do Whisky.
International News Co.	10 pkgs Periodicals.
Van Ingen, E.H.	1 parcel.
Stearns, R.H. & Co.	1 cse Cretonne
Downing, R.F. & Co.	1 cse Iron Jacks,
	1 do Bulbs.
Jacobson, James.	1 cse Hosiery.
Carbon Machinery Equipment Co.	1 cse Clothing.
Sanger, R. & Co.	8 cs Hairnets.
Fleitmann & Co.	1 cse Silk Goods.
Rusch & Co.	1 cse Tissues.
New York Merchandise Co.	1 cse Hairnets.
Blum, J.A.	2 cs Silk Goods.
Tiedeman, T. & Sons.	3 cs Silk Goods.
Costa, F.	1 cse Silk Goods.
Tolson, A.M. & Co.	1 cse Gloves.
Matthews, G.T. & Co.	30 pkgs Tea.
Richards, C.B. & Co.	2 cs Books and Lace.
Tice & Lynch.	5 cs Books, 1 bag Frames,
	1 cse Cotton,
	2 cs Stationery.
US Express Co.	1 cse Scientific Instruments,
	1 cse Sundries,
	3 cs Test Cords,
	1 cse Briar Pipes,
	1 cse Sundries,
	2 cs Printed Matter.

Papa, Chas. & Co.	1196 bags Potatoes.
Bauer, J.P. & Co.	318 bags Potatoes.
Rusch & Co.	1 cse Velvets.
Mallouk, H.	1 cse Laces.
Bardwill Bros.	8 cs Laces.
Heyliger, A.V.	1 cse Velvet.
Peabody, H.W. & Co.	18 bales Straw Goods.
Simon, A.L. & Co.	1 cse Raw Feathers.
Wilson, P.K. & Sons.	2 cs Linens.
Manhattan Shirt Co.	3 cs Tissue.
Broadway Trust Co.	3 cs Coney Skins.
Prost, G.	1 cse Auto Parts.
Young Bros.	1 cse Feathers.
Wimpfhelmer, A. Co.	3 cs Leather.
Brown Bros. & Co.	15 cs Rabbit Hair.
Goldrier, Morris.	11 cs Feathers.
Cobb, G.H.	1 cse Tissue.
Andaffren Ref. Mach. Co.	11 cs Refrigerating Machinery.
Sutar, Alfred.	18 cs Machinery.
Amer. Express Co.	1 cse Packed Packages,
	3 cse Tissue,
	2 bbls Mercury,
	1 bbl Earth,
	2 bbls Glassware,
	3 cs Printed Matter,
	1 cse Straw Braids,
	1 cse Straw Hats,
	1 cse Cheese.
Meadows, Tho. & Co.	3 cs Hosiery.
Urchs & Hegnoer.	3 cs Silk Goods.
Cauvigny Brush Co.	1 cse Brushware.
Johnson, J.G. & Co.	2 cs Ribbons.
Judkins & McCormick.	2 cs Flowers.
Spielman Co.	1 cs Gloves.
American Express Co.	18 cs Merchandise.
Wakem & McLaughlin.	6 bales Cork.
Acker, Merrell & Condit.	75 cs Anchovies,

	1 cse Liqueur,
	225 cs Mustard.
Engs, P.W. & Sons.	190 cs Liqueur, 25 cs Syrups.
Schall & Co.	25 cs Preserves.
N.Y. & Cuba Mail S.S. Co.	12 cs Butter, 18 cs Oil,
	2 hhds Vinegar,
	6 cs Preserves,
	19 cs Vinegar,
	8 cs Dry Fruit,
	10 bndls 2 cs Wine.
DuBois, Geo. C.	16 hhds Wine.
Hollander, H.	185 cs Wine, 110 cs Brandy.
Van Renssaller, C.A.	10 hhds Wine, 15 cs Cognac.
Brown Bros. & Co.	100 cs Shelled Walnuts.
Bernard, Judas & Co.	70 bdls Cheese.
American Express Co.	20 bdls Cheese, 2 cs Cognac.
Mouquin Wine Co.	1 cse Liqueur, 38 cs Oil.
Kanuth, Nachod & Kuhne.	107 cs Mushrooms,
	1 cse Pamphlets.
Lazard Freres.	25 cs Sardines,
	8 cs Preserves.
Acker, Merrell & Condit.	50 cs Wine.
DuBois, Geo. F.	6 casks Vermouth,
	4 cs Wine.
Heidelbach, Ickelheimer & Co.	11 cs Shelled Walnuts.
Brown Bros. & Co.	100 bls Shelled Walnuts.
1st. Nat'l Bank of Chicago.	300 cs Shelled Walnuts.
Bischoff, H. & Co.	35 bags Rough Wood.
Baumert, F.X. & Co.	50 bdls Cheese.
Erie Despatch Co.	5 bdls Cheese.
Galle, B. & Co.	50 bdls Cheese.
Rathenberger & Co.	190 bdls Cheese.
Haupt & Burgi.	50 bdls Cheese.
Sheldon & Co.	10 bdls Cheese.
Percival, C.	50 bdls Cheese.
Stone, C.D. & Co.	30 bdls Cheese.
Phoenix Cheese Co.	30 bdls Cheese.
Reynolds & Dronig.	15 bdls Cheese.

Fougera, E.	41 cs Filter Paper.
Munroe, J. & Co.	22 cs Mushrooms,
	15 cs Peas,
	8 cs Beans, 13 cs Peas,
	10 cs Mixed Vegetables,
	25 cs Olives, 12 bdls Capers,
	10 cs Fish, 20 cs Mdse.
Austin, Nichols & Co.	25 cs Olive Oil,
	14 cs Mushrooms.

Order – 14 cs Factice, 18 do Gum, 14 casks Gum, 225 casks
Tea, 3 bls Skins, 4 cs Opium, 3 cs Window Frames, 8 bls Skins,
8 pkgs Skins, 1 cse Skins, 2 cs Horse Hair, 2 cs Silk Goods,
8 bls Raw Silk, 6 pkgs Hair Nets, 200 pkgs Tea, 246 cs Sardines,
30 rolls Jute Bagging, 1961 bags Potatoes, 7 cs Raw Feathers,
10 cs Hatters Fur, 3 cs Tissue, 1 cs Rabbit Hair, 31 pkgs Crude
Rubber, 7 cs Vegetables, 5 cs Fish, 10 cs Syrups, 2 cs Liqueurs,
150 cs Shelled Walnuts, 15 bdls Cheese, 8 bls Buchu,
2 cs Grandfathers Clocks, 2 cs Leather . . .

Holders original Bill of Lading.
19 bls Goat Skins, 15 cs Calabashes, 5 bls Buchu, 4 cs Calabash
Bowls, 3 bls Sheep Skins, 2 cs Embroidery, 8 octs(?) Wine,
22 cs Ostrich Feathers, 3 bls Skins, 33 bags Argols, 3 bls Sheep
Skins.

This copy of the *Titanic*'s manifest was delivered via Registered
Mail on Cunard Steamship Lines *Mauretania* in New York on
Friday 19 April 1912.

ON BOARD PROVISIONS
HEAD CHEF: C. PROCTOR

Fresh meat	75,000 pounds	Bacon and	6,000 pounds
Poultry	25,000 pounds	ham	
Fresh fish	11,000 pounds	Sausages	2,500 pounds
Salt and dried fish	4,000 pounds		
		Fresh eggs	35,000

Fresh milk	1,500 gallons	Apples	180 boxes
Fresh cream	1,200 quarts	Oranges	(36,000)
Condensed milk	600 gallons		180 boxes
		Grapefruit	50 boxes
Fresh butter	6,000 pounds	Lemons	(16,000)
			50 boxes
Flour	250 barrels	Hothouse grapes	1,000 pounds
Sugar	5 tons		
Salt, black and red pepper	Quantities unknown	Jams & Jellies	1,120 pounds
		Coffee	2,200 pounds
Cereals	10,000 pounds	Tea	1,000 pounds
Potatoes	40 tons	Sweet breads	1,000
Onions	3,500	Ice cream	1,750 quarts
Lettuce	7,000 heads		
Fresh Asparagus	800 bundles	Ale and Stout	15,000 bottles
		Wines	1,000 bottles
Fresh green peas	2,500 pounds	Spirits	850 bottles
		Minerals	1,200 bottles
Tomatoes	3,500 pounds	Cigars	8,000

SERVICEWARE AND LINEN LIST

Breakfast cups	4,500	Flower vases	500
Tea cups	3,000	Ice cream plates	5,500
Coffee cups	1,500	Dinner plates	12,000
Beef tea cups	3,000	Coffee pots	1,200
Cream jugs	1,000	Tea pots	1,200
Breakfast plates	2,500	Breakfast saucers	4,500
Dessert plates	2,000	Tea saucers	3,000
Soup plates	4,500	Coffee saucers	1,500
Pie dishes	1,200	Soufflé dishes	1,500
Beef tea dishes	3,000	Wine glasses	2,000
Cut tumblers	8,000	Champagne glasses	1,500
Water bottles	2,500	Cocktail glasses	1,500
Crystal dishes	1,500	Liqueur glasses	1,200
Celery glasses	300	Claret jugs	300

Salt shakers	2,000	Salt spoons	1,500
Salad bowls	500	Mustard spoons	1,500
Pudding dishes	1,200	Grape scissors	100
Sugar basins	400	Asparagus tongs	400
Fruit dishes	400		
Finger bowls	1,000	LINENS	
Butter dishes	400		
Vegetable dishes	400	Single sheets	15,000
Entree dishes	400	Double sheets	3,000
Meat dishes	400	Pillow slips	15,000
Dinner forks	8,000	Blankets	7,500
Fruit forks	1,500	Bed covers	3,600
Fish forks	1,500	Eiderdown quilts	800
Oyster forks	1,000	Counterpanes	3,000
Butter knives	400	Bath towels	7,500
Sugar tongs	400	Fine towels	25,000
Fruit knives	1,500	Lavatory towels	8,000
Fish knives	1,500	Roller towels	3,500
Table and dessert knives	8,000	Pantry towels	6,500
Nut crackers	300	Tablecloths	6,000
Toast racks	400	Glass cloths	2,000
Dinner spoons	5,000	Table napkins	45,000
Dessert spoons	3,000	Cooks cloths	3,500
Egg spoons	2,000	Aprons	4,000
Tea spoons	6,000	Miscellaneous	40,000

Appendix Two

'Some Unmentioned Morals' by George Bernard Shaw, and correspondence between Shaw and A. Conan Doyle

On May 14th 1912, under the heading 'Some Unmentioned Morals', Bernard Shaw wrote to the *Daily News and Leader*:

'Why is it that the effect of a sensational catastrophe on a modern nation is to cast it into transports, not of weeping, not of prayer, not of sympathy with the bereaved nor congratulation of the rescued, not of poetic expression of the soul purified by pity and terror, but of wild defiance of inexorable Fate and undeniable Fact by an explosion of outrageous romantic lying?

'What is the first demand of romance in a shipwreck? It is the cry of Women and Children first. No male creature is to step into a boat as long as there is a woman or child on the doomed ship. How the boat is to be navigated and rowed by babies and women occupied in holding the babies is not mentioned. The likelihood that no sensible woman would trust either herself or her child in a boat unless there was a considerable percentage of men on board is not considered. Women and Children first: that is the romantic formula. And never did the chorus of solemn delight at the strict observance of this formula by the British heroes on board the *Titanic* rise to sublimer strains than in the papers containing the first account of the wreck by a surviving eye-witness, Lady Duff Gordon. She described how she escaped in the captain's boat. There was one other woman in it, and ten men: twelve all told. One woman for every five men. Chorus: "Not once or twice in our rough island story," etc. etc.

'Second romantic demand. Though all the men (except the foreigners, who must all be shot by stern British officers in attempting to rush the boats over the bodies of the women and children) must be heroes, the Captain must be a super-hero, a magnificent seaman, cool, brave, delighting in death and danger, and a living guarantee that the wreck was nobody's fault, but, on the contrary, a triumph of British navigation.

'Such a man Captain Smith was enthusiastically proclaimed on the day when it was reported (and actually believed, apparently) that he had shot himself on the bridge, or shot the first officer, or been shot by the first officer, or shot anyhow to bring the curtain down effectively. Writers who had never heard of Captain Smith to that hour wrote of him as they would hardly write of Nelson. The one thing positively known was that Captain Smith had lost his ship by deliberately and knowingly steaming into an ice field at the highest speed he had coal for. He paid the penalty; so did most of those for whose lives he was responsible. Had he brought them and the ship safely to land, nobody would have taken the smallest notice of him.

'Third romantic demand. The officers must be calm, proud, steady, unmoved in the intervals of shooting the terrified foreigners. The verdict that they had surpassed all expectations was unanimous. The actual evidence was that Mr Ismay was told by the officer of his boat to go to hell, and that boats which were not full refused to go to the rescue of those who were struggling in the water in cork jackets. Reason frankly given: they were afraid. The fear was as natural as the officer's language to Mr Ismay: who of us at home dare blame them or feel sure that we should have been any cooler or braver? But is it necessary to assure the world that only Englishmen could have behaved so heroically, and to compare their conduct with the hypothetic dastardliness which lascars or Italians or foreigners generally – say Nansen or Amundsen or the Duke of Abruzzi – would have shown in the same circumstances?

'Fourth romantic demand. Everybody must face death without a tremor; and the band, according to the *Birkenhead* precedent, must play "Nearer, my God, to Thee" as an accompaniment to the invitation to Mr Ismay to go to hell. It was duly proclaimed that thus exactly it fell out. Actual evidence: the Captain and officers were so afraid of a panic that, though they knew the ship was sinking, they did not dare to tell the passengers so – especially the third-class passengers – and the band played Rag Times to reassure the passengers, who, therefore, did not get into the boats, and did not realize their situation until the boats were gone and the ship was standing on her head before plunging to the bottom. What happened then Lady Duff Gordon has related, and the witnesses of the American enquiry could hardly bear to relate.

'I ask, What is the use of all this ghastly, blasphemous, inhuman, braggartly lying? Here is a calamity which might well make the proudest man humble, and the wildest joker serious. It makes us vainglorious, insolent and mendacious. At all events, that is what our journalists assumed. Were they right or wrong? Did the press really represent the public? I am afraid it did. Churchmen and statesmen took much the same tone. The effect on me was one of profound disgust, almost of national dishonour. Am I mad? Possibly. At all events, that is how I felt and how I feel about it. It seems to me that when deeply moved men should speak the truth. The English nation appears to take precisely the contrary view. Again I am in the minority. What will be the end of it? – for England, I mean. Suppose we came into conflict with a race that had the courage to look facts in the face and the wisdom to know itself for what it was. Fortunately for us, no such race is in sight. Our wretched consolation must be that any other nation would have behaved just as absurdly.'

Conan Doyle replied on May 20:

'Sir, – I have just been reading the article by Mr Bernard Shaw upon the loss of the *Titanic*, which appeared in your issue of May 14th. It is written professedly in the interests of truth, and accuses everyone around him of lying. Yet I can never remember any production which contained so much that was false within the same compass. How a man could write with such looseness and levity of such an event at such a time passes all comprehension. Let us take a few of the points. Mr Shaw wishes – in order to support his perverse thesis, that there was no heroism – to quote figures to show that the women were not given priority in escape. He picks out, therefore, one single boat, the smallest of all, which was launched and directed under peculiar circumstances, which are now matter for enquiry. Because there were ten men and two women in this boat, therefore there was no heroism or chivalry; and all talk about it is affectation. Yet Mr Shaw knows as well as I know that if he had taken the very next boat he would have been obliged to admit that there were 65 women out of 70 occupants, and that in nearly all the boats navigation was made difficult by the want of men to do the rowing. Therefore, in order to give a false impression, he has deliberately singled out one boat; although he could not but be aware that it entirely misrepresented the general situation. Is this decent controversy, and has the writer any cause to accuse his contemporaries of misstatement?

'His next paragraph is devoted to the attempt to besmirch the conduct of Capt. Smith. He does it by his favourite method of "Suggestio falsi" – the false suggestion being that the sympathy shown by the public for Capt. Smith took the shape of condoning Capt. Smith's navigation. Now everyone – including Mr Bernard Shaw – knows perfectly well that no defence has ever been made of the risk which was run, and that the sympathy was at the spectacle of an old and honoured sailor who has made one terrible mistake, and who deliberately gave his life in reparation, discarding his lifebelt, working to the last for those whom he had unwillingly injured, and finally swimming with a child to a boat into which he himself refused to enter. This is the fact, and Mr Shaw's assertion that the wreck was hailed as a "triumph of British navigation" only shows – what surely needed no showing – that a phrase stands for more than truth with Mr Shaw. The same remark applies to his "wrote of him as they would hardly write of Nelson". If Mr Shaw will show me the work of any responsible journalist in which Capt. Smith is written of in terms of Nelson, I will gladly send £100 to the Fabian Society.

'Mr Shaw's next suggestion – all the more poisonous because it is not put into so many words – is that the officers did not do their duty. If his vague words mean anything, they can only mean this. He quotes as if it were a crime the words of Lowe to Mr Ismay when he interfered with his boat. I could not imagine a finer example of an officer doing his duty than that a subordinate should dare to speak thus to the managing director of the Line when he thought that he was impeding his life-saving work. The sixth officer went down with the Captain, so I presume that even Mr Shaw could not ask him to do more. Of the other officers I have never heard or read any cause for criticism. Mr Shaw finds some cause for offence in the fact that one of them discharged his revolver in order to intimidate some foreign emigrants who threatened to rush the boats. The fact and the assertion that these passengers were foreigners came from several eye-witnesses. Does Mr Shaw think it should have been suppressed? If not what is he scolding about? Finally, Mr Shaw tries to defile the beautiful incident of the band by alleging that it was the result of orders issued to avert panic. But if it were, how does that detract either from the wisdom of the orders or from the heroism of the musicians? It was right to avert panic, and it was wonderful that men could be found to do it in such a way.

'As to the general accusation that the occasion has been used for the glorification of British qualities, we should indeed be a lost people if we did not honour courage and discipline when we see it in its highest form. That our sympathies extend beyond ourselves is shown by the fact that the conduct of the American male passengers, and very particularly of the much-abused millionaires, has been as warmly eulogised as any single feature in the whole wonderful epic. But surely it is a pitiful sight to see a man of undoubted genius using his gifts in order to misrepresent and decry his own people, regardless of the fact that his words must add to the grief of those who have already had more than enough to bear.'

Shaw's reply was printed on May 22:

'Sir, – I hope to persuade my friend Sir Arthur Conan Doyle, now that he has got his romantic and warm-hearted protest off his chest, to read my article again three or four times, and give you his second thoughts on the matter; for it is really not possible for any sane man to disagree with a single word that I have written.

'I again submit that when news of a shipwreck arrives without particulars, and journalists immediately begin to invent particulars, they are lying. It is nothing to the point that authentic news may arrive later on, and may confirm a scrap or two of their more obvious surmises. The first narratives which reached us were those by an occupant of a boat in which there were ten men, two women, and plenty of room for more, and of an occupant of another boat which, like the first, refused to return to rescue the drowning because the people in it were avowedly afraid. It was in the face of that information, and of that alone, that columns of raving about women and children first were published. Sir Arthur says that I "picked out" these boats to prove my case. Of course I did. I wanted to prove my case. They did prove it. They do prove it. My case is that our journalists wrote without the slightest regard to the facts; that they were actually more enthusiastic in their praise of the *Titanic* heroes on the day when the only evidence to hand was evidence of conduct for which a soldier would be shot and a Navy sailor hanged than when later news came in of those officers and crew who did their best; and that it must be evident to every reasonable man that if there had not been a redeeming feature in the whole case, exactly the same "hogwash" would have been lavished on the veriest dastards as upon a crew of Grace Darlings. The Captain positively lost popularity when the deliberate and calumnious lie that he had shot himself was dropped. May I ask what value real heroism has in a country which responds to these inept romances invented by people who can produce nothing after all but stories of sensational cowardice? Would Sir Arthur take a medal from the hands of the imbecile liars whom he is defending?

'Sir Arthur accuses me of lying; and I must say that he gives me no great encouragement to tell the truth. But he proceeds to tell, against himself, what I take to be the most thundering lie ever sent to a printer by a human author. He first says that I "quoted as if it were a crime" the words used by the officer who told Mr Ismay to go to hell. I did not. I said the outburst was very natural, though not in my opinion admirable or heroic. If I am wrong, then I claim to be a hero myself; for it has occurred to me in trying circumstances to lose my head and temper and use the exact words attributed (by himself) to the officer in question. But Sir Arthur goes on to say: "I could not imagine a finer example of an officer doing his duty than that a subordinate should dare to speak thus to the managing director of the Line when he thought he was impeding his life-saving work." Yes you could, Sir Arthur; and many a page of heroic romance from your hand attests that you often have imagined much finer examples. Heroism has not quite come to that yet; nor has your imagination contracted or your brain softened to the bathos of seeing sublimity in a worried officer telling even a managing director (godlike being!) to go to hell. I would not hear your enemy libel you so. But now that you have chivalrously libelled yourself, don't lecture me for reckless mendacity; for you have captured the record in the amazing sentence I have just quoted.

'I will not accept Sir Arthur's offer of £100 to the Fabian Society for every hyper-Nelson eulogy of the late Captain Smith which stands in the newspapers of those first days to bear out my very moderate description of them. I want to see the Fabian

Society solvent, but not at the cost of utter destitution to a friend. I should not have run the risk of adding to the distress of Captain Smith's family by adding one word to facts that speak only too plainly for themselves if others had been equally considerate. But if vociferous journalists will persist in glorifying the barrister whose clients are hanged, the physician whose patients die, the general who loses battles, and the captain whose ship goes to the bottom, such false coin must be nailed to the counter at any cost. There have been British captains who have brought their ships safely through icefields by doing their plain duty and carrying out their instructions. There have been British captains who have seen to it that their crews knew their boats and their places in their boats, and who, when it became necessary to take to those boats, have kept discipline in the face of death, and not lost one life that could have been saved. And often enough nobody has said "Thank you" to them for it, because they have not done mischief enough to stir the emotions of our romantic journalists. These are the men whom I admire and with whom I prefer to sail.

'I do not wish to imply that I for a moment believe that the dead man actually uttered all the heartbreaking rubbish that has been put into his mouth by fools and liars; nor am I forgetting that a captain may not be able to make himself heard and felt everywhere in these huge floating (or sinking) hotels as he can in a cruiser, or rally a mob of waiters and dock labourers as he could a crew of trained seamen. But no excuse, however good, can turn a failure into a success. Sir Arthur cannot be ignorant of what would happen had the *Titanic* been a king's ship, or of what the court-martial would have said and done on the evidence of the last few days. Owing to the fact that a member of my family was engaged in the Atlantic service, and perhaps also that I happen to know by personal experience what it is like to be face to face with death in the sea, I know what the risk of ice means on a liner, and know also that there is no heroism in being drowned when you cannot help it. The Captain of the *Titanic* did not, as Sir Arthur thinks, make "a terrible mistake". He made no mistake. He knew perfectly well that ice is the only risk that is considered really deadly in his line of work, and, knowing it, he chanced it and lost the hazard. Sentimental idiots, with a break in the voice, tell me that "he went down to the depths": I tell them, with the impatient contempt they deserve, that so did the cat. Heroism is extraordinarily fine conduct resulting from extraordinarily high character. Extraordinary circumstances may call it forth and may heighten its dramatic effect by pity and terror, by death and destruction, by darkness and a waste of waters; but none of these accessories are the thing itself; and to pretend that they are is to debase the moral currency by substituting the conception of sensational misfortune for inspiring achievement.

'I am no more insensible to the pity of the catastrophe than anyone else; but I have been driven by an intolerable provocation of disgusting and dishonourable nonsense to recall our journalists to their senses by saying bluntly that the occasion has been disgraced by a callous outburst of romantic lying. To this I now wish to add that if, when I said this, I had read the evidence elicited by Lord Mersey's inquiry as to the *Californian* and the *Titanic*'s emergency boat, I should probably have expressed myself much more strongly. I refrain now only because the facts are beating the hysterics without my help.'

Conan Doyle closed the discussion on May 25:

'Sir – Without continuing a controversy which must be sterile, I would touch on only one point in Mr Shaw's reply to my letter. He says that I accused him of lying. I have been guilty of no such breach of the amenities of the discussion. The worst I think or say of Mr Shaw is that his many brilliant gifts do not include the power of weighing evidence; nor has he that quality – call it good taste, humanity, or what you will – which prevents a man from needlessly hurting the feelings of others.'

Book List

Selected Sources

Wreck Commissioner's Court. Formal Investigation into the Loss of the SS Titanic. Evidence, Appendices, and Index. London: HMSO, 1912.

Shipping Casualties (Loss of the steamship 'Titanic'). Report of a Formal Investigation into the circumstances attending the foundering on 15th April, 1912, of the British Steamship 'Titanic' of Liverpool, after striking ice in or near Latitude 41° 46'N. Longitude 50° 14'W., North Atlantic, whereby loss of life ensued (Cd. 6352). London: HMSO, 1912.

US Congress, Senate, Hearings of a Subcommittee of the Senate Commerce Committee pursuant to S. Res. 283, to Investigate the Causes leading to the Wreck of the White Star liner 'Titanic', 62d Cong., 2d sess., 1912, S. Doc. 463 (6179). Washington. Government Printing Office.

US Congress, Senate, Report of the Senate Committee on Commerce pursuant to S. Res. 283, Directing the Committee to Investigate the Causes of the sinking of the 'Titanic', with speeches by William Alden Smith and Isidor Rayner, 62d Cong., 2d sess., 28 May 1912, S. Rept. 806 (6127). Washington. Government Printing Office.

These are the four indispensable sources of information about the *Titanic*.

Filson Young, *Titanic* (Grant Richards, London, 1912). Useful guide to contemporary attitudes.

Philip Gibbs, *The Deathless Story of the Titanic* (Lloyds Weekly News, London, 1912). Contains early lists of the crew, those saved, and those drowned.

Lawrence Beesley, *The Loss of the SS Titanic: Its Story and its Lessons* (Heinemann, London, 1912). One of the basic texts, written with an earnest desire to be fair and accurate.

Shan F. Bullock, *A Titanic Hero; Thomas Andrews, shipbuilder* (Maunsel, Dublin and London, 1912).

Archibald Gracie, *The Truth about the Titanic* (Mitchell, Kennerley, New York, 1913). The best of the contemporary acounts.

C. H. Lightoller, *Titanic and Other Ships* (Nicholson and Watson, London, 1935). Primary source, both for the disaster and for an honest man's attitude to pre-*Titanic* navigational practices.

Viscount Mersey, *A Picture of Life* 1872–1940 (John Murray, London, 1941). Contains a valuable account of the background and character of the first Lord Mersey.

Walter Lord, *A Night to Remember* (Holt, Rinehard, & Winston, New York, 1955). Racy and dramatic account of the disaster itself, and much criticized by the supporters of Captain Lord.

W. J. Oldham, *The Ismay Line* (Journal of Commerce, Liverpool, 1961). Primary source on Ismay father and son; it includes letters written by J. Bruce Ismay not available elsewhere.

Peter Padfield, *The Titanic and the Californian* (Hodder, London, 1965). Impassioned defence of Captain Lord, showing that the story was more complicated than either the Senate or the British inquiries supposed.

Mercantile Marine Service Association, *The Californian Incident;* text of second petition addressed to the President of the Board of Trade. Liverpool: the Association, 1968. Contains Beesley's statutory declaration of February 1963.

Geoffrey Marcus, *The Maiden Voyage* (George Allen and Unwin, London, 1969). Particularly useful on wireless operations; fiercely critical of the Board of Trade inquiry's 'whitewash'. Marcus has no doubt about Lord's culpability.

Wyn Craig Wade, *The Titanic, End of a Dream* (Ranson, Wade, New York, 1979). Corrective, written by a Michigan psychologist, to the view that the American inquiry was, in Lightoller's words, 'a complete farce'.

Patrick Stenson, *'Lights', The Odyssey of C.H. Lightoller* (The Bodley Head, London, 1984). Careful account of an adventurous life, which helps to explain the attitudes of the *Titanic*'s officers.

Arnold and Betty Watson, *Roster of Valor; the Titanic-Halifax Legacy* (7 C's Press Inc., Riverside, Connecticut, 1984). Contains a revised alphabetical list of the *Titanic*'s crew, addresses, and jobs.

The Titanic Commutator, published quarterly by the Titanic Historical Society Inc., of P.O. Box 53, Indian Orchard, Massachusetts 01151-0053, USA, is the essential modern source of *Titanic* information. The spring, 1983, issue contains the results of research in Halifax, Nova Scotia, by John P. Eaton and Charles Haas; the fall, 1985, issue describes the discovery of the *Titanic* and includes detailed interviews by Karen Childs with Dr Ballard and Captain Bowen of the research vessel *Knorr*.

Oceanus, the journal of the Woods Hole Oceanographic Institution, vol. 28, no. 4, contains accounts and pictures of the discovery of the *Titanic*, and includes Dr Ballard's statement before the House Merchant Marine and Fisheries Committee of 29 October 1985.

The National Geographic Magazine of December 1985 contains a first-hand account of the search for the *Titanic* written by Dr Ballard and Jean-Louis Michel.

Index

History – now available in Grafton Books

Frederick Engels
The Condition of the Working Class in England   £1.95 ☐

Field Marshal Lord Carver
The Seven Ages of the British Army (illustrated)   £4.95 ☐

Christopher Farman
The General Strike (illustrated)   £1.95 ☐

Sir Arthur Bryant
Samuel Pepys: The Man in the Making   £3.95 ☐
Samuel Pepys: The Years of Peril   £3.95 ☐
Samuel Pepys: Saviour of the Navy   £3.95 ☐

Larry Collins and Dominique Lapierre
Freedom at Midnight (illustrated)   £3.95 ☐
O Jerusalem (illustrated)   £3.95 ☐

Angus Calder
The People's War (illustrated)   £3.95 ☐

Thomas Pakenham
The Year of Liberty   £1.95 ☐

Antony Bridge
The Crusaders (illustrated)   £3.95 ☐

Joyce Marlow
The Tolpuddle Martyrs (illustrated)   £2.95 ☐

John Erickson
The Road to Stalingrad (illustrated)   £6.95 ☐
The Road to Berlin   £8.95 ☐

Robert Fisk
In Time of War (illustrated)   £4.95 ☐

To order direct from the publisher just tick the titles you want
and fill in the order form.   **GM781**

Books of historical interest now available in Grafton Books

David Daiches
Edinburgh (illustrated)   £1.95 ☐
Glasgow (illustrated)   £3.95 ☐

 Paul Johnson
The National Trust Book of British Castles (illustrated)   £4.95 ☐

 Nigel Nicolson
The National Trust Book of Great Houses (illustrated)   £4.95 ☐

 Frank Delaney
James Joyce's Odyssey (illustrated)   £2.95 ☐

 Stan Gébler Davies
James Joyce: A Portrait of the Artist (illustrated)   £2.50 ☐

To order direct from the publisher just tick the titles you want
and fill in the order form.   **GM681**

All these books are available at your local bookshop or newsagent, or can be ordered direct from the publisher.

To order direct from the publishers just tick the titles you want and fill in the form below.

Name _____

Address _____

_____

Send to:
Grafton Cash Sales
PO Box 11, Falmouth, Cornwall TR10 9EN.

Please enclose remittance to the value of the cover price plus:

UK 60p for the first book, 25p for the second book plus 15p per copy for each additional book ordered to a maximum charge of £1.90.

BFPO 60p for the first book, 25p for the second book plus 15p per copy for the next 7 books, thereafter 9p per book.

Overseas including Eire £1.25 for the first book, 75p for second book and 28p for each additional book.

Grafton Books reserve the right to show new retail prices on covers, which may differ from those previously advertised in the text or elsewhere.